POL MARTIN

EASY COOKING FOR TODAY

Graphic Design and Layout
Zapp

Photographs by
Melissa du Fretay, Pol Martin (Ontario) Ltd. Studio

Coordinator
Josée Halna du Fretay

BRIMAR PUBLISHING INC.
338 St. Antoine St. East
Montreal, Canada
H2Y 1A3
Telephone: (514) 954-1441
Fax: (514) 954-5086

ISBN 2- 89433- 111- 8

Printed and bound in Canada

CONTENTS

POL MARTIN: A MESSAGE

Dear Friends,

Relax, experiment, enjoy — not the words you would expect to hear from a chef! Yet it is almost that simple to cook well and eat well. I have always believed that eating well, and enjoying it too, is within everyone's reach. Wonderful cuisine does not depend on an elaborately equipped kitchen or endless hours of preparation. All you need is a good chef's knife, a cutting board and a trusty frying pan. It's that simple!

I urge you to improvise, to let your imagination run free. TRY is a key word in cooking, as in most things in life. Trial and error helps form our opinions and is often the best way to learn. Try substituting your favourite ingredients, or those that are freshest in your area. If a recipe calls for broccoli and you prefer cauliflower, try it with cauliflower. I'm not watching you through the pages, so feel free.

Eating well is a constant concern in our society. How true it is that "We eat to live, but live to eat." I take great pleasure in eating, but I am the first to admit that eating properly takes a conscious effort. We want nutritionally-balanced meals, and I provide nutritional data for every recipe. But the numbers do not always tell us what we want to hear. Cake is cake is cake. Take away the fattening ingredients and cake is no longer cake. My answer, for my body, is moderation and exercise. It works for me.

From the many letters I receive, I know how much you value a cookbook that is versatile and practical. My aim is to provide you with a cooking source that you can depend on. The recipes have been carefully written to be precise and informative. The accompanying photographs are a helpful visual reference and show the actual recipe when it was tested in my studio.

I really hope EASY COOKING FOR TODAY becomes your best friend in the kitchen. I have had a great deal of fun creating it and am excited at the prospect of sharing these recipes with you.

Until we meet again, have fun...Bon appetit!

SOME TIPS AND HINTS FROM POL

"The art of cooking is essentially the understanding of techniques. Once you know the techniques, you can cook. Once you can cook, you can experiment."

- It is not necessary to follow a recipe to the letter. What is important is to follow the techniques used in a recipe.

- If you heat the pan before adding oil, you will need less oil.

- Using alcohol can give a special added flavour. Reducing the liquid over high heat will evaporate the alcohol while leaving the flavour.

- Choose the freshest produce available, making substitutions if need be. For example, if green peppers look better than red peppers, then buy the green ones.

- Wonderful meals can be made with inexpensive cuts of meat (Lamb Shoulder Stew, for example) if the proper cooking technique is used.

- One good quality knife is better than 3 or 4 inexpensive ones.

- Cooking should be a fun adventure for the entire family. All children should learn the basics as soon as they are able.

- With the proper guidance, good cooking is very simple. The more fun you have in the kitchen, the more you will want to try. The more you practice, the better you will become.

So have fun, my friends!

SUPER STARTERS

*A bite here, a taste there—
teasers to set the
mood of your menu*

Julienne of Vegetable Soup

serves 4

30 g	(*1 oz*) butter
1	onion, finely chopped
3	carrots, peeled and cut into fine julienne
½	turnip, peeled and cut into fine julienne
1.2 litres	(*2¼ pt*) beef stock, heated
5 ml	(*1 tsp*) chopped fresh parsley
	salt and pepper

Heat butter in large saucepan over low heat. Add onion and cover; cook 5 minutes.

Add carrots and turnip; mix well and season. Cover and continue cooking 10 minutes.

Pour in beef stock, mix well and simmer soup 5 to 6 minutes.

Sprinkle with parsley and serve.

This soup is an ideal start to a fine luncheon.

1 serving	114 calories	13 g carbohydrate
2 g protein	6 g fat	2.7 g fibre

George's Hearty Cabbage Soup

serves 4–6

30 g	(*1 oz*) butter
1	large onion, diced
1	celery stick, diced large
150 g	(*5 oz*) shredded cabbage
3	potatoes, peeled and sliced thick
1.5 litres	(*2¾ pt*) chicken stock, heated
15 ml	(*1 tbsp*) freshly chopped dill
30 ml	(*2 tbsp*) flour
150 ml	(*¼ pt*) soured cream
	salt and pepper

Heat butter in large saucepan over medium heat. Add onion, celery and cabbage; season well. Partly cover and cook 10 minutes over low heat.

Add potatoes, chicken stock and dill; correct seasoning. Stir and bring to boil and continue cooking, partly covered, 20 minutes over low heat.

Mix flour with soured cream in small bowl. Add 150 ml (*¼ pt*) of soup stock to bowl and incorporate, then pour into soup. Mix well and serve.

1 serving	190 calories	20 g carbohydrate
5 g protein	10 g fat	3.0 g fibre

9

Winter Lentil Soup

serves 6

30 g	(*1 oz*) butter	
2	medium onions, chopped	
2	carrots, peeled and chopped	
2 litres	(*3½ pt*) beef stock, heated	
40 ml	(*2½ tbsp*) tomato purée	
400 g	(*14 oz*) lentils, washed	
5 ml	(*1 tsp*) chervil	
2	bay leaves	
15 ml	(*1 tbsp*) freshly chopped parsley	
	salt and pepper	

Heat butter in large saucepan over medium heat. Add onions and carrots; cook 5 minutes.

Add beef stock and tomato purée; mix well and season. Stir in lentils, chervil and bay leaves.

Bring to boil, then reduce heat to low and cook 1½ hours, partly covered, over low heat.

Sprinkle with parsley and serve.

1 serving	125 calories	15 g carbohydrate
5 g protein	5 g fat	7.7 g fibre

Royal Cream of Turnip

serves 4

45 g	(*1½ oz*) butter
½	onion, chopped
2	celery sticks, thinly sliced
2	potatoes, peeled, halved and thinly sliced
½	large turnip, peeled and sliced
½	seedless cucumber, thinly sliced
15 ml	(*1 tbsp*) chopped fresh parsley
5 ml	(*1 tsp*) marjoram
1.2 litres	(*2¼ pt*) chicken stock, heated
45 ml	(*3 tbsp*) double cream
	salt and pepper

Melt butter in large saucepan over low heat. Add onion and celery; cover and cook 5 minutes.

Add remaining vegetables and season with salt and pepper. Sprinkle in parsley and marjoram; mix well. Cover and continue cooking 5 minutes.

Pour in chicken stock and bring to boil. Reduce heat to medium and cook, partly covered, 25 to 30 minutes or until vegetables are done.

Purée soup in food processor, mix in cream and serve. If desired, decorate portions by swirling a little extra cream into soup with fork.

1 serving	161 calories	9 g carbohydrate
2 g protein	13 g fat	1.5 g fibre

Cream of Broccoli Soup

serves 4

1	head of broccoli
45 g	(*1½ oz*) butter
1	small onion, chopped
40 g	(*1¼ oz*) flour
1.2 litres	(*2¼ pt*) chicken stock, heated
2 ml	(*½ tsp*) basil
1	bay leaf
15 ml	(*1 tbsp*) freshly chopped parsley
	juice 1 lemon
	salt and pepper

Place broccoli in large bowl and cover with cold water. Add lemon juice and let stand 1 hour. Drain and chop broccoli.

Heat butter in large saucepan over medium heat. Add onion and cook 3 minutes, partly covered.

Add chopped broccoli and season well. Partly cover and continue cooking 7 minutes. Stir during cooking process.

Mix in flour until well incorporated. Cook 3 minutes, uncovered, over medium heat.

Add remaining ingredients and mix well. Cook soup, partly covered, 30 minutes over low heat. Use food processor or blender to purée soup. Correct seasoning and serve.

1 serving	163 calories	12 g carbohydrate
4 g protein	11 g fat	2.0 g fibre

1. Add lemon juice to broccoli in cold water. Let stand 1 hour before chopping.

2. Cook onion 3 minutes, partly covered, then add chopped broccoli. Season well, partly cover, and continue cooking 7 minutes; stir occasionally.

3. Mix in flour until well incorporated. Cook 3 minutes over medium heat. Add remaining ingredients.

4. After soup has cooked 30 minutes over low heat, blend in food processor.

Cream of Mushroom with Yellow Pepper *serves 4*

45 g	(*1½ oz*) butter
1	shallot, finely chopped
450 g	(*1 lb*) fresh mushrooms, cleaned* and sliced
1	yellow pepper, thinly sliced
2 ml	(*½ tsp*) tarragon
40 g	(*1¼ oz*) flour
1.1 litres	(*2 pt*) chicken stock, heated
60 ml	(*4 tbsp*) double cream
	salt and pepper
dash	paprika

Heat butter in large saucepan over low heat. Add shallot, mushrooms, yellow pepper and tarragon; mix well. Cover and cook 8 to 10 minutes.

Stir in flour until well incorporated. Cook 2 to 3 minutes, uncovered, over low heat.

Pour in chicken stock, mix well with whisk and correct seasoning. Pour in cream and bring to boil.

Cook soup, partly covered, 18 to 20 minutes over medium heat. Sprinkle with paprika before serving.

This soup will keep for 2 days if covered with buttered greaseproof paper and refrigerated.

* Remember to clean mushrooms without using water. Use a soft brush or cloth.

1 serving	194 calories	13 g carbohydrate
4 g protein	14 g fat	3.6 g fibre

Wintery Clam Chowder

serves 4

45 g	(*1½ oz*) butter
2	onions, diced small
1	celery stick, diced small
30 g	(*1 oz*) flour
1 litre	(*1¾ pt*) fish stock, heated
3	potatoes, peeled and diced small
60 ml	(*4 tbsp*) double cream
150 g	(*5 oz*) canned baby clams
	juice from clams
	salt and pepper
pinch	celery seeds
pinch	thyme
dash	paprika
dash	ginger

Melt butter in large saucepan. Add onions and celery; cover and cook 2 minutes over medium heat.

Mix in flour until well incorporated. Cook 3 minutes, uncovered, over low heat.

Pour in fish stock and juice from clams; season and mix well. Add all seasonings and bring to boil.

Stir in potatoes, bring to boil again and reduce heat to medium. Cook 20 to 25 minutes, uncovered, stirring frequently.

Pour in cream and add clams to soup. Mix and cook 4 minutes over low heat. Do not allow liquid to boil.

Serve in large soup tureen.

1 serving	266 calories	27 g carbohydrate
8 g protein	14 g fat	3.3 g fibre

Cream of Pepper Soup

serves 4

45 g	(*1½ oz*) butter
½	onion, finely chopped
1	celery stick, diced
1	yellow pepper, diced
1	red pepper, diced
15 ml	(*1 tbsp*) chopped fresh parsley
2 ml	(*½ tsp*) chervil
40 g	(*1¼ oz*) flour
1.1 litres	(*2 pt*) chicken stock, heated
45 ml	(*3 tbsp*) double cream
	salt and pepper
dash	paprika

Heat butter in large saucepan over low heat. Add onion, cover and cook 4 minutes.

Stir in celery, cover and continue cooking 5 to 6 minutes.

Add yellow and red peppers, season and add parsley, chervil and paprika. Cover and cook 5 to 6 minutes over medium heat.

Mix in flour until well incorporated. Cook 3 minutes, uncovered, over low heat.

Pour in chicken stock, correct seasoning and mix well. Bring to boil; reduce heat to medium and cook soup, partly covered, 20 minutes.

Purée soup in food processor, incorporate cream and serve.

1 serving	165 calories	10 g carbohydrate
2 g protein	13 g fat	1.1 g fibre

1. After cooking onion for 4 minutes, add celery and continue cooking, covered, 5 to 6 minutes over low heat.

2. Add yellow and red peppers, season and add parsley, chervil and paprika. Cover and cook 5 to 6 minutes over medium heat.

3. Mix in flour until well incorporated. This will help to thicken soup.

4. After flour has cooked for several minutes, pour in chicken stock, correct seasoning and mix well. Bring to boil and finish cooking.

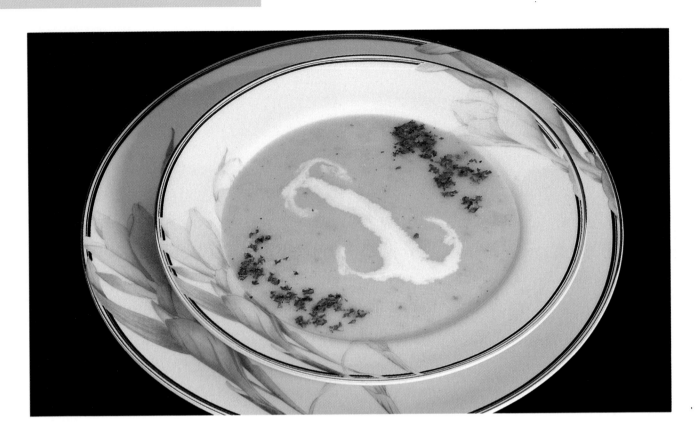

Classic Vichyssoise

serves 4

3	leeks, white part of stalk only
15 g	(*½ oz*) butter
1	onion, thinly sliced
5	medium-large potatoes, peeled and thinly sliced
1 ml	(*¼ tsp*) thyme
2 ml	(*½ tsp*) marjoram
1	bay leaf
1.2 litres	(*2¼ pt*) chicken stock, heated
60 ml	(*4 tbsp*) double cream
	salt and pepper

It is important to wash leeks properly. Slit the stalk of the leek lengthways, leaving 1 cm (½ in) of uncut leek at the base to keep the leaves intact. Make another slit in the same manner to further free the leaves for a thorough washing. You will discover traces of sand and grit deep inside that might otherwise have gone unnoticed. Slice cleaned leeks and set aside.

Melt butter in large saucepan over low heat. Add leeks and onion; cover and cook 10 minutes.

Add potatoes and season well with salt and pepper. Sprinkle in all seasonings and stir well. Cover and continue cooking 12 minutes.

Pour in chicken stock and bring to boil. Cook soup, partly covered, 30 minutes over medium heat.

Purée soup in food processor. Transfer to bowl and set aside to cool. Chill in refrigerator.

When ready to serve, incorporate cream. You can also serve this soup warm, if desired.

1 serving	276 calories	46 g carbohydrate
5 g protein	8 g fat	5.8 g fibre

Lemony Cream of Broccoli Soup

serves 4

1.2 litres	(*2¼ pt*) water
2	lemons, halved
45 g	(*1½ oz*) butter
½	onion, chopped
1	head broccoli, separated into florets and well washed in warm water
30 g	(*1 oz*) flour
60 ml	(*4 tbsp*) double cream
	salt and pepper

Pour water into saucepan. Drop in lemon halves and season with salt; bring to boil and continue boiling for 15 minutes.

Meanwhile, heat butter in large saucepan. Add onion, cover and cook 4 to 5 minutes over low heat.

Add broccoli and season well. Cover and continue cooking 7 to 8 minutes.

Mix in flour until well incorporated. Cover and continue cooking 2 minutes.

Remove lemon halves from boiling water and discard. Slowly incorporate liquid to broccoli in saucepan while stirring with wooden spoon.

Season well and stir in cream; bring to boil. Reduce heat to low and cook soup, partly covered, for 20 minutes.

Purée soup in food processor and serve.

1 serving	*210 calories*	*15 g carbohydrate*
6 g protein	*14 g fat*	*6.6 g fibre*

Curried Apple Soup

serves 4

45 g	(*1½ oz*) butter	
½	onion, chopped	
1	celery stick, chopped	
4	large apples, peeled, cored and thinly sliced	
30 ml	(*2 tbsp*) curry powder	
30 g	(*1 oz*) flour	
1 litre	(*1¾ pt*) chicken stock, heated	
30 ml	(*2 tbsp*) double cream	
	salt and pepper	

Melt butter in large saucepan over low heat. Add onion, cover and cook 5 minutes.

Add celery; continue cooking, covered, 3 to 4 minutes.

Mix in apples and sprinkle in curry powder. Stir well, cover and cook 5 minutes over medium-low heat.

Mix in flour until well incorporated. Cover and continue cooking 2 minutes over low heat.

Pour in chicken stock, mix well and bring to boil. Cook soup, partly covered, 15 minutes over low heat.

Transfer contents to food processor and blend no more than 15 seconds. Incorporate cream, season lightly if needed and serve.

1 serving	220 calories	27 g carbohydrate
1 g protein	12 g fat	3.5 g fibre

Cream of Mushroom Soup

serves 4–6

60 g	**(2 oz) butter**
350 g	**(3/4 lb) fresh mushrooms, cleaned**
1	**large onion, diced small**
2	**shallots, finely chopped**
1	**celery stick, diced small**
15 ml	**(1 tbsp) freshly chopped parsley**
2 ml	**(1/2 tsp) basil**
1	**bay leaf**
50 g	**(1 3/4 oz) flour**
1.2 litres	**(2 1/4 pt) chicken stock, heated**
	few drops lemon juice
	salt and pepper
pinch	**thyme**

Heat 5 ml (*1 tsp*) butter in small saucepan over medium heat. Dice 125 g (*4 oz*) of mushrooms and add to pan with few drops lemon juice. Cook 3 minutes over low heat; set aside.

Place remaining butter in larger saucepan over medium heat. When hot, add onion, shallots and celery; cover and cook 3 minutes over low heat.

Slice remaining mushrooms and add to vegetables in saucepan. Season well and add parsley, basil, bay leaf and thyme. Mix well and add few more drops lemon juice. Cover and cook 6 minutes over medium heat.

Mix in flour until well incorporated. Cook 2 minutes, uncovered, then pour in chicken stock and correct seasoning; bring to boil.

Reduce heat to low and cook soup, partly covered, 30 minutes.

Pass soup through sieve into bowl. Garnish with reserved diced mushrooms and croutons, if desired.

1 serving	167 calories	13 g carbohydrate
4 g protein	11 g fat	2.8 g fibre

Cream of Potato and Red Pepper

serves 4

2	leeks
45 g	(*1½ oz*) butter
2	onions, thinly sliced
1	celery stick, sliced
1	red pepper, diced
5	potatoes, peeled and thinly sliced
5 ml	(*1 tsp*) herbes de Provence
5 ml	(*1 tsp*) marjoram
2 ml	(*½ tsp*) thyme
1	bay leaf
1.2 litres	(*2¼ pt*) chicken stock, heated
60 ml	(*4 tbsp*) double cream
15 ml	(*1 tbsp*) freshly chopped parsley
	salt and pepper

Cut off and discard green part of leeks. Slit white stalks lengthways twice, almost to base. Let leeks soak in cold water 5 minutes, then wash thoroughly to remove sand and grit. Remove and slice thinly.

Heat butter in large saucepan over medium heat. Add leeks, onions and celery; season well. Partly cover and cook 15 minutes.

Add red pepper and potatoes; mix well and continue cooking 3 minutes. Add all seasonings and mix again; pour in chicken stock and bring to boil.

Cook soup, partly covered, 30 minutes over medium heat.

Purée contents of saucepan with blender. Incorporate cream, correct seasoning and sprinkle with parsley. Serve.

1 serving	*318 calories*	*41 g carbohydrate*
7 g protein	*14 g fat*	*6.0 g fibre*

Hearty Vegetable Soup

serves 4

30 g	*(1 oz)* butter
2	large carrots, peeled and diced small
2	celery sticks, diced small
2	small onions, cubed small
½	turnip, peeled and diced small
2	potatoes, peeled and diced small
5 ml	*(1 tsp)* sweet basil
2 ml	*(½ tsp)* chervil
1 ml	*(¼ tsp)* thyme
50 ml	*(2 fl oz)* dry white wine
1.2 litres	*(2¼ pt)* chicken stock, heated
150 g	*(5 oz)* fresh green peas
60 g	*(2 oz)* grated Gruyère cheese
	salt and pepper

Melt butter in large saucepan over medium heat. Add carrots, celery, onions, turnip and potatoes; cover and cook 8 minutes.

Sprinkle in all seasonings; pour in wine and chicken stock. Mix well and correct seasoning. Cover and continue cooking 30 minutes.

Add peas; cover and cook another 8 minutes.

Mix in cheese and serve at once. Accompany with slices of fresh French bread, if desired.

Baked White Wine and Onion Soup

serves 4

30 g	(*1 oz*) butter
4 to 5	medium onions, thinly sliced
150 ml	(*¼ pt*) dry white wine
1 litre	(*1¾ pt*) beef stock, heated
1	bay leaf
1 ml	(*¼ tsp*) thyme
1 ml	(*¼ tsp*) marjoram
4	rounds toasted French bread
125 g	(*4 oz*) grated Gruyère cheese
	salt and pepper

Melt butter in large, deep frying pan. When hot, add onions and cook, uncovered, 30 minutes over medium-low heat. Stir 7 or 8 times during cooking.

Pour in wine and mix well. Cook over medium heat to reduce wine by half (about 3 to 4 minutes).

Pour in beef stock, mix well and add bay leaf and all seasonings. Mix well and cook, uncovered, 35 minutes over low heat.

Preheat oven to 230°C (*450°F, gas mark 8*).

Ladle soup into individual onion-soup bowls. Cover with toasted rounds of bread and top with grated cheese. Bake about 15 minutes or until cheese is nicely melted and bubbly brown. Serve.

1 serving	319 calories	22 g carbohydrate
15 g protein	19 g fat	2.9 g fibre

1. Begin cooking sliced onions in hot butter in large, deep frying pan. Stir 7 or 8 times during the 30 minutes of cooking to help brown onions evenly.

2. After 30 minutes, onions should be nicely browned and tender.

3. Add wine and continue cooking to reduce liquid by half.

4. Add beef stock, bay leaf and all seasonings. Simmer over low heat for 35 minutes to marry all the flavours.

Cooked Leek Salad

serves 4–6

8	medium leeks
2	tomatoes, cored, peeled and cut in wedges
3	hard-boiled eggs, sliced
15 ml	(*1 tbsp*) Dijon mustard
1	egg yolk
45 ml	(*3 tbsp*) red wine vinegar
125 ml	(*4 fl oz*) olive oil
15 ml	(*1 tbsp*) freshly chopped parsley
	salt and pepper

Cut off green tops from leeks and discard or reserve for other uses. Slit white stalks lengthways twice, almost to base. With leaves now parted, wash thoroughly in cold water.

Place leeks in saucepan containing boiling water and cook 20 minutes over high heat. Remove and cool under running water. Drain well. Note: The leeks must be completely cold.

Slice leeks crossways and place in large bowl. Add tomatoes and hard-boiled eggs; season well.

Place mustard, egg yolk, vinegar and oil in small bowl. Season and, using whisk, mix well.

Pour dressing over vegetables in bowl and sprinkle with parsley. Serve.

1 serving	394 calories	32 g carbohydrate
8 g protein	26 g fat	7.2 g fibre

Bean Salad

serves 4

275 g	(*10 oz*) canned chick peas, drained
125 g	(*4 oz*) French green beans, cooked and cut in 2
125 g	(*4 oz*) French yellow beans, cooked and cut in 2
2	shallots, chopped
25 ml	(*1½ tbsp*) Dijon mustard
1	garlic clove, smashed and chopped
30 ml	(*2 tbsp*) wine vinegar
90 ml	(*6 tbsp*) olive oil
15 ml	(*1 tbsp*) freshly chopped parsley
1 ml	(*¼ tsp*) tarragon
	salt and pepper

Place chick peas and French beans in mixing bowl; season well.

Place shallots, mustard, garlic, vinegar and oil in small bowl. Season and, using whisk, mix well until thick.

Pour dressing over salad ingredients and mix well. Add parsley and tarragon; mix again. Marinate 15 minutes at room temperature, mixing once during this time. Serve.

1 serving	309 calories	23 g carbohydrate
7 g protein	21 g fat	6.3 g fibre

Avocado Shades of Green

serves 4

10	**fresh asparagus stems, cleaned**
2	**canned hearts of palm, drained and diced**
6 to 8	**stoned black olives, chopped**
15 ml	**(*1 tbsp*) chopped fresh parsley**
60 ml	**(*4 tbsp*) mayonnaise**
90 g	**(*3 oz*) frozen green peas, cooked**
30 ml	**(*2 tbsp*) pickled hot banana peppers, chopped**
2	**ripe avocados*, halved, stoned and basted with lemon juice**
	few drops lemon juice
	few drops Pickapeppa sauce**
	salt and pepper
	lettuce leaves or bean sprouts

Cook asparagus in salted boiling water until tender. Drain and set aside.

Mix hearts of palm, olives and parsley together in bowl. Dice asparagus and add to bowl, mixing well.

Spoon in mayonnaise and sprinkle with lemon juice; mix until well incorporated.

Add Pickapeppa sauce, season well and mix again. Stir in green peas and pickled banana peppers; mix again.

Arrange avocado halves on serving platter with several leaves of lettuce or bean sprouts. This attractive finishing touch will complete the shades of green.

Spoon filling into shells and serve.

* It might be tricky to find 2 perfectly ripe avocados, so plan ahead and let them ripen at home. Leave them on the counter in a brown paper bag and check them each day for ripeness. As soon as they yield easily to the slightest pressure from your finger, they are ready to be turned into "shades of green".

** Pickapeppa sauce is a hot pepper sauce from Jamaica.

1 serving	332 calories	15 g carbohydrate
5 g protein	28 g fat	6.0 g fibre

Green Pepper and Roast Beef Salad
serves 4

4	**5-mm (¼-in) thick slices roast beef, cut into strips**
1	**shallot, chopped**
15 ml	**(1 tbsp) chopped fresh parsley**
½	**red pepper, cut into strips**
1	**green pepper, cut into strips**
30 ml	**(2 tbsp) wine vinegar**
15 ml	**(1 tbsp) Dijon mustard**
30 ml	**(2 tbsp) olive oil**
1 ml	**(¼ tsp) tarragon**
	few drops hot pepper sauce
	salt and pepper
	romaine lettuce leaves, well washed and dried

Place beef strips, shallot, parsley and peppers in bowl; toss together.

Add vinegar and mustard; mix well.

Pour in oil and mix; season to taste. Add tarragon and hot pepper sauce; mix very well. Correct seasoning.

Arrange lettuce leaves on serving platter and add salad. Accompany with a variety of vegetables such as sliced tomatoes, spring onions and marinated mushrooms.

Cheesy Macaroni Salad

serves 6–8

550 g	(*19 oz*) cooked macaroni, cold
60 g	(*2 oz*) grated Cheddar cheese
45 ml	(*3 tbsp*) grated red onion
½	green pepper, finely chopped
½	red pepper, finely chopped
60 ml	(*4 tbsp*) mayonnaise
45 ml	(*3 tbsp*) soured cream
5 ml	(*1 tsp*) dry mustard
15 ml	(*1 tbsp*) freshly chopped parsley
	juice ½ lemon
	salt and pepper

Place macaroni in bowl and add cheese; mix together. Set aside.

In separate bowl, mix together onion, both peppers, mayonnaise, soured cream and mustard. Add parsley, lemon juice and season well; mix again.

Pour over macaroni and cheese, and mix to combine. Serve on lettuce leaves, if desired.

1 serving	171 calories	22 g carbohydrate
5 g protein	7 g fat	0.2 g fibre

Last-Minute Appetizer

serves 4

1	**small cantaloupe melon**
1	**avocado**
8	**slices prosciutto**
	salt and pepper
	lemon juice

Cut melon in half across the width; scoop out and discard seeds and fibres. Cut halves into 4 equal slices, remove skins, season and set aside.

Cut avocado in half lengthways and carefully pry halves apart, twisting slightly if needed. Remove stone with the help of small knife. Peel fruit and slice each half into 4 equal pieces; immediately brush with lemon juice to prevent discolouring.

Pair slice of melon with slice of avocado; wrap with slice of prosciutto. Secure bundles with toothpicks.

Serve on pretty glass plates.

1 serving	*186 calories*	*15 g carbohydrate*
9 g protein	*10 g fat*	*2.4 g fibre*

Vegetable-Stuffed Artichoke Bottoms *serves 4*

30 ml	(*2 tbsp*) vegetable oil
1	shallot, chopped
1	courgette, diced small
¼	aubergine, peeled and diced small
125 g	(*4 oz*) canned crabmeat, well drained
125 g	(*4 oz*) grated mozzarella cheese
400 g	(*14 oz*) canned artichoke bottoms
30 ml	(*2 tbsp*) breadcrumbs
	salt and pepper
	butter

Heat oil in large frying pan over medium heat. Add shallot, courgette and aubergine; season well. Cover and cook 10 to 12 minutes.

Mix in crabmeat and season well; continue cooking 4 to 5 minutes.

Stir in cheese and finish cooking another 2 minutes.

Meanwhile, warm artichoke bottoms in ovenproof baking dish with a bit of butter.

Stuff artichoke bottoms with vegetable mixture and top each with breadcrumbs. Grill in oven 1 to 2 minutes or until browned.

Serve at once.

1 serving	300 calories	14 g carbohydrate
16 g protein	20 g fat	2.4 g fibre

Clam-Stuffed Artichoke Bottoms

serves 4

30 g	(*1 oz*) butter
2	spring onions, chopped
6	large fresh mushroom caps, cleaned and chopped
30 ml	(*2 tbsp*) flour
250 ml	(*8 fl oz*) milk
150 g	(*5 oz*) canned clams, drained
8	artichoke bottoms, heated
60 g	(*2 oz*) grated cheese of your choice
	salt and pepper
pinch	nutmeg
pinch	paprika

Melt butter in frying pan over medium heat. Add spring onions and mushrooms; season well. Cover and cook 5 minutes.

Mix in flour until well incorporated. Cook 1 minute, uncovered. Pour in milk, mix thoroughly and season with nutmeg and paprika. Continue cooking 5 minutes over low heat.

Mix in clams, cover and cook 2 to 3 minutes over very low heat.

Stuff artichoke bottoms and top with cheese. Sprinkle with more paprika if desired. Grill 3 minutes in oven.

Serve on paper doilies.

1 serving	246 calories	15 g carbohydrate
15 g protein	14 g fat	1.5 g fibre

Pickled Button Mushrooms

serves 4

45 ml	(*3 tbsp*) olive oil
3	garlic cloves, smashed and chopped
1	onion, chopped
450 g	(*1 lb*) fresh button mushrooms, well cleaned
1 ml	(*¼ tsp*) thyme
2 ml	(*½ tsp*) marjoram
5 ml	(*1 tsp*) tarragon
1	bay leaf
3	parsley sprigs
1	slice lemon, halved
250 ml	(*8 fl oz*) dry white wine
30 ml	(*2 tbsp*) wine vinegar
	salt and pepper

Heat oil in saucepan over medium heat. Add garlic and onion; cook 4 to 5 minutes, stirring several times.

Mix in button mushrooms and season with salt and pepper. Sprinkle in all seasonings, bay leaf, parsley and lemon. Mix well and add wine and vinegar; cover and cook 10 minutes over medium heat.

Remove cover and let mushrooms cool in saucepan.

Serve with other tasty starters.

1 serving	156 calories	9 g carbohydrate
3 g protein	12 g fat	3.7 g fibre

Grilled Stuffed Mushroom Caps

serves 4

30 ml	(*2 tbsp*) olive oil
16	large fresh mushroom caps, cleaned
30 g	(*1 oz*) butter
3	shallots, finely chopped
45 ml	(*3 tbsp*) chopped fresh parsley
16	canned snails, rinsed and drained
15 ml	(*1 tbsp*) green peppercorns, crushed
30 ml	(*2 tbsp*) breadcrumbs
	salt and pepper
	lemon slices

Heat oil in frying pan over medium-high heat. Add mushroom caps and season; cook 2 to 3 minutes each side. Remove mushrooms from pan and set aside on ovenproof platter.

Add butter to pan. Cook shallots, parsley, snails and peppercorns 2 to 3 minutes over high heat. During cooking, season well with pepper but do not add salt.

Fill mushroom caps with mixture and sprinkle with breadcrumbs. Grill 2 to 3 minutes or until browned.

Serve with lemon slices.

1 serving	128 calories	9 g carbohydrate
5 g protein	8 g fat	3.2 g fibre

Adventurous Aubergine Sandwiches

serves 4

8	5-mm (¼-in) thick slices aubergine
150 g	(5 oz) seasoned flour
1 ml	(¼ tsp) paprika
2	eggs
250 ml	(8 fl oz) milk
45 ml	(3 tbsp) peanut oil
15 g	(½ oz) butter
125 g	(¼ lb) fresh mushrooms, cleaned and chopped
1	shallot, chopped
5 ml	(1 tsp) chopped fresh parsley
5 ml	(1 tsp) flour
150 g	(5 oz) canned crabmeat, well drained and finely chopped
125 ml	(4 fl oz) double cream
60 g	(2 oz) grated Gruyère cheese
	salt and pepper

Dredge aubergine slices in flour; season with paprika and set aside.

Place eggs and milk in bowl; whisk well and season. Dip aubergine slices in mixture and set aside. Heat peanut oil in large frying pan and cook aubergine slices 3 to 4 minutes each side, seasoning when turning over. It is best to do this in several batches or use more than one pan. When all aubergine slices have been browned, remove from pan and place 4 on ovenproof platter; set others aside on a plate.

Melt butter in saucepan over medium-low heat. Add mushrooms, shallot and parsley; cover and cook 3 to 4 minutes. Mix in 5 ml (1 tsp) flour until incorporated; cook 1 minute, uncovered. Stir in crabmeat and season well. Continue cooking 2 to 3 minutes. Pour in cream, correct seasoning and cook 4 to 5 minutes. Add half of cheese, mix well and cook 2 minutes. Divide half of crabmeat mixture onto 4 aubergine slices on ovenproof platter. Close sandwiches with other aubergine slices and top with remaining filling.

Sprinkle with remaining cheese, adding more if needed, and grill 5 to 6 minutes in oven.

Serve with plenty of napkins.

1 serving	544 calories	33 g carbohydrate
22 g protein	36 g fat	2.3 g fibre

1. Dredge aubergine slices in seasoned flour; sprinkle with paprika, adding more if desired.

2. Dip slices in mixture of egg and milk to coat thoroughly.

3. Cook aubergine slices in hot peanut oil for 3 to 4 minutes each side. It is important not to overcrowd pan; the best method is to cook them in several batches.

4. Have bottom slices ready on ovenproof platter and top with some of crabmeat filling. Close sandwich with other aubergine slice and prepare to top with more filling and remaining cheese before grilling.

Elegant Asparagus with Vinaigrette

serves 4

2	large bunches fresh asparagus
15 ml	(*1 tbsp*) Dijon mustard
1	egg yolk
45 ml	(*3 tbsp*) white wine vinegar
125 ml	(*4 fl oz*) olive oil
30 ml	(*2 tbsp*) double cream
5 ml	(*1 tsp*) green peppercorns, crushed
	salt and pepper
	few drops hot pepper sauce

Slice off 2.5 cm (*1 in*) of stalk from base of asparagus. Peel and wash thoroughly to remove all traces of sand.

Cook asparagus in salted boiling water for 7 to 8 minutes. Cool under cold running water and drain well; set aside.

Place mustard in bowl. Add egg yolk and vinegar; whisk together. Season well.

Incorporate oil in thin stream while whisking constantly. Pour in cream, mixing constantly with electric beater.

Add crushed peppercorns, mix well and season with hot pepper sauce.

To serve, pour vinaigrette into gravy boat or an attractive bowl. Gather asparagus in a neat pile and place between folds of napkin, which will absorb any excess moisture.

Guests should help themselves to several asparagus at a time and dip them in vinaigrette.

1 serving	337 calories	6 g carbohydrate
4 g protein	33 g fat	2.0 g fibre

Pub-Style Courgette Sticks

serves 4

2	courgettes
1	garlic clove, smashed and chopped
150 g	(*5 oz*) plain flour
2	beaten eggs
150 g	(*5 oz*) seasoned breadcrumbs
	olive oil
	soy sauce
	peanut oil

Slice courgettes with skin into sticks of uniform size. Wash in cold water then drain and pat dry.

Place courgette sticks in bowl with garlic; sprinkle with olive oil and soy sauce. Marinate 30 minutes.

Preheat plenty of peanut oil in deep-fryer set at 190°C (*375°F*).

Dredge courgette sticks in flour then dip in beaten eggs. Be sure sticks are well covered. Coat completely in breadcrumbs.

Deep-fry until golden brown. Drain on absorbent kitchen paper before serving.

1 serving	427 calories	61 g carbohydrate
12 g protein	15 g fat	3.4 g fibre

Cheesy Deep-Fried Potato Skins

serves 4-6

4	baked potatoes
60 g	(*2 oz*) grated Cheddar or your choice of cheese
	salt and pepper

Preheat plenty of peanut oil in electric deep-fryer set at 190°C (*375°F*).

Slice potatoes in half lengthways and scoop out most of flesh, which can be reserved for use in other recipes.

Cut remaining potato skins into smaller pieces suitable for finger eating. Deep-fry 5 to 6 minutes or adjust time depending on how much potato flesh is left on skins.

Drain well on absorbent kitchen paper and transfer peels to ovenproof plate. Top with cheese and season; grill 2 minutes to melt cheese and serve at once.

This recipe is sure to be a winner when served to "tide them over" during soccer season.

1 serving	160 calories	11 g carbohydrate
4 g protein	11 g fat	1.0 g fibre

Potato-Skin Crowd Pleaser

serves 4–6

30 g	(*1 oz*) bacon fat
1	onion, thinly sliced
1	green pepper, thinly sliced
12	large fresh mushrooms, cleaned and thinly sliced
5	baked potatoes, halved lengthways
5	rashers crisp cooked bacon, chopped
125 g	(*4 oz*) grated cheese (mozzarella or Cheddar or both, if desired)
	salt and freshly ground pepper

Heat bacon fat in saucepan. Add onion, green pepper and mushrooms; season well. Cook 5 to 6 minutes over medium heat.

Mix well and continue cooking another 8 minutes over low heat.

Meanwhile, scoop out about ¾ of potato flesh from each half. Reserve for use in other recipes. Arrange skins on large serving platter and warm in oven if not already hot.

Fill potatoes with vegetable mixture and top with bacon and your choice of cheese; season well.

Grill 5 to 6 minutes in oven until cheese is bubbly. Serve as halves or cut into slices for a larger group of people.

1 serving	414 calories	30 g carbohydrate
6 g protein	30 g fat	1.4 g fibre

Muscovite Tomatoes

serves 4

8	**small tomatoes**
4	**hard-boiled eggs**
3	**anchovy fillets, puréed**
15 ml	(*1 tbsp*) **Dijon mustard**
5 ml	(*1 tsp*) **Worcestershire sauce**
15 ml	(*1 tbsp*) **wine vinegar**
45 ml	(*3 tbsp*) **olive oil**
	salt and pepper
	few drops hot sauce
	lettuce leaves

Using small knife, cut out top from each tomato. Remove most of pulp inside and reserve for use in other recipes. Season cavities and set tomato shells aside.

Slice eggs in half and force yolks through fine sieve into bowl. Also reserve whites for use in other recipes. Add anchovy purée and mustard; mix well.

Add Worcestershire sauce and wine vinegar; mix well. Incorporate oil while mixing constantly with whisk. Season with hot sauce and spoon into tomato shells.

Serve on bed of lettuce leaves.

1 serving	192 calories	4 g carbohydrate
8 g protein	16 g fat	1.0 g fibre

1. Cut out top from each tomato and, using spoon, scoop out most of pulp. Season cavities.

2. Force egg yolks through fine sieve into bowl. Add anchovy purée and mustard; mix well.

3. After incorporating Worcestershire sauce and vinegar, pour in oil slowly while whisking.

4. Finished mixture should have quite a thick consistency. Spoon into tomato shells.

Tomato Canapés Parmesano

serves 6–8

30 ml	(*2 tbsp*) olive oil
1	garlic clove, smashed and chopped
4	tomatoes, sliced 1 cm (*½ in*) thick
24	slices toasted French bread
125 g	(*4 oz*) grated Parmesan cheese
	salt and pepper

Heat olive oil in frying pan over medium heat. Add garlic and cook 2 minutes.

Add tomatoes, placing them flat in pan without crowding and cook 1 minute each side. Cook in two batches if necessary.

Place each tomato slice on round of bread. Set all on baking sheet and top with grated cheese. Grill 3 minutes and serve.

1 serving	274 calories	34 g carbohydrate
12 g protein	10 g fat	2.9 g fibre

Cheese Canapés

serves 8–10

¹/₂	celery stick, diced small
1	shallot, chopped
125 g	(*4 oz*) canned crabmeat, well drained
12	stoned black olives
225 g	(*8 oz*) full fat soft cheese
30 ml	(*2 tbsp*) plain yogurt
	few drops Pickapeppa sauce
	few drops Tabasco sauce
	salt and pepper

Place celery, shallot, crabmeat, olives and cheese in food processor. Blend 1 minute.

Add Pickapeppa sauce and Tabasco sauce; blend again 20 seconds.

Add yogurt, salt and pepper; blend to combine. Pour into bowl, cover and chill 1 hour.

Spread over crackers or toasted bread, or serve as dip for fresh vegetables.

1 serving	*110 calories*	*1 g carbohydrate*
4 g protein	*10 g fat*	*0.2 g fibre*

Aioli

serves 4–6

6	garlic cloves, peeled
2	egg yolks
175 ml	(6 fl oz) olive oil
	salt and pepper
	cayenne pepper to taste
	few drops hot pepper sauce
	few drops lemon juice
	toasted French bread

Place garlic cloves in mortar and season with salt, pepper and cayenne pepper. Grind with pestle until garlic becomes almost paste-like.

Add egg yolks and continue mixing and grinding with pestle until well combined.

Begin adding oil very slowly, preferably drop by drop, while mixing constantly with pestle. The oil must incorporate perfectly to obtain a silky smooth aioli sauce.

Season with hot pepper sauce and lemon juice to taste. Mix again.

Serve aioli on slices of toasted French bread or, if preferred, on thick, crunchy crackers. Not surprisingly, aioli is very hot and spicy, so it is best served with a cool drink.

1 serving	414 calories	30 g carbohydrate
6 g protein	30 g fat	1.4 g fibre

1. Preparing aioli really requires a mortar and pestle. If you don't have one you might consider it a worthwhile investment. It will come in handy for other recipes as well.

2. Grind seasoned garlic cloves with pestle until paste-like.

3. Add egg yolks and continue mixing and grinding until well combined and smooth.

4. Incorporating the oil takes some patience as it must be added very slowly to ensure that the sauce does not separate. Be sure to mix constantly while adding the oil drop by drop.

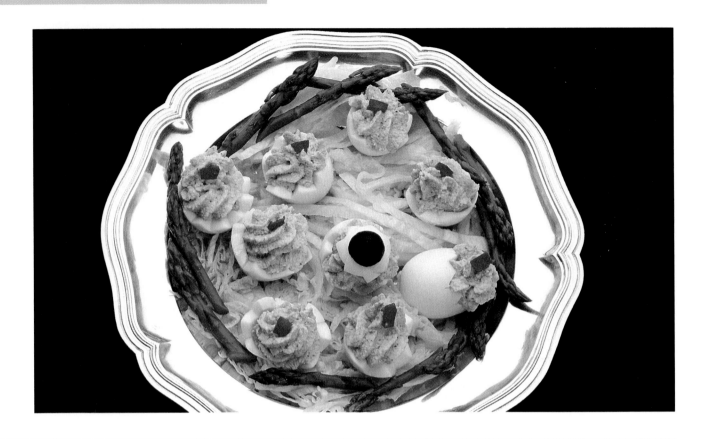

Curried Stuffed Eggs

serves 4

10	hard-boiled eggs
45 ml	(*3 tbsp*) mayonnaise
15 ml	(*1 tbsp*) curry powder
15 ml	(*1 tbsp*) Dijon mustard
dash	paprika
	salt and pepper
	few drops Pickapeppa sauce
	tiny pieces pimiento for decoration
	shredded lettuce

Using small sharp knife, cut around middle of 8 eggs in a zigzag design. Carefully pry whites apart and remove yolks. Cut remaining 2 eggs in half.

Place all yolks from 10 eggs into wire sieve. Also add the whites from the plainly cut eggs. Force through into bowl.

Mix in mayonnaise, curry powder, mustard and paprika. Season with salt, pepper and Pickapeppa sauce; mix well until smooth.

Spoon mixture into piping bag fitted with star nozzle and stuff decoratively cut egg whites. Decorate with pimiento.

Arrange some shredded lettuce on serving platter and place eggs on top. Serve.

1 serving	258 calories	0 g carbohydrate
15 g protein	22 g fat	0.1 g fibre

Stuffed Hard-Boiled Eggs

serves 4–6

12	hard-boiled eggs, peeled
15 ml	(*1 tbsp*) Dijon mustard
45 ml	(*3 tbsp*) mayonnaise
1 ml	(*¼ tsp*) lemon juice
6	canned bamboo shoots, cut into 5-mm (*¼-in*) lengths
60 ml	(*4 tbsp*) vinaigrette
5 ml	(*1 tsp*) chopped fresh parsley
	salt and pepper
	paprika to taste
	sliced black olives

Carefully slice eggs in half lengthways. Remove cooked yolks and force through wire sieve into bowl. This method will eliminate any lumps in the stuffing.

Add mustard and mayonnaise to egg yolks and mix well until thoroughly incorporated. Taste and add more mayonnaise, if desired.

Sprinkle in lemon juice and season well; mix again. Spoon mixture into piping bag fitted with star nozzle and stuff egg whites.

Arrange stuffed eggs on attractive platter or bed of shredded lettuce. Sprinkle with paprika to taste and decorate with black olives.

In a small bowl, toss sliced bamboo shoots with vinaigrette and serve alongside eggs. Sprinkle with parsley.

If desired, cover eggs with cling film and refrigerate up to 6 hours before serving.

1 serving	259 calories	3 g carbohydrate
13 g protein	23 g fat	0.4 g fibre

Stuffed Eggs Surprise on Watercress Bed *serves 4*

4	**hard-boiled eggs**
150 ml	**(¼ pt) mayonnaise**
1	**bunch fresh watercress, washed and well dried**
	juice 1 lemon
	few drops Tabasco sauce
	salt and pepper

Slice eggs in half lengthways and carefully remove yolks. Force them through wire sieve into bowl. Set whites aside.

Add 60 ml (*4 tbsp*) mayonnaise, few drops lemon juice, Tabasco sauce and season well. Mix until incorporated, then spoon into egg whites. Reshape into whole eggs and set aside.

Place watercress in saucepan with 300 ml (*½ pt*) water and few drops lemon juice; season. Bring to boil and cook 3 minutes.

Remove watercress from pan and drain well. Transfer to blender and purée. Add remaining mayonnaise, mix well and correct seasoning.

To serve, spoon portion of watercress purée on each plate and top with stuffed egg.

1 serving	228 calories	5 g carbohydrate
7 g protein	20 g fat	0.8 g fibre

1. Force yolks through wire sieve into bowl. Set whites aside.

2. After mayonnaise and seasonings have been incorporated, spoon yolk mixture back into whites and reshape into whole eggs. Set aside.

3. Cook watercress in boiling water with hint of lemon juice for 3 minutes. Drain well and purée in food processor.

4. Add remaining mayonnaise and blend to incorporate.

Irresistible Deep-Fried Camembert Wedges *serves 4*

2	**200-g (7-*oz*) Camembert cheese wheels, chilled**
150 g	**(*5 oz*) seasoned flour**
5 ml	**(*1 tsp*) olive oil**
3	**beaten eggs**
225 g	**(*8 oz*) breadcrumbs**
	peanut oil for frying

Scrape off some of rind from cheese and cut each wheel into triangular wedges. Dredge in flour.

Add oil to beaten eggs, mixing well, and carefully dip pieces of cheese in mixture.

Dredge moistened cheese in flour again; then dip in beaten egg mixture again.

Finish by coating in breadcrumbs. Place all wedges on plate and transfer to freezer for 10 minutes.

Meanwhile, preheat plenty of peanut oil in electric deep-fryer set at 190°C (*375°F*).

Deep-fry cheese wedges in hot oil about 2 minutes or until golden brown. Drain on absorbent kitchen paper before serving. If desired, accompany with raspberry sauce (available in gourmet shops).

1 serving	913 calories	65 g carbohydrate
35 g protein	57 g fat	3.0 g fibre

Croque-Monsieur New York Style

serves 4

45 g	(1½ oz) butter
1	small green pepper, halved and thinly sliced
8	thin slices French bread
8	slices Gruyère cheese
4	slices Black Forest ham
	freshly ground pepper

Heat 15 g (½ oz) butter in small saucepan. Add green pepper and cover; cook 15 minutes over low heat.

Arrange slices of bread on cutting board to form sandwiches. Begin by covering bottom slice with piece of cheese generously seasoned with pepper.

Divide cooked green pepper among sandwiches and top with slice of ham. Cover with second piece of cheese and close sandwiches.

Place nonstick pan (two may be necessary) over medium-high heat. Spread 15 g (½ oz) butter over one side of sandwiches, and when pan is hot add them, buttered side down.

Cook first side about 3 to 4 minutes or until golden brown. Meanwhile butter other side of bread.

Turn sandwiches over, continue cooking until nicely browned and serve. Slice in half, in sticks or in triangles.

1 serving	472 calories	18 g carbohydrate
28 g protein	32 g fat	1.0 g fibre

Crusty Spicy Sausage Bites

serves 4

15 ml	(*1 tbsp*) olive oil
1	onion, chopped
1	garlic clove, smashed and chopped
350 g	(*¾ lb*) spicy sausage, sliced
400 ml	(*⅔ pt*) canned tomato sauce
1	French bread, sliced thick and toasted
125 g	(*4 oz*) grated Gruyère cheese
	salt and pepper
	few drops Pickapeppa sauce

Heat oil in frying pan over medium heat. Add onion and garlic; cook 4 minutes.

Add sausage slices, season well and continue cooking 7 to 8 minutes.

Pour in tomato sauce, correct seasoning and cook another 6 to 8 minutes.

Transfer contents to food processor and blend. Spread mixture over slices of toasted bread and place on ovenproof platter.

Top with cheese, sprinkle with Pickapeppa sauce and grill in oven until bubbly and lightly browned.

Serve at once with cool drinks.

1 serving	706 calories	56 g carbohydrate
35 g protein	38 g fat	3.4 g fibre

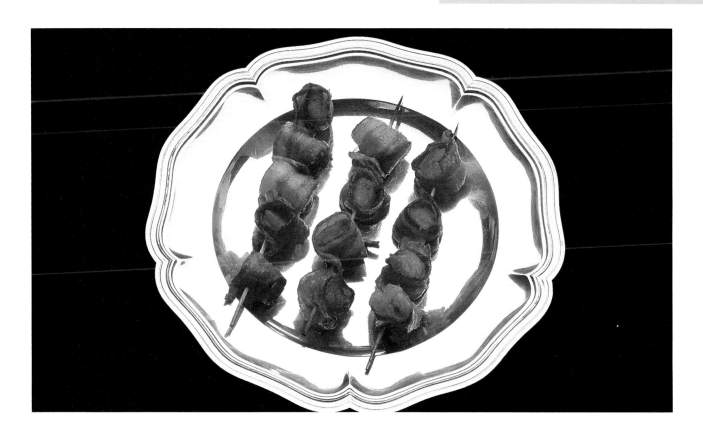

Bacon-Wrapped Pineapple on Skewers   *serves 4*

400 g	**(*14 oz*) canned large pineapple chunks, drained**
150 ml	**(*¼ pt*) your favourite barbecue sauce**
5 ml	**(*1 tsp*) teriyaki sauce**
60 ml	**(*4 tbsp*) honey**
8	**rashers bacon, precooked 3 minutes**
	pepper

Place pineapple chunks in bowl. Add barbecue sauce, teriyaki sauce and honey; season with pepper. Marinate 15 minutes.

Cut bacon rashers in half and use each half to wrap a piece of pineapple. Carefully thread on wooden skewers.

Grill 1 to 2 minutes. Serve with cocktail sauce.

1 serving	*203 calories*	*30 g carbohydrate*	**55**
5 g protein	*7 g fat*	*0.8 g fibre*	

Ham Cones with Vegetable Aspic

serves 4

1	celery stick, diced small
1	carrot, peeled and diced small
1	potato, peeled and diced small
90 g	(3 oz) frozen sweet green peas
½	courgette, diced small
300 ml	(½ pt) canned beef consommé
7 g	(¼ oz) unflavoured powdered gelatine
50 ml	(2 fl oz) boiling water
30 ml	(2 tbsp) mayonnaise
8	thin slices cooked ham
	shredded lettuce

Cook vegetables in salted boiling water for 8 to 10 minutes or until tender.

Meanwhile, heat consommé in small saucepan. Dilute gelatine in 50 ml (2 fl oz) boiling water and add to consommé; cook 2 minutes, stirring frequently. Remove and chill.

Drain vegetables, cool under running water and drain again. Pat dry with absorbent kitchen paper.

Place vegetables in mixing bowl, add mayonnaise and stir to incorporate.

Pour 50 ml (2 fl oz) of cooled consommé mixture into bowl containing vegetables; mix very well.

Cupping ham slices in hand, roll into cone shapes and secure with toothpick. Fill with vegetable mixture.

Carefully place cones on stainless-steel wire rack set over large plate or baking sheet. Brush cones with consommé gelatine mixture and place in refrigerator for 15 minutes.

Baste cones again; chill another 15 minutes.

Repeat above procedure. Be sure to place the consommé gelatine mixture back in the refrigerator each time.

Serve cones on chilled serving platter on bed of shredded fresh lettuce. If desired, decorate with cubed pieces of leftover consommé gelatine.

1 serving	201 calories	12 g carbohydrate
18 g protein	9 g fat	4.7 g fibre

Baked Chicken Wings

serves 4

12	large chicken wings
15 ml	(*1 tbsp*) olive oil
30 ml	(*2 tbsp*) honey
30 ml	(*2 tbsp*) soy sauce
2	garlic cloves, smashed and chopped
30 ml	(*2 tbsp*) breadcrumbs
	juice ¼ lemon
	salt and pepper

Snip off tips from wings and cut each into 2 pieces. Place in large bowl and add oil, honey, soy sauce, garlic and lemon juice. Season well and toss; marinate 1 hour.

Preheat oven to 230°C (*450°F, gas mark 8*).

Thread wings on skewers and place on baking sheet. Bake 10 minutes.

Turn skewers over and continue baking another 8 minutes.

Change oven setting to grill.

Sprinkle breadcrumbs over wings and grill 5 minutes. Serve.

1 serving	209 calories	12 g carbohydrate
20 g protein	9 g fat	0.1 g fibre

Buffalo Style Deep-Fried Wings

serves 4

900 g	(*2 lb*) chicken wings
300 g	(*11 oz*) seasoned flour
3	beaten eggs
5 ml	(*1 tsp*) vegetable oil
225 g	(*8 oz*) seasoned breadcrumbs
	salt and pepper
	paprika to taste
	peanut oil for frying

Preheat plenty of peanut oil in electric deep-fryer set at 190°C (*375°F*).

Snip off tips from wings and cut each into two. Parboil 10 to 12 minutes. Drain well.

Dredge wings in flour. Dip wings in beaten eggs mixed with vegetable oil; then coat with breadcrumbs. Season with salt, pepper and paprika.

Deep-fry 5 to 6 minutes or until golden brown. Serve with your favourite hot, spicy sauce.

1 serving	282 calories	23 g carbohydrate
18 g protein	13 g fat	1.1 g fibre

Chicken Spiced with Apple in Pastry

serves 4

30 g	(*1 oz*) butter
1	celery stick, diced
2	apples, peeled, cored and diced large
45 ml	(*3 tbsp*) flour
1 ml	(*¼ tsp*) paprika
500 ml	(*17 fl oz*) chicken stock, heated
2	whole chicken breasts, cooked and skinned, diced large
30 ml	(*2 tbsp*) soured cream
4	cooked vol-au-vent shells*, hot
	salt and pepper
	chopped walnuts

Melt butter in frying pan over low heat. Add celery and apples; cover and cook 5 minutes.

Stir in flour until well incorporated. Season and sprinkle in paprika. Cook 2 minutes, uncovered, over low heat.

Pour in chicken stock and bring to boil. Cook, uncovered, 8 to 10 minutes over medium heat.

Mix in cooked chicken and simmer 2 minutes to heat. Mix in soured cream and spoon mixture into pastry shells. Sprinkle with nuts and serve.

* Commercial frozen pastry dough is quite suitable for this recipe.

1 serving	565 calories	35 g carbohydrate
32 g protein	33 g fat	2.2 g fibre

Chicken Fingers in Beer Batter

serves 4

150 g	(5 oz) flour
300 ml	(½ pt) beer
125 ml	(4 fl oz) water
1	egg yolk
1	egg white, beaten stiff
1	whole chicken breast, skinned, boned and cut in large strips
	salt
	few drops Worcestershire sauce
	few drops hot sauce
	peanut oil for frying

Place flour in bowl. Add salt, mix and pour in beer. Whisk well and pour in water; whisk again until smooth.

Incorporate egg yolk; then incorporate beaten egg white. Whisk again until well blended and refrigerate batter 2 hours before using.

Preheat plenty of peanut oil in electric deep-fryer set at 190°C (375°F).

Place chicken strips in bowl and marinate in Worcestershire and hot sauces for about 10 minutes while oil is heating.

Dip chicken in batter and deep-fry about 7 to 8 minutes or according to thickness of strips.

Drain on absorbent kitchen paper before serving and accompany with dipping sauce.

1 serving	345 calories	29 g carbohydrate
19 g protein	15 g fat	1.2 g fibre

Cold Chicken Salad

serves 2

½	cantaloupe melon, flesh scooped out into balls
1	whole chicken breast, cooked, skinned and diced large
5 ml	(*1 tsp*) cumin
½	shallot, chopped
1	celery stick, diced
15 ml	(*1 tbsp*) chutney
15 ml	(*1 tbsp*) mayonnaise
15 ml	(*1 tbsp*) soured cream
	salt and pepper
	few drops lemon juice

Toss together melon balls, chicken, cumin, shallot, celery and chutney; season well.

Add mayonnaise and soured cream; mix until evenly coated.

Sprinkle in lemon juice and serve on lettuce leaves, if desired.

1 serving	258 calories	14 g carbohydrate
28 g protein	10 g fat	1.9 g fibre

Chicken Liver Pâté

serves 4

450 g	(*1 lb*) chicken livers, cleaned
30 g	(*1 oz*) butter
2	onions, chopped
2	garlic cloves, smashed and chopped
1	celery stick, chopped
2 ml	(*½ tsp*) savory
5 ml	(*1 tsp*) chervil
2 ml	(*½ tsp*) grated lemon zest
50 ml	(*2 fl oz*) dry white wine
30 ml	(*2 tbsp*) cognac
60 ml	(*4 tbsp*) soured cream
pinch	thyme
	salt and pepper

Slice chicken livers in half and remove fat; set aside.

Melt butter in large frying pan over medium heat. Cook onions, garlic and celery, covered, 4 to 5 minutes.

Add livers and all seasonings. Stir in lemon zest; cover and cook 15 minutes over medium heat. Stir occasionally during cooking process.

Pour in wine and cognac; cover and continue cooking 5 to 6 minutes.

Transfer mixture to food processor and blend until well incorporated and smooth.

Add soured cream and continue mixing several minutes. Pour into serving bowl and chill overnight.

Serve on toasted French bread or on crackers. Accompany with various condiments.

1 serving	262 calories	8 g carbohydrate
26 g protein	14 g fat	1.3 g fibre

1. Clean chicken livers and slice in half to remove fat.

2. Cook onions, garlic and celery in hot butter, covered, for 4 to 5 minutes.

3. Add livers and all seasonings. Stir in lemon zest and continue cooking, covered, 15 minutes.

4. Pour in wine, then cognac; resume cooking.

Lobster in Cream Sauce on Toast

serves 4

30 g	(*1 oz*) butter
1	shallot, chopped
1	green pepper, diced small
1	courgette, diced small
450 g	(*1 lb*) canned frozen lobster meat, thawed and drained
30 g	(*1 oz*) flour
400 ml	(*⅔ pt*) chicken stock, heated
50 ml	(*2 fl oz*) double cream
	salt and pepper
dash	paprika
	toasted bread

Melt butter in frying pan over medium-low heat. Add shallot, green pepper and courgette; cover and cook 8 minutes.

Stir in lobster and season well; sprinkle in paprika. Cook 3 minutes, uncovered. Remove lobster and set aside.

Add flour to vegetables in pan and mix until well incorporated. Cook 2 minutes over low heat.

Pour in chicken stock, mix and bring to boil. Cook 4 to 5 minutes over medium-low heat.

Add cream, stir and correct seasoning. Cook 2 to 3 minutes over low heat. Return lobster to sauce, stir and spoon over toasted bread.

1 serving	342 calories	26 g carbohydrate
28 g protein	14 g fat	2.4 g fibre

Lobster Coquilles in Tomato Sauce

serves 4

30 g	(*1 oz*) butter
2	garlic cloves, smashed and chopped
2	shallots, chopped
450 g	(*1 lb*) canned frozen lobster meat, thawed and drained
800 g	(*1¾ lb*) canned tomatoes, drained and chopped
5 ml	(*1 tsp*) oregano
60 g	(*2 oz*) grated mozzarella cheese
	salt and pepper

Melt butter in frying pan over low heat. Add garlic and shallots and cook 2 to 3 minutes.

Mix in lobster meat and cook 2 to 3 minutes over high heat. Remove lobster and set aside.

Add tomatoes and oregano to pan; season well. Cook 8 to 10 minutes over medium heat.

Return lobster to sauce, stir and add cheese. Cook 2 minutes; then transfer to individual scallop dishes. Serve at once.

1 serving	269 calories	9 g carbohydrate
29 g protein	13 g fat	1.7 g fibre

Escargots with Garlic Butter*

serves 4

225 g	(½ lb) unsalted butter
15 ml	(1 tbsp) chopped fresh parsley
3	garlic cloves, smashed and chopped
3	shallots, chopped
24	snail shells
24	canned snails, well washed and drained
	salt and pepper
	few drops Tabasco sauce
	few drops Worcestershire sauce
	juice ¼ lemon

Place butter, parsley, garlic and shallots in food processor. Season with salt and blend until well combined.

Add Tabasco sauce, Worcestershire sauce, ground pepper and lemon juice. Blend again and set aside.

Preheat oven to 200°C (400°F, gas mark 6) and have ready four escargot dishes, tongs and forks.

Place a small bit of garlic butter in each shell and add a snail. Cover snail with more butter until it is level with top of shell. Place shells in escargot dishes; place dishes on baking sheet and cook 3 minutes in oven.

Change oven setting to grill and set snails on oven rack about 15 cm (6 in) from top element. Grill 2 to 3 minutes or until butter is hot and bubbly.

It is essential that snails be served immediately. They are usually accompanied by thick slices of fresh French bread. (This recipe is not exactly a dieter's dream!)

* Should you need garlic butter for another recipe or just want to have some on hand, feel free to double the ingredients. Garlic butter freezes very well if shaped in a cylindrical tube and wrapped tightly in foil.

1 serving	453 calories	0 g carbohydrate
3 g protein	49 g fat	0 g fibre

1. Garlic butter is easy to make with the help of a food processor. It can also be prepared by hand if you are willing to exert the necessary muscle power.

2. Add the garlic and shallots to the butter and parsley already in bowl of food processor.

3. Season with salt and blend until well combined.

4. Add Tabasco sauce, Worcestershire sauce, ground pepper and lemon juice. Blend again for a few seconds. Then set aside until ready to use.

Aubergine Quiche

serves 4

30 ml	(*2 tbsp*) vegetable oil
1	aubergine, peeled and diced
2	garlic cloves, smashed and chopped
1	courgette, diced
225 g	(*½ lb*) canned tomatoes, drained and chopped
2 ml	(*½ tsp*) tarragon
15 ml	(*1 tbsp*) sweet basil
125 g	(*4 oz*) grated Emmenthal cheese
1	egg
2	egg yolks
250 ml	(*8 fl oz*) double cream
	pastry dough
	salt and black pepper
pinch	nutmeg
pinch	cayenne pepper

Preheat oven to 190°C (*375°F, gas mark 5*). Roll out dough on floured surface and line 23-cm (*9-in*) flan tin. Prick bottom of dough with fork and let rest 1 hour.

Meanwhile, heat oil in frying pan over medium heat. Add aubergine, garlic and courgette; season well. Cook 15 minutes.

Stir in tomatoes and continue cooking another 15 to 20 minutes.

Add tarragon and basil; mix in 60 g (*2 oz*) of cheese. Cook 2 minutes and correct seasoning.

Pour filling into pastry shell and set quiche on baking sheet.

Place whole egg and additional yolks in bowl. Add nutmeg, cayenne pepper, salt and black pepper to taste. Pour in cream and whisk well.

Pour egg mixture into pastry shell and carefully mix with fork to help liquid drain to bottom.

Top with remaining cheese and bake 35 minutes in oven.

Let stand several minutes before slicing.

1 serving	685 calories	24 g carbohydrate
19 g protein	57 g fat	2.6 g fibre

1. Cook aubergine, garlic and courgette in hot oil for 15 minutes over medium heat.

2. Stir in tomatoes and continue cooking another 15 to 20 minutes.

3. Add seasonings and half of cheese; mix well and continue cooking another 2 minutes.

4. Fill oven-ready quiche crust with mixture and prepare to bake in oven.

Bacon and Onion Quiche

serves 4

5	rashers crisp cooked bacon
2	onions, thinly sliced and cooked
15 ml	(*1 tbsp*) chopped fresh parsley
125 g	(*4 oz*) grated Gruyère cheese
1	egg
2	egg yolks
250 ml	(*8 fl oz*) double cream
	pastry dough
	freshly ground pepper
pinch	paprika
pinch	nutmeg

Preheat oven to 190°C (*375°F, gas mark 5*). Roll out dough on floured surface and line 23-cm (*9-in*) flan tin. Prick bottom of dough with fork and let rest 1 hour.

Arrange bacon rashers in bottom of pastry shell. Cover with cooked onions and sprinkle with parsley. Add half of cheese and season with pepper.

Place whole egg and additional yolks in bowl. Pour in cream and add paprika and nutmeg; beat with whisk.

Pour egg mixture into pastry shell and top with remaining cheese. Place quiche on baking sheet and bake 35 minutes in oven.

Let stand several minutes before slicing.

1 serving	662 calories	23 g carbohydrate
21 g protein	54 g fat	1.2 g fibre

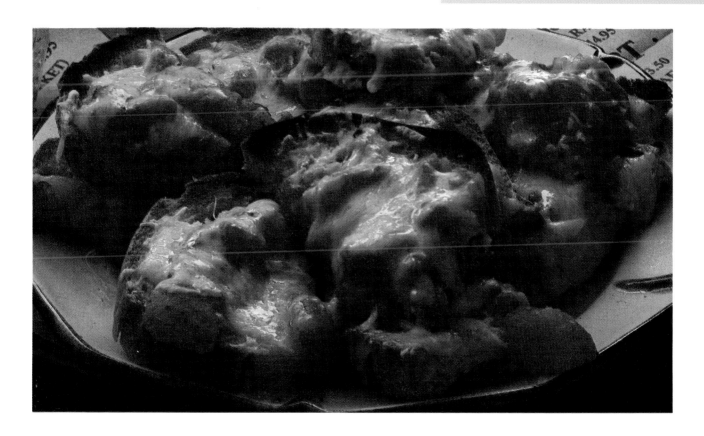

Cheesy Crusty Bread

serves 6–8

30 ml	(*2 tbsp*) olive oil
3	garlic cloves, smashed and chopped
6	medium tomatoes, peeled and diced
15 ml	(*1 tbsp*) oregano
8	large slices lightly toasted crusty bread
175 g	(*6 oz*) grated mozzarella cheese
	salt and freshly ground pepper

Preheat oven to 190°C (*375°F, gas mark 5*).

Heat oil in frying pan over medium heat. When hot, add garlic, tomatoes and oregano; season well and cook 10 minutes.

Arrange bread on baking sheet and top with tomato mixture. Cover with cheese. Change oven setting to grill and cook crusty bread until cheese is melted and bubbly.

Season pieces with freshly ground pepper, slice in half and serve.

1 serving	260 calories	27 g carbohydrate
11 g protein	12 g fat	3.2 g fibre

71

Bruschetta

serves 4

30 ml	(*2 tbsp*) vegetable oil
½	green pepper, chopped
1	onion, chopped
2	garlic cloves, smashed and chopped
50 ml	(*2 fl oz*) dry white wine
800 g	(*1¾ lb*) canned tomatoes, drained and chopped
2 ml	(*½ tsp*) basil
1	fresh French bread
15 ml	(*1 tbsp*) tomato purée
175 g	(*6 oz*) grated Gruyère cheese
pinch	thyme
dash	paprika
	salt and pepper

Heat oil in large frying pan over medium-high heat. Add green pepper, onion and garlic; cook 3 to 4 minutes.

Pour in wine and cook 3 to 4 minutes over high heat.

Add tomatoes and all seasonings. Cook 15 minutes over high heat, stirring several times.

Meanwhile, slice bread into 2 pieces lengthways and cut each half into 4 equal pieces. Toast on both sides in oven.

Add tomato purée to cooking tomato mixture; continue cooking 3 to 4 minutes over medium heat.

Stir in cheese, correct seasoning and spread over toasted bread. Grill 1 minute or so in oven; serve at once.

1 serving	610 calories	57 g carbohydrate
28 g protein	30 g fat	4.5 g fibre

1. Cook green pepper, onion and garlic in hot oil for 3 to 4 minutes over medium-high heat.

2. Add wine and cook 3 to 4 minutes over high heat to reduce liquid by about half.

3. Add tomatoes and all seasonings. Cook 15 minutes over high heat.

4. Add cheese and spread over toasted French bread.

Blue Cheese Dip

150 g	(5 oz) blue cheese
12	stoned black olives
15 ml	(1 tbsp) soured cream
1 ml	(¼ tsp) paprika
30 ml	(2 tbsp) chutney
	salt and pepper
	celery sticks, well washed and cut into 3 pieces

Blend cheese and olives together in food processor for about 1 minute.

Add soured cream and continue blending until combined. Season and sprinkle in paprika.

Add chutney and blend again until smooth. Pour dip into bowl; cover and chill 2 hours.

Spoon dip into piping bag fitted with star nozzle. Stuff celery sticks, or other vegetables if desired. Serve.

1 serving	186 calories	6 g carbohydrate
9 g protein	14 g fat	1.9 g fibre

RISE AND SHINE

*A glorious celebration
to start the day*

Mixed Fruit Salad in Cantaloupe Shells   *serves 2*

1	cantaloupe melon
225 g	(*½ lb*) cubed watermelon
1	orange, peeled and sectioned
90 g	(*3 oz*) mixed green and purple seedless grapes
50 ml	(*2 fl oz*) light rum
30 ml	(*2 tbsp*) chopped walnuts
	juice 1 lime

Cut cantaloupe melon in half using small knife in zigzag cutting motion. Remove seeds and discard. Remove most of flesh and chop; place in bowl.

Add remaining fruits to bowl containing cantaloup melon; sprinkle in rum and mix well. Marinate 15 to 20 minutes.

Sprinkle with lime juice, toss and spoon back into shells. Top with nuts and serve.

1 serving	*329 calories*	*50 g carbohydrate*
5 g protein	*6 g fat*	*6.1 g fibre*

Kiwi Salad with Raspberry Sauce

serves 4

200 g	(7 oz) fresh raspberries, washed
30 ml	(2 tbsp) sugar
50 ml	(2 fl oz) vodka
4	kiwis, peeled and sliced

Drain raspberries well and place in saucepan with sugar and half of vodka. Cover and cook 6 to 8 minutes over medium heat.

Transfer mixture to food processor; blend. Set aside to cool.

Meanwhile, place kiwi slices in bowl and marinate in remaining vodka for 15 minutes.

When ready to serve, spoon kiwi slices into dessert bowls and top with raspberry sauce. If desired, garnish with whipped cream.

1 serving	131 calories	23 g carbohydrate
1 g protein	1 g fat	3.6 g fibre

Grapefruit Salad

serves 4

2	large grapefruit, halved
2	large seedless oranges, halved
90 g	(*3 oz*) mixed green and purple seedless grapes
150 g	(*5 oz*) strawberries, washed, hulled and halved
15 ml	(*1 tbsp*) sugar
	juice 1 orange
	juice 1 lemon

Using paring knife, cut along inside of grapefruit shell to remove entire half in one piece. Set shells aside and section fruit as shown in technique; place in bowl.

Section oranges in same way as grapefruit and add to bowl. Toss in remaining fruit and sugar. Sprinkle in fruit juices and mix lightly.

Spoon fruit back into shells and serve with croissants for a quick, satisfying breakfast.

1 serving	132 calories	31 g carbohydrate
2 g protein	0 g fat	3.3 g fibre

1. Using paring knife, cut along inside of grapefruit shell to remove entire half in one piece.

2. Spoon out any remaining flesh or juice from shells and discard; set shells aside. Take whole grapefruit halves that have been removed and section fruit as shown in picture 4.

3. Remove rind from oranges using a knife. Try to avoid cutting off too much of the flesh.

4. Section fruit by cutting on either side of the casing supporting the segments.

Grilled Pears in Egg Sauce

serves 4

4	egg yolks
100 g	(3½ oz) granulated sugar
375 ml	(13 fl oz) hot milk
30 ml	(2 tbsp) vodka
4	poached pears
30 ml	(2 tbsp) brown sugar
	fresh berries for decoration

Place egg yolks and granulated sugar in stainless-steel bowl; beat together well.

Whisk in milk until well incorporated. Place bowl over saucepan containing hot water. Cook over medium heat, stirring constantly until cream coats back of wooden spoon.

Mix in vodka and set aside to cool.

Place drained poached pears in baking dish. Pour in cooked cream and sprinkle with brown sugar. Grill 1 minute in oven.

Decorate with fresh berries and serve.

1 serving	344 calories	61 g carbohydrate
7 g protein	8 g fat	2.9 g fibre

Strawberries in Red Wine

serves 4

350 g	(¾ *lb*) strawberries, washed and hulled
30 ml	(*2 tbsp*) sugar
300 ml	(½ *pt*) dry red wine
150 ml	(¼ *pt*) whipped cream

Make sure that strawberries are well drained and place in bowl. Sprinkle in sugar and toss gently.

Pour in wine and marinate 2 hours on counter.

Drain strawberries, transfer to clean bowl and decorate with whipped cream.

Purée of Fruit

serves 4

15 g	(½ oz) butter
3	apples, peeled, cored and sliced
30 ml	(2 tbsp) maple syrup
5 ml	(1 tsp) cinnamon
90 g	(3 oz) sultana raisins
300 ml	(½ pt) double cream, whipped
	juice ½ orange
	fresh blackberries for decoration

Melt butter in saucepan over medium heat. Add apples, maple syrup, cinnamon and orange juice; cook 6 minutes, stirring occasionally.

Mix in raisins and continue cooking 3 to 4 minutes.

Transfer contents to food processor and blend until puréed. Set aside to cool.

When ready to serve, fold whipped cream into fruit mixture and spoon into dessert bowls. Decorate with fresh berries.

1 serving	397 calories	41 g carbohydrate
2 g protein	25 g fat	3.5 g fibre

Watermelon Salad in Pineapple Boats

serves 2

1	**fresh ripe pineapple**
170 g	**(*6 oz*) chopped seeded watermelon**
30 ml	**(*2 tbsp*) seedless golden raisins**
5 ml	**(1 tsp) your favourite liqueur**

Slice pineapple in half lengthways using sharp knife. Separate halves and remove centre core from each. Decoratively cut flesh in zigzag pattern to make room for fruit filling.

Chop some of pineapple and place in bowl with watermelon and raisins. Sprinkle in liqueur and toss; let stand 15 minutes.

Fill pineapple boats with fruit filling and serve chilled.

1 serving	*173 calories*	*39 g carbohydrate*
2 g protein	*1 g fat*	*3.9 g fibre*

Poached Pears in Light Syrup

serves 4

225 g	(*½ lb*) granulated sugar
600 ml	(*1 pt*) water
4	pears, cored and peeled
30 ml	(*2 tbsp*) brown sugar
5 ml	(*1 tsp*) butter
5 ml	(*1 tsp*) cinnamon
125 ml	(*4 fl oz*) orange juice
30 ml	(*2 tbsp*) chopped walnuts
	juice 1 lime
	zest 1 orange and 1 lime, cut into julienne

Place granulated sugar, water and lime juice in small saucepan. Bring to boil over high heat and continue cooking 3 minutes. Do not stir.

Meanwhile, place pears, brown sugar, butter and fruit zests in another saucepan. Sprinkle in cinnamon and add orange juice.

Pour in syrup and cook 10 to 12 minutes over medium heat.

Remove saucepan from heat and let pears cool in syrup mixture.

Serve cold with chopped walnuts.

1 serving	292 calories	62 g carbohydrate
2 g protein	4 g fat	3.2 g fibre

1. Peel and core pears neatly to enhance their final appearance.

2. While syrup is being made, place pears in another saucepan.

3. Add brown sugar and butter; sprinkle in julienned fruit zest.

4. Add cinnamon, orange juice and syrup. Cook 10 to 12 minutes over medium heat.

Healthy Banana-Nut Muffins

serves 6–8

150 g	(5 oz) plain flour
150 g	(5 oz) wholemeal flour
125 g	(4 oz) brown sugar
60 g	(2 oz) chopped walnuts
10 ml	(2 tsp) baking powder
5 ml	(1 tsp) cinnamon
2 ml	(½ tsp) salt
2	medium bananas, mashed
2	large eggs
250 ml	(8 fl oz) milk
75 ml	(5 tbsp) vegetable oil

Preheat oven to 200°C (400°F, gas mark 6).

Mix both flours with brown sugar and walnuts. Stir in baking powder, cinnamon and salt.

Place mashed bananas in separate bowl and add eggs, milk and oil; mix until well combined.

Add wet ingredients to dry, mixing just until moistened. Spoon into lightly greased muffin tins and bake 15 to 20 minutes depending on size.

Check that muffins are done before removing from oven. Cool on wire racks several minutes before serving.

1 serving	307 calories	53 g carbohydrate
8 g protein	7 g fat	3.6 g fibre

Eggs en Cocotte

serves 4

4	**large eggs**
250 ml	**(*8 fl oz*) double cream**
	salt and pepper

Preheat oven to 180°C (*350°F, gas mark 4*).

Have ready deep ovenproof tray filled with 2.5 cm (*1 in*) hot water.

Break eggs into cocotte dishes and divide cream among them. Season and set in tray; bake 10 to 12 minutes in oven.

Serve with toast and jam.

1 serving	*288 calories*	*2 g carbohydrate*
7 g protein	*28 g fat*	*0 g fibre*

Two-in-One

serves 4

225 g	(½ lb) plain flour, sifted
45 ml	(3 tbsp) brown sugar
1 ml	(¼ tsp) salt
250 ml	(8 fl oz) milk
250 ml	(8 fl oz) hot water
12	large eggs
45 ml	(3 tbsp) melted butter
30 g	(1 oz) butter
12	rashers crisp cooked bacon
	pure maple syrup

Sift flour, brown sugar and salt into large bowl. Whisk in milk until well incorporated; then whisk in water.

Add 4 eggs and whisk until smooth. Pour through wire sieve into clean bowl and whisk in melted butter. Cover with cling film, touching surface, and chill 1 hour.*

Make crêpes following technique of Allumettes, page 117.

From the stack of crêpes you have just prepared, take 12 and place them in oven to keep hot. Refrigerate or freeze remaining crêpes for later use.

Heat 15 g (½ oz) butter in each of 2 large nonstick frying pans over medium heat.

Add 4 eggs to each pan; cover and cook 4 to 5 minutes over low heat or until done to taste. The whites should be soft and moist.

Meanwhile, arrange 3 crêpes per person on dinner plates, slightly overlapping but also covering most of plate.

When eggs are ready, carefully place 2 on each plate over crêpes and partly cover whites with sides of crêpe. Arrange bacon around plate and moisten with maple syrup. Serve at once.

* The batter can be made the night before, if preferred.

1 serving	875 calories	96 g carbohydrate
26 g protein	43 g fat	1.8 g fibre

1. Sift flour, brown sugar and salt into large bowl.

2. Whisk in milk until well incorporated; then whisk in water.

3. Add 4 eggs and whisk well until smooth.

4. Pour batter through wire sieve into clean bowl and whisk in butter. Cover with cling film, touching surface, and chill 1 hour.

Baked Eggs

serves 4

30 g	(*1 oz*) butter
8	large eggs
	salt and pepper

Preheat oven to 180°C (*350°F, gas mark 4*).

Divide butter into 4 individual ovenproof egg dishes and place in oven to melt.

Break 2 eggs into each dish and season well. Bake 12 to 15 minutes.

Serve with small rounds of toast.

1 serving	201 calories	0 g carbohydrate
12 g protein	17 g fat	0 g fibre

Home-Style Hash Browns and Sausages   *serves 4*

8	**breakfast-style pork sausage links**
4	**potatoes, boiled in skins***
30 g	(*1 oz*) **butter**
2	**shallots, chopped**
15 ml	(*1 tbsp*) **chopped fresh parsley**
5 ml	(*1 tsp*) **chopped fresh chives**
	salt and pepper
	nutmeg to taste

Prepare sausage links for grilling by first cooking them in boiling water for 3 minutes. This technique will remove some of the fat. Drain well and set aside.

Peel potatoes and chop. Heat butter in cast-iron frying pan (or substitute if not available). Add potatoes and cook 20 minutes over low heat, stirring occasionally.

Meanwhile, grill sausages in oven until skins are crisp and insides thoroughly cooked.

Add remaining ingredients to potatoes; mix thoroughly. Cook another 3 to 4 minutes.

Serve sausages with hash browns and accompany with your favourite style of eggs.

* Do not overcook potatoes. For this recipe, they are better if still a little firm.

1 serving	*462 calories*	*52 g carbohydrate*
14 g protein	*22 g fat*	*2.5 g fibre*

Aubergine Baked Eggs

serves 2

30 g	(*1 oz*) butter
1	spring onion, chopped
1/2	small onion, chopped
1	garlic clove, smashed and chopped
1/2	aubergine, peeled and diced
5 ml	(*1 tsp*) chopped fresh parsley
2 ml	(*1/2 tsp*) oregano
1 ml	(*1/4 tsp*) thyme
1	ripe tomato, cored and chopped
60 g	(*2 oz*) grated Cheddar cheese
10 ml	(*2 tsp*) melted butter
4	eggs
	salt and pepper
pinch	sugar
	slices toasted French bread

Melt 30 g (*1 oz*) butter in frying pan over medium heat. Add both onions and garlic; cook 3 minutes.

Stir in aubergine, parsley, oregano and thyme; mix well. Season, cover and cook 15 minutes, stirring frequently.

Add tomato and sugar; correct seasoning and mix well. Cover and continue cooking 10 minutes.

Meanwhile, preheat oven to 180°C (*350°F, gas mark 4*).

Add cheese to aubergine mixture, mix well and cook 1 to 2 minutes. Set aside.

Divide melted butter between two individual ovenproof egg dishes. Place in oven for several minutes to heat.

Cover bottom of dishes with aubergine mixture and return to oven 5 to 6 minutes.

Break 2 eggs into each dish over aubergine and season well. Bake 12 to 15 minutes.

Serve with toast.

1 serving	*494 calories*	*16 g carbohydrate*
22 g protein	*38 g fat*	*2.5 g fibre*

Scrambled Eggs and Mixed Vegetables   *serves 4*

30 g	(*1 oz*) butter
1	cooked carrot, diced
18	fresh mushrooms, cleaned and diced
1	green pepper, diced
1	yellow pepper, diced
5 ml	(*1 tsp*) freshly chopped chives
1	shallot, chopped
8	large eggs
30 ml	(*2 tbsp*) single cream
	salt and pepper

Heat half of butter in nonstick frying pan over medium heat. Add all vegetables, season and cook 3 to 4 minutes over medium-high heat.

Add chives and shallot; continue cooking 1 minute over low heat.

Beat eggs together with cream; season with pepper.

Add remaining butter to vegetables in frying pan and mix. Pour eggs in pan and cook 1 minute at medium-high heat. Stir quickly; cook 1 minute.

Stir quickly; continue cooking until eggs are still soft on top.

1 serving	*276 calories*	*9 g carbohydrate*
15 g protein	*20 g fat*	*3. 7 g fibre*

Scrambled Eggs in Baked Tomatoes

serves 2

1	**large tomato**
10 ml	**(*2 tsp*) garlic butter**
4	**large eggs**
30 ml	**(*2 tbsp*) single cream**
5 ml	**(*1 tsp*) freshly chopped parsley**
30 ml	**(*2 tbsp*) grated Gruyère cheese**
15 g	**(*½ oz*) butter**
	salt and pepper

Preheat oven to 200°C (*400°F, gas mark 6*).

Neatly core tomato and, using zigzag cutting pattern, divide into halves crossways.

Place tomato halves, cut side up, in baking dish and spread 5 ml (*1 tsp*) garlic butter over each. Bake 10 minutes.

Beat eggs together with cream and parsley; season. Sprinkle in cheese and mix again.

Heat butter in nonstick frying pan over medium heat. Pour in eggs and cook 30 seconds. Stir quickly; cook 30 seconds. Stir quickly; continue cooking until eggs are soft on top.

Spoon eggs over tomatoes and serve.

1 serving	345 calories	6 g carbohydrate
15 g protein	29 g fat	1.5 g fibre

1. Core tomato and, using zigzag cutting pattern, divide into halves crossways.

2. Place tomato halves in baking dish and top with garlic butter. Bake 10 minutes.

3. Meanwhile, beat eggs with cream, parsley and cheese. Scramble eggs in nonstick frying pan over medium heat.

4. Spoon eggs over tomatoes and serve.

Scrambled Eggs With Prawns

serves 4

45 g	(*1½ oz*) butter
350 g	(*¾ lb*) medium-size raw prawns, peeled, deveined and sliced into 3
1	shallot, chopped
15 ml	(*1 tbsp*) freshly chopped parsley
30 ml	(*2 tbsp*) flour
250 ml	(*8 fl oz*) hot milk
6	large eggs
30 ml	(*2 tbsp*) single cream
	salt and pepper
pinch	nutmeg

Heat 5 ml (*1 tsp*) butter in saucepan over medium heat. Add prawns, shallot and parsley; season. Cook 5 to 6 minutes over very low heat.

Meanwhile, heat 25 ml (*1½ tbsp*) butter in second saucepan over medium heat. Sprinkle in flour and mix rapidly. Cook 1 minute. Pour in milk, mix well and season with nutmeg. Cook sauce 7 minutes over low heat, stirring occasionally.

Add prawns to white sauce, mixing well, and simmer over very low heat until eggs are done.

Prepare eggs by beating with cream; season with pepper. Heat rest of butter in large nonstick frying pan over medium heat. Pour in eggs and cook 1 minute.

Stir quickly; cook 1 minute. Stir quickly; continue cooking until eggs are soft on top.

Serve with prawns in sauce.

1 serving	375 calories	8 g carbohydrate
34 g protein	23 g fat	0.3 g fibre

Scrambled Eggs with Cheese

serves 4

6	large eggs
30 ml	(*2 tbsp*) single cream
30 ml	(*2 tbsp*) chopped fresh chives
125 g	(*4 oz*) grated well-aged white Cheddar cheese
30 g	(*1 oz*) butter
	salt and pepper
dash	paprika

Beat eggs with cream, chives and cheese, using fork. Season well.

Heat butter in large nonstick frying pan over medium-high heat.

When butter is bubbling, pour in eggs and cook 15 seconds without stirring. Stir gently with wooden spoon to give eggs shape; let cook another 15 seconds without stirring.

Monitor heat carefully — if heat is too high, eggs will become rubbery.

When eggs are cooked but still soft and moist, immediately remove from stove, sprinkle with paprika and serve. Accompany with slices of raisin bread and fresh fruit.

1 serving	310 calories	2 g carbohydrate
17 g protein	26 g fat	0 g fibre

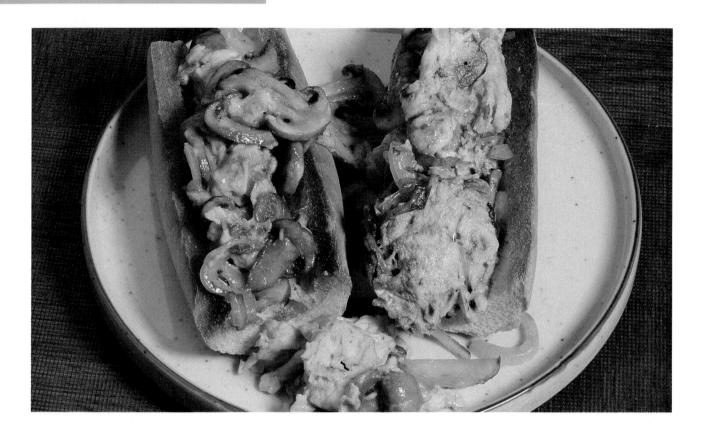

Scrambled Mushroom Eggs on Quarter Loaves   *serves 4*

30 g	(*1 oz*) butter
1/2	Spanish onion, thinly sliced
225 g	(*1/2 lb*) fresh mushrooms, cleaned and sliced
6	large eggs
2 ml	(*1/2 tsp*) celery seeds
1	French bread
	salt and pepper
pinch	paprika
pinch	nutmeg

Heat butter in nonstick frying pan over low heat. Add onion and cook 8 to 10 minutes or until soft.

Add mushrooms and all seasonings; continue cooking 3 to 4 minutes over medium heat.

Beat eggs with fork, pour into pan with mushrooms and proceed to scramble.

Meanwhile, cut French bread in half and then cut each piece into two again lengthways, for a total of 4 pieces. Toast lightly under grill.

Serve scrambled eggs over quarter loaves.

1 serving	429 calories	51 g carbohydrate
18 g protein	17 g fat	4.3 g fibre

Scrambled Eggs à la Française

serves 6–8

8	**large eggs**
50 ml	**(2 fl oz) single cream**
60 g	**(2 oz) grated Swiss cheese**
30 g	**(1 oz) butter**
	salt and pepper

Beat eggs with cream and cheese, using fork. Season with pepper.

Place stainless steel bowl over saucepan containing 750 ml (1¼ pt) boiling water set over medium heat.

Add butter to bowl and let melt. Pour in beaten egg mixture and whisk gently and constantly until eggs are softly scrambled. If you stop stirring, eggs will probably stick to bowl.

Serve, buffet style, with Rösti Potatoes (page 122) or Home-Style Hash Browns and Sausages (page 91).

1 serving	*144 calories*	*0 g carbohydrate*	**99**
9 g protein	*12 g fat*	*0 g fibre*	

Soft-Boiled Eggs in Crêpe Bundles

serves 4

4	large eggs, at room temperature
8	crêpes*
60 g	(2 oz) grated well-aged white Cheddar cheese
	salt and pepper

Using spoon, carefully immerse eggs in saucepan filled with gently boiling water. Boil 5 minutes.

Remove eggs from water and quickly cool in cold water for 1 minute only.

Carefully peel shells and set each egg on 2 stacked crêpes. Wrap into bundles and place in baking dish.

Sprinkle with cheese and grill 2 minutes. Serve at once. Have salt and pepper at table for seasoning.

* See Crêpes Stuffed with Veal, page 224.

1 serving	436 calories	35 g carbohydrate
20 g protein	24 g fat	1.4 g fibre

1. Using spoon, carefully immerse eggs in saucepan filled with gently boiling water. Boil 5 minutes.

2. Remove eggs from water and quickly cool in cold water for 1 minute only just long enough to stop cooking process.

3. Carefully peel shells and set each egg on 2 stacked crêpes. Finish recipe as directed.

4. A properly cooked soft-boiled egg should have a runny yolk similar to this one.

Soft-Boiled Eggs

serves 4

4	**large eggs**
4	**slices toasted bread, cut into sticks**

Have eggs ready at room temperature. Bring plenty of water to boil in saucepan.

Add eggs and boil 3 to 4 minutes or a little longer, depending on your taste.

Remove eggs from water and place in egg cups. Carefully slice off top of each egg and serve with toast.

1 serving	118 calories	8 g carbohydrate
8 g protein	6 g fat	0.4 g fibre

Soft-Boiled Eggs with Mushroom Garnish   *serves 2*

4	large eggs, at room temperature
30 g	(*1 oz*) butter
225 g	(*½ lb*) fresh mushrooms, cleaned and sliced
3	shallots, chopped
15 ml	(*1 tbsp*) chopped fresh chives
1	garlic clove, smashed and chopped
60 g	(*2 oz*) grated Emmenthal cheese
	salt and pepper

Using spoon, carefully immerse eggs in saucepan filled with gently boiling water. Boil 5 minutes.

Remove eggs from water and quickly cool in cold water for 1 minute only.

Carefully peel shells and set 2 eggs in each individual egg plate. Set aside.

Heat butter in large frying pan over medium-high heat. Add remaining ingredients except cheese and cook 3 to 4 minutes.

Spoon mushroom garnish over eggs, season and top with cheese. Grill in oven until melted.

1 serving	*465 calories*	*6 g carbohydrate*
27 g protein	*37 g fat*	*3.1 g fibre*

Eggs Bretonne

serves 4

30 g	(*1 oz*) butter
1	onion, thinly sliced
1	leek*, white stalk washed and thinly sliced
225 g	(*½ lb*) fresh mushrooms, cleaned and sliced
400 ml	(*⅔ pt*) white sauce, heated
4	hard-boiled eggs, sliced
60 g	(*2 oz*) grated Cheddar cheese
	paprika
	salt and pepper

Preheat oven to 200°C (*400°F, gas mark 6*).

Heat butter in frying pan over medium-high heat. Add onion and leek; season with paprika. Cook 3 to 4 minutes.

Add mushrooms and season well; continue cooking 5 to 6 minutes. Remove pan from heat.

Spoon half of white sauce in medium-size baking dish. Add vegetable mixture from frying pan.

Cover with layer of sliced eggs and top with remaining white sauce. Sprinkle with Cheddar cheese and season.

Bake 8 minutes in oven. Serve.

* Slit stalk lengthways twice almost to base. With leaves now parted, wash thoroughly in cold water to remove sand and grit.

1 serving	344 calories	20 g carbohydrate
12 g protein	24 g fat	3.1 g fibre

Mixed Pepper and Mushroom Omelette   *serves 2*

30 g	(*1 oz*) butter
⅓	green pepper, thinly sliced
⅓	yellow pepper, thinly sliced
8	large fresh mushrooms, cleaned and sliced
1	shallot, chopped
15 ml	(*1 tbsp*) freshly chopped parsley
4	large eggs, beaten
	salt and pepper

Heat half of butter in medium-size nonstick frying pan over medium heat. Add vegetables, shallot and parsley; season well. Cook 3 minutes, stirring once during process.

Add remaining butter, let melt, then pour in beaten eggs. Increase heat to medium-high and cook 30 seconds.

Using wooden spoon, stir middle of omelette. Pat eggs back into shape and continue cooking 1 minute or longer until eggs are set but still soft.

Fold omelette in 3 (first right side, then left) and turn out onto heated platter. Cut in half and serve.

1 serving	287 calories	6 g carbohydrate
14 g protein	23 g fat	2.6 g fibre

Apple-Raisin Omelette

serves 2

30 g	(*1 oz*) butter
2	apples, peeled, cored, quartered and sliced
30 ml	(*2 tbsp*) brown sugar
30 ml	(*2 tbsp*) sultana raisins
15 ml	(*1 tbsp*) plum jelly
4	large eggs
30 ml	(*2 tbsp*) single cream
15 ml	(*1 tbsp*) granulated sugar

Preheat oven to 120°C (*250°F, gas mark ½*).

Heat 15 g (*½ oz*) butter in nonstick frying pan. Cook apples and brown sugar, covered, 4 minutes over medium heat.

Stir in raisins and continue cooking 2 minutes. Add jelly, mix well and finish cooking 3 to 4 minutes, uncovered. Transfer to ovenproof dish and keep hot in oven.

Heat remaining butter in nonstick frying pan over medium-high heat. Meanwhile, beat eggs and cream together with fork.

Pour eggs into hot butter and let cook 30 seconds without stirring.

Gently stir middle of omelette to help eggs set. Continue cooking 30 seconds or until eggs have taken shape but are still soft. Then, using spatula, start rolling omelette from right to left while tilting pan in direction of roll. Sprinkle sugar on underside of omelette to glaze.

Turn omelette out onto heated platter and slit middle as shown on facing page. Stuff with some of apple mixture and spoon remainder over omelette. Slice and serve.

1 serving	481 calories	51 g carbohydrate
13 g protein	25 g fat	3.4 g fibre

1. Cook apples and brown sugar, covered, in nonstick frying pan 4 minutes over medium heat.

2. Stir in raisins and continue cooking 2 minutes.

3. Add plum jelly, mix well and finish cooking 3 to 4 minutes, uncovered.

4. Once omelette is made, slit middle with knife and stuff with some of apple mixture. Spoon remaining mixture over omelette.

Strawberry Omelette

serves 2

150 g	(5 oz) strawberries, washed and hulled
45 ml	(3 tbsp) sugar
15 ml	(1 tbsp) very finely chopped lemon zest
4	large eggs
30 ml	(2 tbsp) single cream
15 g	(½ oz) butter
	fresh strawberries for decoration

Place strawberries, sugar and lemon zest in saucepan. Cook 3 to 4 minutes over medium heat, stirring once.

Transfer contents to food processor; blend until puréed. Set aside.

Beat eggs with cream in small bowl. Heat butter in medium-size nonstick frying pan over medium heat.

Increase heat to medium-high and pour in eggs; let cook 30 seconds without stirring.

Gently stir middle of omelette to help eggs set. Continue cooking 30 seconds, or until eggs have taken shape but are still soft.

Spoon 60 ml (4 tbsp) of strawberry sauce over eggs and begin rolling omelette from right to left using spatula, tilting pan in direction of roll.

Turn omelette out onto heated platter and serve with remaining sauce. Decorate with fresh strawberries.

1 serving	327 calories	26 g carbohydrate
13 g protein	19 g fat	2.2 g fibre

Banana-Filled Omelette

serves 2

45 g	(1½ oz) butter
2	bananas, sliced
30 ml	(2 tbsp) brown sugar
4	large eggs
50 ml	(2 fl oz) milk or single cream
30 ml	(2 tbsp) rum

Heat 15 g (½ oz) butter in small frying pan over medium heat. Add bananas and brown sugar; cook 2 to 3 minutes. Set aside.

Beat eggs with milk and rum; set aside.

Heat remaining butter in nonstick frying pan over medium-high heat. When hot, pour in eggs and let cook 30 seconds without stirring.

Gently stir middle of omelette to help eggs set. Continue cooking 30 seconds or until eggs have taken shape but are still soft.

Spread half of bananas over eggs and begin rolling omelette from right to left using spatula, tilting pan in direction of roll.

Turn nicely browned omelette out onto heated platter and decorate with remaining bananas.

1 serving	509 calories	37 g carbohydrate
14 g protein	30 g fat	3.9 g fibre

Western Omelette

serves 2

30 g	(*1 oz*) butter
1/2	onion, chopped
1	spring onion, chopped
1/2	green pepper, chopped
75 g	(*2 1/2 oz*) leftover cooked ham, diced
4	eggs
	salt and pepper

Heat butter in medium-size nonstick frying pan over medium heat. Add vegetables and ham; cook 4 minutes. Season well.

Beat eggs with fork and season. Increase heat to medium-high and pour eggs over vegetables. Let cook 1 minute without stirring.

Gently stir middle of omelette to help eggs set. Continue cooking 1 to 2 minutes, or until eggs have taken shape but are still soft. Then, using spatula, start to roll omelette from the right side towards the left, tilting pan in direction of roll.

Keep heat on while you are rolling to finish cooking eggs — the underside should be nicely browned. When omelette is rolled to far edge of pan, position plate against edge and turn frying pan upside-down, spilling omelette out onto plate. This technique takes some practice, but once you have acquired the skill all your omelettes will be perfectly shaped.

Slice omelette and serve at once.

1 serving	321 calories	4 g carbohydrate
20 g protein	25 g fat	0.7 g fibre

Poached Eggs with Hollandaise Sauce serves 4

2	**egg yolks**
30 ml	(*2 tbsp*) **cold water**
250 ml	(*8 fl oz*) **clarified butter**
4	**small slices toasted bread**
4	**slices Black Forest ham, heated**
4	**poached eggs, hot**
	few drops lemon juice
	salt and pepper

Place egg yolks in stainless steel bowl. Add water and set bowl over saucepan containing 750 ml (*1¼ pt*) hot water. Do not place over heat.

Whisk egg yolks until very thick. Then incorporate clarified butter in thin stream while whisking constantly.

Add few drops lemon juice and season to taste.

Arrange plates with toasted bread covered with ham and topped with poached egg. Pour sauce over and serve immediately.

1 serving	602 calories	8 g carbohydrate
12 g protein	58 g fat	0.4 g fibre

Cheese Soufflé

serves 4

175 g	(*6 oz*) grated Gruyère, Emmenthal or mozzarella cheese
60 g	(*2 oz*) butter
40 g	(*1¼ oz*) flour
300 ml	(*½ pt*) cold milk
4	egg yolks, room temperature
5	egg whites, beaten stiff at room temperature
	salt and pepper
	extra butter for mould

Preheat oven to 190°C (*375°F, gas mark 5*). Butter 1.5-litre (*2¾-pt*) soufflé mould; sprinkle sides and bottom with cheese.

Melt butter in saucepan over very low heat. Mix in flour using wooden spoon and cook 3 to 4 minutes.

Pour in half of milk and stir 2 minutes over medium heat. Gradually add remaining milk while stirring constantly to make smooth paste.

Add salt and slowly bring to boil, stirring constantly until mixture starts to adhere slightly to pan. This should take about 3 to 4 minutes. Remove from heat and let cool slightly.

Add egg yolks, one by one, mixing with wooden spoon between additions. Add cheese and pepper.

Incorporate large spoonful of beaten egg white to yolk mixture. Then pour yolks into bowl containing whites. Use spatula to fold together until batter is an even colour.

Pour batter into mould and run thumb around inside edge, about 1 cm (*½ in*) deep into batter. This will form an extra little top. Bake 35 minutes.

1 serving	455 calories	11 g carbohydrate
24 g protein	35 g fat	0.3 g fibre

1. Prepare soufflé mould by greasing well with butter and sprinkling sides and bottom with grated cheese; set aside.

2. Melt butter in saucepan over low heat. Mix in flour and incorporate, using wooden spoon. Cook 3 to 4 minutes over very low heat.

3. Pour half of milk into saucepan and stir several minutes while cooking over medium heat. Continue incorporating milk a little at a time, stirring to make smooth paste.

4. When time, add egg yolks one by one, mixing well with wooden spoon between additions. Notice that saucepan has been removed from heat.

Potato Soufflé

serves 4

30 g	(*1 oz*) grated mozzarella cheese
450 g	(*1 lb*) white potatoes, peeled
45 g	(*1½ oz*) butter
1 ml	(*¼ tsp*) nutmeg
125 ml	(*4 fl oz*) single cream, heated
4	egg yolks, room temperature
6	egg whites, room temperature
	salt and pepper
dash	paprika
dash	savory
dash	cayenne pepper
	extra butter for mould

Preheat oven to 190°C (*375°F, gas mark 5*).

Butter a 1.5-litre (*2¾-pt*) soufflé mould and sprinkle sides and bottom with mozzarella cheese; set aside.

Cut potatoes into small pieces to decrease cooking time and place in saucepan filled with water; season with salt. Boil until just cooked — do not overcook!

Drain potatoes well and return to saucepan. Place over low heat and dry several minutes. Purée through potato ricer into large bowl.

Stir in butter until well incorporated. Add all seasonings and mix well. Pour in cream and incorporate. Mixture should have consistency of mashed potatoes.

Using wooden spoon, beat in all egg yolks at the same time. Set bowl aside.

Beat egg whites until stiff, using copper bowl if available, and spoon a bit of white into egg yolk mixture. Incorporate well.

Fold egg yolk mixture into egg whites, using rubber spatula to incorporate evenly. Rotate bowl while folding and continue until no trace of white is left.

Pour batter into mould and run thumb around inside edge, about 1 cm (*½ in*) deep into batter. This will form an extra little top. Bake 35 minutes.

1 serving	296 calories	18 g carbohydrate
11 g protein	20 g fat	2.4 g fibre

Crêpe Bouchées

serves 6–8

45 g	(*1½ oz*) butter
2	shallots, finely chopped
125 g	(*4 oz*) fresh button mushrooms, cleaned and finely chopped
15 ml	(*1 tbsp*) finely chopped fresh parsley
5 ml	(*1 tsp*) herbes de Provence
30 ml	(*2 tbsp*) flour
375 ml	(*13 fl oz*) milk
60 g	(*2 oz*) grated Gruyère cheese
8	crêpes*
	few drops Tabasco sauce
dash	paprika
	salt and pepper
	several large oranges (optional)

Heat butter in frying pan over medium heat. Cook shallots, button mushrooms and seasonings, including herbs, 3 to 4 minutes to evaporate moisture from mushrooms.

Season well and stir in flour. Mix and continue cooking 2 minutes over low heat.

Pour in milk while mixing with wooden spoon. Increase heat to medium-low and season. Continue cooking 3 to 4 minutes or until smooth.

Add cheese and mix well. Remove sauce from heat and set aside to cool.

Spread mushroom mixture over each crêpe, covering whole surface. Roll loosely and place on plate; cover lightly with cling film. Chill 2 hours.

Slice crêpe rolls into pieces about 2.5 cm (*1 in*) long. Serve cold or, if preferred, warm several minutes under grill.

Use oranges for creative presentation, if desired.

* See Crêpes Stuffed with Veal, page 224.

1 serving	121 calories	5 g carbohydrate
5 g protein	9 g fat	0.5 g fibre

Crêpes Savoyardes

serves 4

8	**crêpes***
8	**thin slices Black Forest ham**
8	**thin slices Gruyère cheese or 175 g (*6 oz*) grated cheese**
30 ml	(*2 tbsp*) **melted butter**
dash	**paprika**
	pepper

Preheat oven to 180°C (*350°F, gas mark 4*).

Stack ham and cheese on each crêpe. Season with paprika and pepper lightly. Roll and place in baking dish.

Baste crêpes with melted butter and bake 10 to 15 minutes in oven.

* See Crêpes Stuffed with Veal, page 224.

1 serving	*560 calories*	*50 g carbohydrate*
27 g protein	*28 g fat*	*1.4 g fibre*

Allumettes

serves 6–8

225 g	(½ lb) plain flour
1 ml	(¼ tsp) salt
250 ml	(8 fl oz) cold milk
3	eggs
250 ml	(8 fl oz) beer
45 ml	(3 tbsp) melted butter
	your favourite jam
	granulated sugar

Place flour and salt in large bowl. Whisk in milk. Add eggs; mix very well.

Mix in beer until batter is smooth. Strain batter and stir in butter. Cover with sheet of cling film touching surface; chill 1 hour.

Lightly butter crêpe pan and place over high heat. Mix batter well. When butter is hot, pour in small ladle of batter. Tilt pan and rotate, causing batter to cover bottom of pan. Cook 1 minute over medium-high heat until underside is lightly browned.

Turn crêpe over; cook 30 seconds. Stack crêpes on plate as they are cooked and monitor heat. Grease pan if needed.

To serve, spread opened crêpe with jam. Roll and place on ovenproof platter; sprinkle with granulated sugar. Grill 3 minutes.

1 serving	295 calories	50 g carbohydrate
6 g protein	7 g fat	1.1 g fibre

Croque-Madame

serves 4

8	**thick slices bread, toasted**
4	**slices cooked ham**
125 g	**(*4 oz*) grated Gruyère cheese**
300 ml	**(*½ pt*) white sauce*, heated**
	salt and pepper

Arrange 4 slices of bread on large ovenproof platter. Cover each with slice of ham and top with 60 g (*2 oz*) cheese. Season well.

Close sandwiches with remaining bread and spoon white sauce over each.

Top with remaining cheese and grill 5 to 6 minutes in oven until bubbly and light brown.

Slice and serve.

* See Poached Salmon with Egg Sauce, page 324.

1 serving	*476 calories*	*39 g carbohydrate*
26 g protein	*24 g fat*	*1.6 g fibre*

1. Arrange 4 slices of bread on large ovenproof platter and cover each with ham.

2. Top with grated cheese, reserving half. Be sure to season well.

3. Close sandwiches with remaining bread.

4. Spoon white sauce over each sandwich; sprinkle with remaining cheese before grilling in oven.

Apple-Raisin Sauté for French Toast

serves 4

30 g	(*1 oz*) butter
3	apples, peeled, cored, quartered and sliced
90 g	(*3 oz*) sultana raisins
1 ml	(*¼ tsp*) cinnamon
30 ml	(*2 tbsp*) maple syrup
dash	nutmeg

Heat butter in frying pan over medium heat. Add apples, raisins, cinnamon and nutmeg; mix well. Cook 8 to 10 minutes.

Stir in maple syrup and continue cooking another 5 minutes.

Serve with French toast, pancakes or eggs.

1 serving	*206 calories*	*37 g carbohydrate*
1 g protein	*6 g fat*	*3.4 g fibre*

Delicious French Toast

serves 4

5	large eggs
50 ml	(*2 fl oz*) single cream
15 ml	(*1 tbsp*) honey
8	thick slices French bread, with crust
45 g	(*1½ oz*) butter
	strawberry jam
	icing sugar

Preheat oven to 110°C (*225°F, gas mark ¼*).

Beat eggs with cream and honey in large bowl.

Dip 4 slices of bread into mixture to coat thoroughly; transfer to plate.

Heat half of butter in large nonstick frying pan. When hot, add first 4 pieces of bread. Cook over medium heat 2 minutes on each side or until nicely browned.

Transfer first batch to ovenproof platter and keep hot.

Repeat above procedure with remaining butter and slices of bread.

Serve with strawberry jam and sprinkle portions with a little icing sugar.

1 serving	483 calories	65 g carbohydrate
13 g protein	19 g fat	1.8 g fibre

Rösti Potatoes

serves 4

4	**large potatoes, boiled in skins***
4	**rashers of bacon, diced small**
30 g	(*1 oz*) **butter**
	salt and pepper

Peel potatoes and grate into long, fine strands; set aside.

Cook bacon in large nonstick frying pan over medium heat until done. Discard bacon pieces, leaving fat in pan.

Quickly add grated potatoes to pan and cook 10 to 12 minutes over medium heat, stirring frequently. Season several times during cooking.

Using wide metal spatula, press potatoes down flat. Lift up corner and slip butter underneath. Continue cooking 6 to 7 minutes or until nicely browned on bottom.

To serve, flip over to show browned side.

* Do not overcook potatoes.

1 serving	205 calories	27 g carbohydrate
4 g protein	9 g fat	2.7 g fibre

1. Peel potatoes and grate into long, fine stands; set aside.

2. Cook bacon in large nonstick frying pan over medium heat until done. Discard bacon pieces, leaving fat in pan.

3. Quickly add grated potatoes to pan and cook 10 to 12 minutes over medium heat, stirring frequently. Season several times during cooking.

4. Using wide spatula, press potatoes down flat. Lift up corner and slip butter underneath. Continue cooking 6 to 7 minutes or until nicely browned on bottom.

Cottage Cheese Pancakes

serves 4

4	eggs, separated
25 ml	(1½ tbsp) sugar
60 ml	(4 tbsp) cottage cheese
40 g	(1¼ oz) plain flour
30 ml	(2 tbsp) melted butter
	extra cottage cheese and maple syrup

Using electric mixer, beat egg whites in small bowl until quite foamy. Add sugar and continue beating until stiff.

Beat yolks in separate bowl and incorporate cheese; blend well.

Add flour to egg yolks; then incorporate beaten whites. Mix batter until quite smooth. Stir in melted butter.

Heat frying pan or griddle with thin film of oil. Cook pancakes over medium-high heat until nicely browned on both sides.

Serve with extra cheese and maple syrup.

1 serving	308 calories	39 g carbohydrate
11 g protein	12 g fat	0.2 g fibre

Cocoa and Whipped Cream

serves 2

300 ml	(*½ pt*) **double cream, chilled**
2 ml	(*½ tsp*) **vanilla**
15 ml	(*1 tbsp*) **icing sugar**
60 ml	(*4 tbsp*) **cocoa**
60 ml	(*4 tbsp*) **granulated sugar**
500 ml	(*17 fl oz*) **scalded milk, still hot**
	grated mint-flavoured chocolate

To make whipped cream, chill stainless steel bowl in refrigerator. Pour cold cream and vanilla into bowl; beat with electric beater until peaks form.

Sprinkle in icing sugar and incorporate, using rubber spatula. Set aside in refrigerator.

In another stainless steel bowl, mix cocoa with granulated sugar. Gradually add milk while whisking constantly.

Pour cocoa into 2 large glasses. Top with whipped cream (use piping bag for ease) and sprinkle each serving with a little grated chocolate.

1 serving	*778 calories*	*58 g carbohydrate*
15 g protein	*54 g fat*	*1.2 g fibre*

Bavarian Coffee

serves 4

125 g	(*4 oz*) semi-sweet chocolate
400 ml	(*⅔ pt*) double cream, whipped
	strong hot black coffee for four
dash	cinnamon

Place chocolate in stainless steel bowl placed over saucepan half-filled with hot water. Heat saucepan so that water is bubbling and melts chocolate.

Place hot coffee into pitcher and mix in melted chocolate. Pour into four Irish-coffee glasses or attractive mugs, being sure to leave at least 2.5 cm (*1 in*) free for cream. Carefully spoon whipped cream into glasses so that it rests on liquid.

Sprinkle with cinnamon and serve at once.

1 serving	518 calories	12 g carbohydrate
5 g protein	50 g fat	0.8 g fibre

RUSH-HOUR COOKING

*Fast, fun cooking
for those on the run*

Gourmet Pitta Pizza

serves 4

15 ml	(*1 tbsp*) olive oil
1	garlic clove, smashed and chopped
15 ml	(*1 tbsp*) chopped fresh parsley
1	onion, chopped
2	shallots, chopped
800 g	(*1¾ lb*) canned tomatoes, drained and chopped
30 ml	(*2 tbsp*) tomato purée
½	jalapeño pepper, chopped
4	large wholemeal or plain pitta breads
½	green pepper, thinly sliced
225 g	(*½ lb*) fresh mushrooms, cleaned and sliced
225 g	(*½ lb*) grated mozzarella cheese
	salt and pepper
pinch	sugar
	sliced pepperoni sausage
dash	paprika

Heat oil in large frying pan. Add garlic, parsley, onion and shallots; cook 5 to 6 minutes over low heat.

Stir in tomatoes and season well; cook 20 minutes over low heat.

Mix in tomato purée and chopped jalapeño pepper. Sprinkle in sugar, stir and finish cooking 7 to 8 minutes over low heat.

At this point, the sauce is ready and may be stored for later use. Let cool and then cover with cling film touching surface. Refrigerate up to 4 days.

To prepare pizza, preheat oven to 200°C (*400°F, gas mark 6*).

Arrange pitta breads on baking sheets. Spread tomato sauce over breads and garnish with green pepper, mushrooms and pepperoni slices.

Top with grated cheese and season with salt, pepper and paprika. Cook 12 minutes in oven.

128

1 serving	854 calories	70 g carbohydrate
40 g protein	46 g fat	4.0 g fibre

1. Begin gourmet tomato sauce by sautéing garlic, parsley, onion and shallots 5 to 6 minutes in hot olive oil.

2. Stir in tomatoes and season well; cook 20 minutes over low heat.

3. Mix in tomato purée and jalapeño pepper. (Decrease amount of hot pepper for a milder sauce.) Sprinkle in sugar to offset bitterness that may be caused by tomato purée; stir well. Finish cooking sauce 7 to 8 minutes over low heat. Prepare to make pizza or cool sauce for refrigeration.

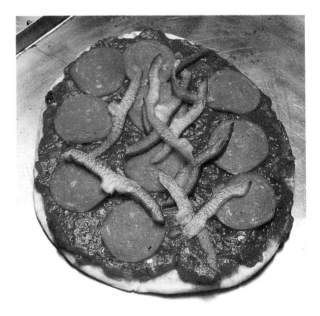

4. Garnish pitta breads with vegetables and pepperoni slices. You can substitute our suggestions with courgette slices, julienned carrot and anything else that might intrigue you.

Quick Prawn Salad on French Bread

serves 2

12	medium prawns
2	slices lemon
1/2	celery stick, chopped
1/4	green pepper, chopped
2	tomato slices, chopped
5 ml	(*1 tsp*) chopped fresh parsley
5 ml	(*1 tsp*) Dijon mustard
30 ml	(*2 tbsp*) mayonnaise
	few drops lemon juice
	salt and pepper
	few drops Tabasco sauce
	fresh French bread

Place prawns in saucepan and pour in enough cold water to cover. Add lemon slices and bring to boil.

Immediately remove pan from heat and let stand 5 to 6 minutes on cutting board. Drain prawns, peel and devein.

Dice prawns and place in bowl with vegetables; toss together. Add parsley, mustard and mayonnaise; mix well.

Season salad with lemon juice, salt, pepper and Tabasco sauce.

Serve on opened slices of French bread.

1 serving	747 calories	95 g carbohydrate
49 g protein	19 g fat	6.4 g fibre

Salad in a Roll

serves 4

200 g	(7 oz) frozen mixed vegetables
4	slices cooked ham, cut into strips
3	hard-boiled eggs, chopped
15 ml	(1 tbsp) chopped fresh chives
45 ml	(3 tbsp) mayonnaise
	salt and pepper
	juice 1 lemon
	wholemeal or kaiser rolls

Cook frozen vegetables according to directions on package. Cool in cold water, drain well and place in bowl.

Add ham and eggs; season with salt and pepper.

Sprinkle in chives and mix in mayonnaise. Add lemon juice and mix well again.

Slice tops off rolls and scoop out most of insides. Spoon vegetable salad into hollow rolls and serve with tops as decoration. If desired, accompany with sliced fresh fruit.

1 serving	360 calories	37 g carbohydrate
17 g protein	16 g fat	2.5 g fibre

Ten-Minute Western Sandwiches for Two   *serves 2*

15 g	(*½ oz*) butter
½	onion, chopped
150 g	(*5 oz*) chopped cooked ham
½	green pepper, chopped
5 ml	(*1 tsp*) chopped fresh parsley
4	large eggs
4	slices toasted bread
	salt and pepper

Melt butter in nonstick frying pan over high heat. Add onion, ham, green pepper and parsley and cook 3 to 4 minutes.

Meanwhile, break eggs into bowl and beat well with fork; season lightly.

Pour eggs over ham mixture in pan. Mix slightly, reduce heat to medium and continue cooking 2 minutes.

Using metal spatula, turn flat omelette over; continue cooking 1 minute.

Slice omelette into 4 pieces and assemble sandwiches. If desired, serve with chips.

1 serving	*454 calories*	*33 g carbohydrate*
31 g protein	*22 g fat*	*1.1 g fibre*

Double Fish Salad

serves 4

2	**cooked sole fillets**
450 g	**(*1 lb*) cooked prawns**
2	**blanched carrots, sliced**
150 g	**(*5 oz*) blanched mangetouts**
2	**large apples, cored and sliced with skin**
1	**spring onion, chopped**
15 ml	**(*1 tbsp*) chopped fresh parsley**
60 ml	**(*4 tbsp*) olive oil**
30 ml	**(*2 tbsp*) red wine vinegar**
	salt and pepper
	lemon juice to taste
	romaine lettuce leaves

Break sole fillets into small pieces and place in bowl with prawns.

Add vegetables and apples; toss ingredients together.

Sprinkle in parsley, oil and vinegar; season well and toss thoroughly.

Season salad with lemon juice to taste and serve on bed of fresh crisp lettuce leaves.

1 serving	376 calories	18 g carbohydrate
40 g protein	16 g fat	5.0 g fibre

133

Hot Chicken and Asparagus Salad

serves 4

1	apple, cored, peeled and sliced
5 ml	(*1 tsp*) lemon juice
2	spring onions, sliced
1	celery stick, chopped
2	boneless half chicken breasts, cooked and still hot
2	tomatoes, cored, halved and sliced
1	endive, separated into leaves
2	bunches fresh asparagus, peeled if needed, cooked and still hot
30 ml	(*2 tbsp*) mayonnaise
30 ml	(*2 tbsp*) double cream
2	fresh mint leaves, chopped
30 g	(*1 oz*) chopped nuts
	salt and pepper

Place apple in large bowl and toss with lemon juice. Add spring onions and celery; season well.

Slice chicken into large strips and add to bowl. Mix in tomatoes and endive leaves.

Cut asparagus stalks into 3 and add to bowl.

Mix in mayonnaise and cream. Season and add chopped mint; mix well. Toss in nuts and serve decorated with slices of fresh fruit.

1 serving	263 calories	14 g carbohydrate
18 g protein	15 g fat	3.9 g fibre

Baby Prawn Salad

serves 4

350 g	(¾ *lb*) cooked baby prawns
1	celery stick, chopped
½	red pepper, chopped
15 ml	(*1 tbsp*) chopped fresh parsley
1	red apple, cored, peeled and coarsely chopped
15 ml	(*1 tbsp*) lemon juice
125 g	(¼ *lb*) French beans, cooked and diced
90 g	(*3 oz*) blanched broccoli florets
1	spring onion, blanched and sliced
60 ml	(*4 tbsp*) mayonnaise
	salt and white pepper
dash	paprika

Rinse prawns in cold water, drain well and pat dry with paper towels.

Place prawns in large bowl with celery, red pepper, parsley and apple. Sprinkle in lemon juice and season well.

Add cooked vegetables and mix well.

Spoon in mayonnaise and season with paprika; mix until thoroughly incorporated.

Correct seasoning and serve.

1 serving	248 calories	12 g carbohydrate
23 g protein	12 g fat	4.8 g fibre

Tomatoes with Sausage-Rice Stuffing

serves 4

4	large tomatoes, well cleaned
15 ml	(*1 tbsp*) vegetable oil
2	garlic cloves, smashed and chopped
1	onion, finely chopped
125 g	(*4 oz*) chopped pork sausagemeat
5 ml	(*1 tsp*) chopped fresh thyme
5 ml	(*1 tsp*) chopped fresh chives
15 ml	(*1 tbsp*) chopped fresh parsley
4	thin slices cooked ham, diced small
225 g	(*8 oz*) cooked long-grain rice
125 g	(*4 oz*) grated well-aged white Cheddar cheese
	salt and pepper
pinch	cayenne pepper

Preheat oven to 190°C (*375°F, gas mark 5*).

Cut off slice from bottom of each tomato so that it stands flat. Using paring knife, cut out top and reserve for decoration. Scoop out about 3/4 of pulp and either discard or keep for other uses.

Season tomato cavities, sprinkle with a few drops oil and set aside in baking dish.

Heat oil in frying pan over medium heat. Cook garlic and onion 3 minutes.

Stir in sausagemeat and fresh herbs; season with salt and pepper. Cook 3 minutes over medium heat.

Add ham, mix well and continue cooking 3 minutes.

Stir in rice, correct seasoning and cook another 3 to 4 minutes.

Incorporate cheese and correct seasoning; sprinkle with cayenne pepper to taste. Cook 2 minutes.

Spoon stuffing into tomatoes and bake 30 minutes in oven or according to size of tomatoes.

Serve with tomato hats as decoration.

1 serving	*339 calories*	*22 g carbohydrate*
20 g protein	*19 g fat*	*2.9 g fibre*

1. Cut off slice from bottom of each tomato. Remove top and reserve for decoration. Scoop out about ¾ of pulp to make room for stuffing. Be sure to leave sturdy shell.

2. Add sausagemeat and fresh herbs to garlic and onion.

3. Mix in ham and continue cooking 3 minutes.

4. Stir in rice, correct seasoning and cook another 3 to 4 minutes.

Welsh Rarebit

serves 2

2	2-cm (*3/4-in*) thick slices bread, toasted
350 g	(*3/4 lb*) grated well-aged Cheddar cheese
1 ml	(*1/4 tsp*) paprika
5 ml	(*1 tsp*) dry mustard
150 ml	(*1/4 pt*) beer
	freshly ground pepper

Set toasted bread aside on serving platter.

Place cheese and paprika in bowl. Pepper to taste. Add mustard and mix well.

Pour beer into nonstick frying pan and bring to boil. Continue cooking to reduce liquid by half.

Add cheese and cook 7 to 8 minutes over medium heat, stirring once or twice.

Spoon over bread and serve.

1 serving	816 calories	22 g carbohydrate
47 g protein	60 g fat	0.8 g fibre

Superstar Hot Dogs

serves 2

15 ml	(*1 tbsp*) vegetable oil
1	onion, thinly sliced
2	hot dog rolls, toasted or steamed
2	beef, pork or veal sausage-type hot dogs, cooked
½	pickled hot banana pepper, thinly sliced
2	slices tomato, halved
	mustard, relish and ketchup

Time the cooking of the onions with the preparation of the rolls and hot dogs so everything is ready and hot at the same time.

Heat vegetable oil in small frying pan. Add onion, cover and cook 15 minutes over medium heat. Stir several times during cooking.

To assemble hot dogs, spoon some of onion mixture into rolls and add hot dog.

Top with condiments to taste followed by remaining onion, sliced banana pepper and tomato.

Serve with pickles and nacho chips.

1 serving	*533 calories*	*38 g carbohydrate*
21 g protein	*33 g fat*	*2.8 g fibre*

Onion Quiche with Mint Seasoning

serves 4–6

30 g	(1 oz) butter
1	large Spanish onion, thinly sliced
15 ml	(1 tbsp) chopped fresh parsley
2	eggs
1	egg yolk
2	fresh mint leaves, chopped
5 ml	(1 tsp) chopped fresh chives
250 ml	(8 fl oz) double cream
125 g	(4 oz) grated Cheddar cheese
	pastry dough
	beaten egg
	salt and pepper

Preheat oven to 190°C (*375°F, gas mark 5*). Roll out dough on floured surface and line 23-cm (*9-in*) flan tin. Prick bottom with fork and brush with beaten egg. Set aside.

Melt butter in frying pan over medium heat. Add onion and parsley; cover and cook 15 minutes.

Remove cover and continue cooking 4 to 5 minutes.

Meanwhile, mix eggs and additional yolk together in small bowl. Add mint, chives and cream; whisk everything together and season generously.

When onions are nicely browned, transfer to bottom of quiche crust. Top with cheese.

Pour egg mixture over cheese and place quiche on baking sheet; bake in oven for 35 minutes.

1 serving	437 calories	15 g carbohydrate
11 g protein	37 g fat	0.8 g fibre

_1._ There are many good-quality prepared pastry doughs available on the market, but if time permits by all means make your own. Be sure to prick the bottom with a fork and brush with beaten egg.

_2._ Cook Spanish onion with parsley in hot butter for 15 minutes over low heat. Cover pan.

_3._ Just before onion is cooked, mix together ingredients for creamy filling that will bind quiche. The chopped mint will lend an interesting flavour.

_4._ Make quiche by filling bottom of crust with onion and topping with Cheddar cheese.

Ham and Apple Stuffed Crêpes

serves 4

2	apples, cored, peeled and diced
45 g	(*1½ oz*) butter
1	red pepper, chopped
3	spring onions, sliced
225 g	(*½ lb*) fresh mushrooms, cleaned and diced
300 g	(*11 oz*) cubed leftover cooked ham
15 ml	(*1 tbsp*) chopped fresh parsley
1 ml	(*¼ tsp*) marjoram
40 g	(*1¼ oz*) flour
500 ml	(*17 fl oz*) chicken stock, heated
200 g	(*7 oz*) grated Gruyère cheese
8	crêpes*
	lemon juice
	salt and pepper
dash	paprika
pinch	nutmeg
	few crushed chillies
pinch	powdered cloves

Place apples in bowl filled with lemony cold water. Set aside.

Reserve 5 ml (*1 tsp*) butter; melt remainder in large frying pan over medium heat. Add red pepper, spring onions and mushrooms; cook 3 to 4 minutes.

Drain apples, add to pan and correct seasoning. Mix in ham, cover and cook 6 minutes over low heat. Add parsley and all seasonings; mix well. Stir in flour until well incorporated; cover and cook 3 minutes over low heat.

Pour in chicken stock, adjust seasoning and bring to boil. Cook 5 to 6 minutes, uncovered, over medium heat.

Mix in half of cheese and cook 2 minutes.

Preheat oven to 200°C (*400°F, gas mark 6*).

Lay crêpes flat on cutting board. Using slotted spoon, divide filling onto crêpes; fold each in half and then in half again to form triangle. Place in large baking dish, pour in remaining sauce and top with rest of cheese.

Dot with 5 ml (*1 tsp*) butter, season with pepper and bake 5 minutes.

* See Crêpes Stuffed with Veal, page 224.

1 serving	825 calories	71 g carbohydrate
43 g protein	41 g fat	4.9 g fibre

1. Cook red pepper, spring onions and mushrooms 3 to 4 minutes in hot butter.

2. Add apples and ham; cover and cook 6 minutes over low heat.

3. Add parsley and all seasonings; mix well. Stir in flour until well incorporated; cover and cook 3 minutes over low heat.

4. Pour in chicken stock, adjust seasoning and bring to boil. Resume cooking.

Baked Ham Slices with Double Mushroom Sauce   *serves 4*

45 g	(*1½ oz*) butter
1	small onion, finely chopped
90 g	(*3 oz*) fresh mushrooms, cleaned and sliced
125 g	(*4 oz*) fresh oyster mushrooms*, cleaned and sliced
1 ml	(*¼ tsp*) nutmeg
30 g	(*1 oz*) flour
500 ml	(*17 fl oz*) milk, heated
8	5-mm (*¼-in*) thick slices cooked ham
2	egg yolks
	salt and pepper

Preheat oven to 180°C (*350°F, gas mark 4*).

Melt butter in frying pan over medium heat. Add onion and cook, covered, 3 minutes.

Add both types of mushrooms and nutmeg; season well. Cover and continue cooking 3 minutes.

Mix in flour until well incorporated. Cook 2 minutes, uncovered, over low heat.

Pour in milk, mix well and season again; continue cooking 8 minutes.

Roll ham slices and place in baking dish.

Remove sauce from heat and add egg yolks; mix very well. Pour sauce over ham and bake 5 to 6 minutes in oven.

Serve with garden salad.

* Oyster mushrooms are a wild variety available most often during the fall and winter months.

1 serving	314 calories	17 g carbohydrate
21 g protein	18 g fat	1.7 g fibre

Scrumptious Potato Omelette

serves 4

45 g	(1½ oz) butter
4	potatoes, peeled, halved and thinly sliced
1	small onion, chopped
15 ml	(1 tbsp) chopped fresh chives
15 ml	(1 tbsp) chopped fresh basil
5 ml	(1 tsp) chopped fresh parsley
15 ml	(1 tbsp) milk
8	beaten eggs
	salt and pepper

The success of an omelette is often determined by the pan. Choose a medium-large nonstick frying pan that has a smooth surface. Add butter and melt over medium heat.

Place potatoes in pan and cover; cook 8 minutes, stirring 2 or 3 times.

Add onion and all fresh herbs; season with salt and pepper. Cook 3 to 4 minutes, uncovered. Check potatoes for doneness and cook a little longer if needed.

Beat milk into eggs. Increase heat to high and pour eggs over potatoes. Season lightly and let cook 1 minute without stirring.

Gently stir omelette to help eggs set and continue cooking 1 to 2 minutes or until eggs have taken shape but are still soft. Then, using spatula, flip omelette over and cook 1 more minute.

Fold omelette in half and serve at once.

1 serving	356 calories	29 g carbohydrate
15 g protein	20 g fat	2.9 g fibre

Ham and Potato Hash Browns

serves 4

30 g	(*1 oz*) butter
1	small onion, finely chopped
450 g	(*1 lb*) leftover cooked ham, chopped
15 ml	(*1 tbsp*) chopped fresh parsley
3	large cooked potatoes, peeled and diced small
15 ml	(*1 tbsp*) chopped fresh chives
	salt and pepper
	vegetable oil, if needed

Melt butter in large frying pan. Add onion, ham and parsley; cook 3 minutes over high heat.

Add potatoes and season well. Continue cooking 8 to 10 minutes, stirring occasionally and adding oil if needed. Toward the end of cooking, start to flatten potatoes with large metal spatula.

Sprinkle chives over potatoes, mix well and finish cooking 2 minutes before serving.

1 serving	407 calories	30 g carbohydrate
29 g protein	19 g fat	2.9 g fibre

Poached Eggs with Chasseur Sauce
serves 4

15 g	(½ oz) butter
3	rashers bacon, diced
1	small onion, chopped
125 g	(¼ lb) fresh mushrooms, cleaned and quartered
30 ml	(2 tbsp) flour
50 ml	(2 fl oz) dry white wine
300 ml	(½ pt) beef stock, heated
5 ml	(1 tsp) tomato purée
8	poached eggs
8	slices toasted French bread
	salt and pepper
	few drops Pickapeppa sauce

Melt butter in small saucepan over medium heat. Add bacon and cook 4 to 5 minutes. Mix in onion and cook another 3 minutes.

Add mushrooms, season and cook 3 to 4 minutes. Mix in flour until well incorporated; cook 2 minutes over low heat.

Pour in wine, stir well and add beef stock, tomato purée and Pickapeppa sauce. Cook 15 minutes over medium heat.

Set each poached egg on slice of toasted bread and top with sauce. Serve at once.

1 serving	330 calories	24 g carbohydrate
18 g protein	18 g fat	2.3 g fibre

Aubergine-Filled Crêpes

serves 4

45 g	(*1½ oz*) butter
1	onion, chopped
1	spring onion, sliced
1	garlic clove, smashed and chopped
1	aubergine, peeled and diced
15 ml	(*1 tbsp*) chopped fresh parsley
2 ml	(*½ tsp*) oregano
2 ml	(*½ tsp*) thyme
1 ml	(*¼ tsp*) tarragon
2	tomatoes, cored and cubed
125 g	(*4 oz*) grated Gruyère cheese
8	crêpes*
	salt and pepper
pinch	sugar

Melt 30 g (*1 oz*) butter in large frying pan over medium heat. Add onion, spring onion and garlic; cook 3 to 4 minutes.

Add aubergine and all seasonings; cover and cook 20 minutes, stirring occasionally.

Stir in tomatoes, season and add sugar. Mix, cover and cook 15 minutes.

Add half of cheese, correct seasoning and cook another 2 minutes.

Preheat oven to 200°C (*400°F, gas mark 6*).

Lay crêpes flat on cutting board. Divide filling onto crêpes; fold each in half and then in half again to form triangle. Place in large baking dish and top with remaining cheese. Dot with leftover butter.

Cook 4 minutes in oven and serve.

* For crepe batter, see Crêpes Stuffed with Veal, page 224. Having a stack of cooked crêpes on hand in your refrigerator or freezer makes it easy to prepare a delicious dinner in very little time.

1 serving	*612 calories*	*58 g carbohydrate*
23 g protein	*32 g fat*	*3.8 g fibre*

1. Cook onion, spring onion and garlic in hot butter 3 to 4 minutes over medium heat.

2. Add aubergine and all seasonings; cover and cook 20 minutes, stirring occasionally.

3. Stir in tomatoes, season and add sugar to offset any bitterness. Mix, cover and cook another 15 minutes.

4. Add half of cheese, correct seasoning and cook 2 minutes. Prepare to stuff crêpes.

Watercress Pesto Pasta

serves 4

90 g	(*3 oz*) fresh watercress, washed and well dried
45 g	(*1½ oz*) fresh parsley, washed and well dried
2	garlic cloves, smashed and chopped
90 g	(*3 oz*) grated Romano cheese
4	portions cooked penne pasta, hot
	olive oil
	freshly ground pepper

Place watercress and parsley in food processor; blend until well chopped.

Add garlic and continue blending several minutes. Add cheese and blend again until incorporated.

Incorporate just enough oil to make paste. Season with pepper to taste and blend once more.

Place hot penne in bowl and add pesto sauce; toss to coat evenly.

Serve immediately.

1 serving	447 calories	43 g carbohydrate
17 g protein	23 g fat	3.3 g fibre

Veal and Vegetable Pasta Toss

serves 4

30 g	(*1 oz*) butter
2	veal cutlets, trimmed of fat and cut into strips
4	large fresh oyster mushrooms, cleaned and sliced thick
½	red pepper, cut into strips
2	spring onions, sliced thick
2	fresh mint leaves, finely chopped
175 ml	(*6 fl oz*) chicken stock, heated
5 ml	(*1 tsp*) cornflour
30 ml	(*2 tbsp*) cold water
4	portions cooked spinach fettuccine, hot
	salt and pepper

Melt butter in large frying pan over high heat. Add strips of veal and cook 2 minutes, browning all sides.

Season meat well, remove and keep hot in oven.

Add all vegetables and chopped mint to frying pan; season well. Cook 3 minutes over high heat, adding a bit of butter if needed.

Remove vegetables from pan and place in oven with meat.

Pour chicken stock into pan and bring to boil. Mix cornflour with water; stir into sauce until well incorporated. Reduce heat and cook 1 minute.

Return meat and vegetables to frying pan with sauce. Simmer several minutes; then toss with hot pasta and serve.

1 serving	382 calories	44 g carbohydrate
20 g protein	14 g fat	2.5 g fibre

Seafood Spirals

serves 4

30 g	(*1 oz*) butter
1	shallot, chopped
225 g	(*½ lb*) fresh mushrooms, cleaned and sliced
15 ml	(*1 tbsp*) chopped fresh parsley
30 ml	(*2 tbsp*) flour
400 ml	(*⅔ pt*) hot milk
125 g	(*4 oz*) canned crabmeat, well drained
4	portions cooked spiral pasta*, hot
	salt and pepper

Melt butter in saucepan over medium heat. Add shallot, mushrooms and parsley; cook 3 to 4 minutes.

Mix in flour until well incorporated. Cook 2 minutes over low heat.

Season well and pour in milk; mix and continue cooking 8 to 10 minutes over low heat.

Add crabmeat, mix well and correct seasoning. Cook 2 minutes over very low heat.

Spoon over pasta and serve.

* You can use leftover pasta by rinsing it in hot water, draining well and sautéing it in a bit of butter before topping with sauce.

1 serving	362 calories	52 g carbohydrate
16 g protein	10 g fat	3.3 g fibre

1. Cook shallot, mushrooms and parsley in hot butter for 3 to 4 minutes over medium heat.

2. Mix in flour until well incorporated. This will help thicken the sauce. Be sure to reduce heat to low and cook flour 2 minutes.

3. After seasoning, pour in milk; mix and continue cooking 8 to 10 minutes over low heat.

4. Add crabmeat, mix well and correct seasoning. Cook 2 minutes over very low heat.

Open-Faced Veal and Mushroom Sandwiches   *serves 2*

2	veal escalopes*
30 g	(*1 oz*) butter
4	thick slices fresh bread, toasted
15 ml	(*1 tbsp*) garlic butter
8	fresh mushrooms, cleaned and sliced
5 ml	(*1 tsp*) chopped fresh parsley
50 ml	(*2 fl oz*) chicken stock, heated
	salt and pepper

Lightly season veal with pepper only. Melt butter in frying pan and cook veal 2 minutes over medium-high heat.

Turn pieces over, season well and continue cooking 2 minutes.

Place 2 slices of bread on each heated dinner plate. Rest veal over bread and keep warm in oven.

Melt garlic butter in frying pan. Add mushrooms and parsley; cook 2 minutes over high heat.

Pour in chicken stock and season; reduce liquid by half.

Pour sauce over open-faced sandwiches and serve.

* Escalopes are pounded pieces of veal cutlet usually about 5 mm (*1/4 in*) thick.

1 serving	576 calories	38 g carbohydrate
34 g protein	32 g fat	4.2 g fibre

Lemon Veal Escalopes

serves 4

4	veal escalopes
30 g	(*1 oz*) butter
50 ml	(*2 fl oz*) chicken stock, heated
15 ml	(*1 tbsp*) chopped fresh parsley
	salt and pepper
	juice 1 lemon
	lemon slices

Lightly season veal with pepper only.

Melt butter in large frying pan over medium-high heat. Add veal and cook 2 minutes.

Turn veal over, season with salt and pepper and continue cooking 2 minutes. Be careful not to overcook veal. Remove and keep warm on hot serving platter covered with foil.

Add chicken stock, parsley and lemon juice to frying pan. Increase heat to high and reduce liquid for 3 minutes.

Immediately pour sauce over veal and garnish with lemon slices. Serve at once and accompany with fresh asparagus, if desired.

1 serving	283 calories	1 g carbohydrate
27 g protein	19 g fat	0.1 g fibre

155

Veal Escalopes with Chinese Flair

serves 4

450 g	(*1 lb*) veal escalopes, trimmed of fat
150 g	(*5 oz*) seasoned flour
30 g	(*1 oz*) butter
1	celery stick, sliced into pieces 5 cm (*2 in*) long
1	courgette, thinly sliced
5 ml	(*1 tsp*) sesame seeds
125 ml	(*4 fl oz*) chicken stock, heated
45 ml	(*3 tbsp*) plum sauce
5 ml	(*1 tsp*) cornflour
30 ml	(*2 tbsp*) cold water
	salt and pepper

Lightly dredge veal in flour. Melt butter in frying pan and add meat; cook 2 minutes over medium heat.

Turn veal over, season well and continue cooking another 2 minutes. Remove veal from pan and set aside.

Add vegetables and sesame seeds to pan. Mix well, cover and cook 3 minutes.

Pour in chicken stock and bring to boil. Stir in plum sauce, reduce heat and cook 2 minutes.

Mix cornflour with water; stir into sauce until well incorporated and cook 1 minute. Reheat veal in sauce 1 minute over low heat. Serve.

1 serving	*453 calories*	*35 g carbohydrate*
31 g protein	*21 g fat*	*2.6 g fibre*

Pan-Fried Veal Escalopes

serves 4

4	large veal escalopes, trimmed of fat
150 g	(5 oz) seasoned flour
2	eggs
250 ml	(8 fl oz) milk
30 ml	(2 tbsp) peanut oil
	breadcrumbs*
	salt and pepper

Preheat oven to 180°C (350°F, gas mark 4).

Lightly dredge veal in flour. Beat eggs with milk and dip pieces of veal in mixture. Thoroughly coat with breadcrumbs, pressing in with fingertips.

Heat oil in large frying pan. When hot, add veal and cook 2 minutes over medium heat. Turn meat over, season and cook another 3 minutes.

Transfer veal to ovenproof platter and cook 4 to 5 minutes in oven. Serve with lemon wedges.

* Choose good quality, tasty breadcrumbs as they are a significant factor in the overall taste of the recipe.

1 serving	529 calories	39 g carbohydrate
37 g protein	25 g fat	3.3 g fibre

Veal Chops Sesame

serves 4

4	2.5-cm (*1-in*) thick veal chops, trimmed of fat
150 g	(*5 oz*) seasoned flour
60 g	(*2 oz*) butter
450 g	(*1 lb*) fresh mushrooms, cleaned and sliced
15 ml	(*1 tbsp*) chopped fresh parsley
	salt and pepper
	sesame oil*

Dredge veal in flour.

Heat half of butter in large frying pan over medium heat. Add veal and cook 5 minutes.

Turn chops over, season well and continue cooking 3 to 4 minutes, depending on size.

Meanwhile, heat remaining butter in separate frying pan and cook mushrooms with parsley about 3 minutes over high heat. Be sure to season well.

Sprinkle mushrooms with sesame oil and continue cooking 1 minute.

When chops are done, serve at once with mushrooms.

* This product can be found in Chinese shops or gourmet specialty stores.

1 serving	536 calories	32 g carbohydrate
30 g protein	32 g fat	4.4 g fibre

Veal Escalopes Marsala

serves 4

4	veal escalopes
40 g	(1¼ oz) butter
50 ml	(2 fl oz) Marsala wine
15 ml	(1 tbsp) chopped fresh parsley
	salt and pepper

Lightly season veal with pepper only.

Melt 30 g (1 oz) butter in large frying pan over medium-high heat. Add veal and cook 2 minutes.

Turn veal over, season with salt and pepper and continue cooking 2 minutes. Be careful not to overcook veal. Remove and keep warm on hot serving platter covered with foil.

Pour wine into frying pan and add remaining butter and parsley. Reduce liquid 3 minutes over high heat.

Pour sauce over veal immediately and serve at once. Accompany with tomatoes or sautéed mushrooms, which take only minutes to prepare.

1 serving	293 calories	0 g carbohydrate
26 g protein	21 g fat	0.1 g fibre

Breaded Pork Cutlets

serves 4

4	pork cutlets, 5 mm (¼ *in*) thick
150 g	(*5 oz*) seasoned flour
250 ml	(*8 fl oz*) double cream
125 g	(*4 oz*) spicy breadcrumbs
30 ml	(*2 tbsp*) peanut oil
300 ml	(*½ pt*) your favourite tomato sauce, heated
	salt and pepper

Preheat oven to 180°C (*350°F, gas mark 4*).

Dredge cutlets in flour; then dip in cream and thoroughly coat with breadcrumbs.

Heat oil in large frying pan over high heat. Add cutlets and cook 2 minutes on each side. Transfer to baking dish and finish cooking 7 minutes in oven.

When ready to serve, spoon tomato sauce over heated dinner plates. Set cutlets on sauce and decorate, if desired, by grating a little hard-boiled egg yolk over meat. Serve with sautéed vegetables.

1 serving	808 calories	53 g carbohydrate
41 g protein	48 g fat	2.6 g fibre

Barbecued Pork Platter

serves 4

4	fresh pork sausages, parboiled 4 minutes
4	small pork chops, trimmed of fat
30 ml	(*2 tbsp*) olive oil
15 ml	(*1 tbsp*) teriyaki sauce
5 ml	(*1 tsp*) lemon juice
1	garlic clove, smashed and chopped
	few drops sesame oil
	freshly ground pepper

Place all ingredients in large bowl and marinate 15 minutes. Meanwhile, preheat barbecue at HIGH and oil grill.

When ready to barbecue, simply place meat on grill. Reduce heat to MEDIUM and cook about 15 minutes or according to size and thickness of meat.

Turn often to avoid charring and baste frequently with any leftover marinade.

Serve with barbecued vegetables, if desired. Accompany with fresh country-style bread.

1 serving	*358 calories*	*1 g carbohydrate*
30 g protein	*26 g fat*	*0 g fibre*

161

Pork Stir-Fry

serves 4

75 ml	(*5 tbsp*) vegetable oil
3	pork chops, trimmed of fat and cut into strips
600 g	(*1¼ lb*) boiled rice
30 ml	(*2 tbsp*) light soy sauce
2	beaten eggs
30 ml	(*2 tbsp*) chopped fresh chives
	salt and pepper

Heat 30 ml (*2 tbsp*) oil in wok or large, heavy frying pan. When oil starts to smoke, add pork and stir-fry 4 to 5 minutes over high heat.

Remove meat and set aside on plate.

Add remaining oil to wok and heat to smoking point. Quickly add rice and cook 7 to 8 minutes, mixing occasionally.

Return pork to wok with rice and season well. Cook another 3 minutes.

Sprinkle in soy sauce, mix well and pour in beaten eggs. Reduce heat to low and stir quickly until eggs are cooked.

Sprinkle with chopped chives and serve.

1 serving	*496 calories*	*40 g carbohydrate*
21 g protein	*28 g fat*	*1.3 g fibre*

Rice and Vegetable Pilaf Dinner

serves 4

15 g	(*½ oz*) butter
2	spring onions, chopped
1	celery stick, chopped
200 g	(*7 oz*) long-grain rice, rinsed and drained
15 ml	(*1 tbsp*) basil
2 ml	(*½ tsp*) oregano
1 ml	(*¼ tsp*) crushed chillies
375 ml	(*13 fl oz*) chicken stock, heated
15 ml	(*1 tbsp*) olive oil
6	cooked asparagus tips, cut into 3
1	carrot, peeled and thinly sliced
1	green pepper, cut into strips
½	seedless cucumber, thinly sliced
1	large tomato, cored and cut into wedges
1	garlic clove, smashed and chopped
	salt and pepper
	sesame oil to taste (optional)

Preheat oven to 180°C (*350°F, gas mark 4*).

Heat butter in ovenproof casserole over medium heat. Add spring onions and celery; cook 2 to 3 minutes.

Add rice and mix well. Season with salt, pepper, basil, oregano and crushed chillies. Cook 2 to 3 minutes or until rice starts to stick to bottom of casserole. Mix well.

Pour in chicken stock; cover and bring to boil. Place in oven and bake 18 minutes, covered.

About 5 minutes before rice is done, begin preparing vegetables. Heat olive oil in frying pan over high heat.

Add vegetables and garlic; season well. Cook 2 to 3 minutes, stirring once. Season with sesame oil if desired.

Serve with rice.

1 serving	159 calories	21 g carbohydrate
3 g protein	7 g fat	2.8 g fibre

163

Calf Liver with Spanish Onion

serves 4

60 g	(*2 oz*) butter
1	large tomato, cored, halved and sliced
1	Spanish onion, halved and sliced
5 ml	(*1 tsp*) chopped fresh basil
4	large slices calf liver
150 g	(*5 oz*) seasoned flour
	salt and pepper

Melt half of butter in frying pan over medium heat. Add tomato, onion and basil; season well and cook 20 to 25 minutes. Stir occasionally.

Dredge liver in flour. Melt remaining butter in frying pan over low heat. Cook liver 3 minutes on first side. Turn pieces over, season and continue cooking 2 minutes.

Serve with tomato and onion mixture.

1 serving	462 calories	38 g carbohydrate
37 g protein	18 g fat	2.7 g fibre

Calf Liver with Mushrooms and Herbs   *serves 4*

4	slices fresh calf liver
45 g	(*1½ oz*) butter
225 g	(*½ lb*) fresh mushrooms, cleaned and quartered
30 ml	(*2 tbsp*) chopped fresh parsley
15 ml	(*1 tbsp*) chopped fresh tarragon
	flour
	salt and pepper

Dredge liver in flour. Melt 30 g (*1 oz*) butter in frying pan over medium heat. Add liver and season; cook 2 to 3 minutes each side.

Transfer liver to heated serving platter and keep hot in oven.

Add remaining butter to pan. Cook mushrooms, parsley and tarragon 2 to 3 minutes over high heat, seasoning generously with salt and pepper.

Serve with liver and, if desired, accompany with steamed asparagus.

Poached Chicken in White Wine

serves 4

30 g	(*1 oz*) butter
2	whole chicken breasts, skinned, boned and split into 2
125 ml	(*4 fl oz*) dry white wine
15 ml	(*1 tbsp*) chopped fresh parsley
6	large fresh oyster mushrooms, cleaned and cut in half
½	seedless cucumber, seeded and sliced thick
300 ml	(*½ pt*) chicken stock, heated
15 ml	(*1 tbsp*) cornflour
30 ml	(*2 tbsp*) cold water
	salt and pepper

Melt butter in large frying pan over low heat. Add chicken, wine and parsley; season well. Cover and cook 10 minutes.

Turn chicken over. Add mushrooms and cucumber; season again. Cover and continue cooking 6 to 7 minutes.

Remove chicken from pan and keep hot in oven.

Add chicken stock to pan and bring to boil, uncovered.

Mix cornflour with water; stir into sauce until well incorporated. Cook 1 minute over low heat.

Ladle sauce over chicken and serve. Accompany with fresh bread.

1 serving	*213 calories*	*5 g carbohydrate*
28 g protein	*9 g fat*	*1.3 g fibre*

Creamed Chicken on Toast

serves 4

2	**whole chicken breasts, skinned and cut into large cubes**
30 g	**(*1 oz*) butter**
125 g	**(*¼ lb*) fresh mushrooms, cleaned and quartered**
2	**shallots, chopped**
5 ml	**(*1 tsp*) chopped fresh parsley**
400 ml	**(*⅔ pt*) chicken stock, heated**
50 ml	**(*2 fl oz*) double cream (optional)**
	flour
	salt and pepper
	toasted bread

Dredge chicken in flour and season cubes generously. Melt butter in frying pan over medium heat. Add chicken pieces, cover and cook 10 minutes, stirring occasionally.

Add mushrooms, shallots and parsley. Season, cover and continue cooking 5 minutes.

Pour in chicken stock and mix well. Add cream and stir; cook 3 to 4 minutes, uncovered.

Spoon over toast and serve. This dish is especially good when a light meal is what you want.

1 serving	*282 calories*	*10 g carbohydrate*
29 g protein	*14 g fat*	*1.2 g fibre*

Cheddar Chicken Surprise

serves 4

2	whole chicken breasts, skinned, boned and split into two
125 g	(*4 oz*) grated well-aged white Cheddar cheese
4	large thin slices Black Forest ham
150 g	(*5 oz*) seasoned flour
2	beaten eggs
125 g	(*4 oz*) breadcrumbs
30 ml	(*2 tbsp*) peanut oil
	salt and pepper

Slice each piece of chicken breast open to form cavity. Stuff with cheese and reshape meat with hands. Wrap in slice of ham.

Carefully dredge chicken in flour and then dip in beaten egg. Thoroughly coat with breadcrumbs. Chicken must be well coated or cheese may leak during cooking.

Preheat oven to 190°C (*375°F, gas mark 5*).

Heat oil in large ovenproof frying pan. When hot, add chicken and cook 2 to 3 minutes on each side over medium-high heat to brown breadcrumbs. Season well when turning over.

Transfer to oven and finish cooking 10 minutes or longer depending on size of breasts.

Serve with fresh rolls if desired.

1 serving	622 calories	46 g carbohydrate
51 g protein	26 g fat	2.1 g fibre

1. Slice each piece of chicken breast open to form cavity for cheese. Stuff and reshape meat with hands.

2. Wrap in slice of ham. The flavour of the ham will have a considerable effect on the taste of the recipe.

3. Dredge in flour, being careful to keep ham taut.

4. Dip in beaten eggs; then coat thoroughly with breadcrumbs.

Sesame-Flavoured Chicken Fry

serves 4

2	**whole chicken breasts, skinned and cut into 5-cm (*2-in*) pieces**
15 ml	**(*1 tbsp*) vegetable oil**
1	**courgette, thinly sliced**
1	**large carrot, peeled and thinly sliced**
1	**red pepper, thinly sliced**
3	**spring onions, cut into sticks**
15 ml	**(*1 tbsp*) soy sauce**
	flour
	salt and pepper
	few drops sesame oil*

Dredge chicken pieces in flour. Heat vegetable oil in frying pan over medium heat. Add chicken, cover and cook 3 to 4 minutes. Remove chicken from pan and set aside.

Stir in courgette and carrot; season well. Cover and cook 6 minutes over medium heat, stirring occasionally.

Add red pepper, spring onions, soy sauce and sesame oil. Return chicken to pan, cover and cook 3 minutes. Serve.

* Look for this product in your local Chinese shop or in gourmet specialty stores. If not available, substitute with a hot pepper sauce such as Tabasco. Although the overall taste will be different, it will be just as nice.

1 serving	231 calories	13 g carbohydrate
29 g protein	7 g fat	2.8 g fibre

Beef Fillet with Oyster Mushrooms

serves 4

15 ml	(*1 tbsp*) vegetable oil
8	slices beef fillet
8	large fresh oyster mushrooms, cleaned and cut into large pieces
1	garlic clove, smashed and chopped
15 ml	(*1 tbsp*) chopped fresh chives
2	tomatoes, cored, halved and sliced
	salt and pepper

Heat oil in frying pan over medium-high heat. Add slices of beef and sear 1 to 2 minutes, depending on thickness. Turn over, season and sear other side 1 minute.

Remove meat from pan and set aside.

Add mushrooms, garlic and chives to pan; cook 3 to 4 minutes.

Add tomatoes and season well; continue cooking 3 to 4 minutes.

Return meat to pan and cook 1 to 2 minutes until reheated. Serve at once.

1 serving	347 calories	5 g carbohydrate
48 g protein	15 g fat	2.2 g fibre

Greek Meatballs

serves 4

15 g	(½ oz) butter
2	onions, chopped
4	slices white bread, crusts trimmed
150 ml	(¼ pt) milk
600 g	(1¼ lb) lean minced beef
1	garlic clove, smashed and chopped
5 ml	(1 tsp) oregano
1	egg
30 ml	(2 tbsp) soured cream
15 ml	(1 tbsp) vegetable oil
dash	paprika
	salt and pepper

Melt butter in small saucepan. Add onions and cook 4 to 5 minutes over medium heat.

Meanwhile, place bread in bowl and pour in milk; set aside to soak.

When onions are done, place in food processor with meat. Add garlic, all seasonings and egg.

Squeeze out excess milk from bread and add bread to food processor. Mix several minutes to combine ingredients well.

Spoon in soured cream and mix again until thoroughly combined. Transfer mixture to bowl and cover with cling film. Refrigerate 1 hour.*

When ready to cook meatballs, take mixture from refrigerator. With oiled hands, shape into small balls.

Heat oil in large frying pan over medium heat. Cook meatballs 3 to 4 minutes on each side or longer, depending on size. Do not crowd pan; cook in batches if necessary.

Serve meatballs with spicy dipping sauce, with pasta in tomato sauce or with a light salad.

* To accommodate your schedule, you can prepare the first half of the recipe in the morning and have the meatballs chill while you are at work.

1 serving	402 calories	19 g carbohydrate
41 g protein	18 g fat	1.9 g fibre

1. Onions should always be precooked before adding them to meatball or hamburger meat mixture. Sautéing them in butter will lend a very nice flavour to the meatballs.

2. When onions are done, place them with meat in food processor. Be sure to put meat on the bottom or onions will be difficult to incorporate. Add garlic, all seasonings and egg.

3. Add soaked bread and blend several minutes until well combined. Add soured cream, blend again and chill.

4. When cooking meatballs, use medium heat. Avoid excess stirring — let each side sear properly before turning.

Ginger-Basted Prawn Kebabs

serves 4

20	large prawns, shelled, deveined and cleaned
3	spring onions, cut into 5-cm (*2-in*) lengths
150 g	(*5 oz*) blanched mangetouts
2	onions, cut into wedges
2	large carrots, peeled, sliced 1-cm (*½-in*) thick and blanched
30 ml	(*2 tbsp*) vegetable oil
30 ml	(*2 tbsp*) teriyaki sauce
15 ml	(*1 tbsp*) lime juice
30 ml	(*2 tbsp*) chopped fresh ginger
	salt and pepper

Alternate prawns and vegetables on skewers.

Mix remaining ingredients together in small bowl and brush over kebabs.

Place skewers in oven about 15 cm (*6 in*) from top element. Grill 3 to 4 minutes on each side, depending on size. If desired, they can be cooked on grill in the same time.

Be sure to baste several times during cooking.

Brandy Prawn Sauté

serves 4

30 g	*(1 oz)* butter
800 g	*(1¾ lb)* medium prawns, shelled, deveined and cleaned
45 ml	*(3 tbsp)* brandy
1	carrot, peeled and finely diced
1	celery stick, finely diced
15 ml	*(1 tbsp)* finely chopped fresh parsley
5 ml	*(1 tsp)* finely chopped fresh tarragon
2	shallots, chopped
250 ml	*(8 fl oz)* dry white wine
250 ml	*(8 fl oz)* double cream
	salt and pepper
	few drops lime juice

Heat butter in large frying pan over high heat. Add prawns and cook 3 minutes, without stirring.

Turn prawns over, season and cook another 3 minutes. Pour in brandy and flambé.

As soon as alcohol has burned off, remove prawns and set aside.

Add vegetables, parsley, tarragon and shallots to pan. Cook 3 to 4 minutes over high heat. Season well.

Pour in wine and continue cooking 3 to 4 minutes to reduce liquid by half.

Add cream and continue cooking, stirring occasionally, until sauce has thickened.

Reduce heat to low and place prawns in sauce. Simmer several minutes until reheated.

Sprinkle with lime juice and serve.

1 serving	393 calories	6 g carbohydrate
27 g protein	29 g fat	0.8 g fibre

175

Tempura Prawns

serves 4

900 g	(*2 lb*) medium prawns
30 ml	(*2 tbsp*) teriyaki sauce
15 ml	(*1 tbsp*) lemon juice
15 ml	(*1 tbsp*) honey
1	garlic clove, smashed and chopped
	salt and pepper
	commercial tempura batter mix
	peanut oil
	lemon slices

Peel and devein prawns, leaving tails intact. Wash thoroughly in cold water, drain and pat dry with absorbent kitchen paper.

Place prawns in bowl; add teriyaki sauce, lemon juice, honey and garlic. Season with pepper and let stand 30 minutes.

Meanwhile, prepare batter according to directions on package.

Preheat plenty of peanut oil in electric deep-fryer set at 190°C (*375°F*).

Coat prawns in batter and deep-fry, in several batches, about 2 to 3 minutes or until golden brown. Drain well on absorbent kitchen paper before serving.

Accompany with lemon slices.

1 serving	374 calories	21 g carbohydrate
32 g protein	18 g fat	0.4 g fibre

ECONOMICAL FARE

Delicious, tempting recipes that will save you money but won't disappoint your palate

Cheryl's Hot Penne Salad

serves 4

15 ml	(*1 tbsp*) olive oil
1	onion, cubed small
1	green pepper, diced
2	celery sticks, sliced
2	carrots, peeled and thinly sliced
15 ml	(*1 tbsp*) chopped fresh ginger
400 g	(*14 oz*) cooked penne, still warm
15 ml	(*1 tbsp*) chopped fresh parsley
30 ml	(*2 tbsp*) olive oil
30 ml	(*2 tbsp*) wine vinegar
15 ml	(*1 tbsp*) Dijon mustard
200 g	(*7 oz*) canned chick peas, drained
	salt and pepper

Heat 15 ml (*1 tbsp*) oil in saucepan over high heat. Add vegetables and ginger; cook 4 to 5 minutes.

Place warm pasta in bowl. Add parsley, 30 ml (*2 tbsp*) oil, vinegar and mustard; toss until well mixed.

Add chick peas and season well; toss again.

Stir in hot vegetables, toss once more and serve in attractive bowl, decorated with lettuce leaves if desired.

1 serving	336 calories	48 g carbohydrate
9 g protein	12 g fat	6.6 g fibre

Penne Abigail

serves 6

30 ml	(**2 tbsp**) olive oil
1	**medium onion, chopped**
2	**shallots, chopped**
½	**hot green pepper, seeded and chopped**
1	**small courgette, diced with skin**
450 g	(**1 lb**) **lean minced beef**
800 g	(**1¾ lb**) **canned tomatoes, drained and chopped**
15 ml	(**1 tbsp**) **chopped fresh parsley**
400 g	(**14 oz**) **canned red kidney beans, drained**
5 ml	(**1 tsp**) **basil**
2 ml	(**½ tsp**) **chilli powder**
700 g	(**1½ lb**) **cooked penne pasta**
125 g	(**4 oz**) **grated mozzarella cheese**
	salt and pepper
	few drops Pickapeppa sauce

Heat oil in large, deep frying pan. Add onion, shallots, hot pepper and courgette; cook 7 to 8 minutes over high heat.

Mix in beef and continue cooking 3 to 4 minutes, stirring several times during cooking.

Season meat well and add tomatoes, parsley and kidney beans. Mix well and sprinkle in basil, chilli powder and Pickapeppa sauce.

Mix again, correct seasoning and cook 8 to 10 minutes over high heat.

Reduce heat to medium and continue cooking 15 minutes.

Stir in penne noodles and cook 3 to 4 minutes. Add cheese and continue cooking another 2 minutes or until cheese is melted.

1 serving	448 calories	38 g carbohydrate
29 g protein	20 g fat	2.5 g fibre

Shell Noodles with Tomato Clam Sauce   *serves 4*

200 g	(*7 oz*) dry shell noodles
5 ml	(*1 tsp*) wine vinegar
30 ml	(*2 tbsp*) olive oil
1	onion, finely chopped
1	garlic clove, smashed and finely chopped
1.2 kg	(*2½ lb*) canned tomatoes, drained and chopped
5 ml	(*1 tsp*) oregano
5 ml	(*1 tsp*) freshly chopped parsley
150 oz	(*5 oz*) canned baby clams, drained and juice reserved
	salt and pepper
	grated Parmesan cheese

Place pasta in boiling, salted water in saucepan. Add vinegar and cook 10 minutes or until "al dente". When done, remove saucepan from heat and set under cold running water for a few seconds. Drain well and set pasta aside.

Heat oil in frying pan over medium heat. Add onion and garlic; cook 3 minutes.

Add tomatoes, oregano and parsley; mix well, season and cook 5 minutes over high heat.

Pour in clam juice, season and cook 8 to 10 minutes over low heat. Mix in clams and cook 2 minutes over very low heat.

Meanwhile, fill large saucepan with salted water and a few drops oil. Bring to boil over high heat. Place pasta in strainer and drop strainer into boiling water for 2 minutes to reheat.

Drain pasta again and serve with sauce and grated cheese.

1 serving	498 calories	69 g carbohydrate
24 g protein	14 g fat	3.5 g fibre

Fettucini with Greens

serves 4

30 ml	(*2 tbsp*) olive oil
4	spring onions, chopped
1	celery stick, thinly sliced
1	red pepper, thinly sliced
10	large fresh mushrooms caps, cleaned and sliced in 3
15	mangetouts, topped and tailed
1	garlic clove, smashed and chopped
15 ml	(*1 tbsp*) freshly chopped fennel
400 ml	(*⅔ pt*) chicken stock, heated
15 ml	(*1 tbsp*) cornflour
45 ml	(*3 tbsp*) cold water
4	portions cooked fettucini, hot
	salt and pepper

Heat oil in large frying pan over medium heat. Add spring onions and celery; cook 4 minutes.

Add remaining vegetables and garlic; season well. Mix and cook 4 minutes over high heat.

Add fennel and chicken stock; cook 4 minutes over medium heat.

Mix cornflour with cold water; stir into vegetable mixture until well incorporated. Correct seasoning and cook 1 minute. Spoon over hot pasta and serve.

1 serving	441 calories	77 g carbohydrate
13 g protein	9 g fat	4.5 g fibre

White Spaghetti and Peas

serves 4

45 g	(*1½ oz*) butter
30 g	(*1 oz*) flour
500 ml	(*17 fl oz*) milk, heated
4	rashers cooked back bacon, cut into thin strips
½	green pepper, cut into strips
15 ml	(*1 tbsp*) chopped lemon zest
175 g	(*6 oz*) frozen green peas, cooked
4	portions cooked spaghetti, hot
125 g	(*4 oz*) grated mozzarella cheese
pinch	nutmeg
	salt and pepper

Melt 30 g (*1 oz*) butter in saucepan over medium heat. Add flour and mix well with wooden spoon; cook 3 minutes over low heat, stirring constantly.

Pour in hot milk and mix well; continue cooking 8 to 10 minutes over low heat. Stir frequently.

Sprinkle in nutmeg, season and set white sauce aside.

Melt remaining butter in frying pan. Add bacon, green pepper and lemon zest; season well. Cook 3 minutes over medium heat.

Stir in peas, pasta and white sauce. Add cheese, mix well and cook 2 minutes over medium heat before serving.

1 serving	559 calories	60 g carbohydrate
28 g protein	23 g fat	3.9 g fibre

Stuffed Cannelloni

serves 4

15 ml	(*1 tbsp*) vegetable oil
1	medium onion, chopped
8	large fresh mushrooms, cleaned and chopped
1	spring onion, chopped
5 ml	(*1 tsp*) chopped lime zest
2 ml	(*½ tsp*) cumin
3	jumbo green olives, chopped
175 g	(*6 oz*) lean minced beef
90 g	(*3 oz*) feta cheese, crumbled
12	cooked cannelloni
300 ml	(*½ pt*) tomato sauce
125 ml	(*4 fl oz*) chicken stock, heated
pinch	paprika
	salt and pepper
	freshly grated Parmesan cheese

Preheat oven to 160°C (*325°F, gas mark 3*).

Heat oil in frying pan. Add chopped onion, mushrooms, spring onion and lime zest; season well.

Sprinkle in all seasonings and cook 4 to 5 minutes over medium heat.

Stir in olives and minced beef; mix well, season again and continue cooking 4 minutes.

Mix in feta cheese and cook 3 more minutes.

Transfer mixture to bowl of food processor and blend. Spoon stuffing into piping bag fitted with plain nozzle.

Stuff cannelloni and place in baking dish. Mix tomato sauce with chicken stock and pour over pasta.

Cover dish with foil and bake 1 hour. Serve with Parmesan cheese.

1 serving	412 calories	45 g carbohydrate
22 g protein	16 g fat	2.7 g fibre

Lamb Shoulder Stew with Carrots

serves 4

1.4 kg	(*3 lb*) boneless lamb shoulder, trimmed of fat
2	shallots, chopped
300 ml	(*½ pt*) dry white wine
15 ml	(*1 tbsp*) olive oil
30 ml	(*2 tbsp*) peanut oil
30 g	(*1 oz*) flour
600 ml	(*1 pt*) beef stock, heated
30 ml	(*2 tbsp*) tomato purée
5 ml	(*1 tsp*) olive oil
1	onion, cut into 6
1	garlic clove, smashed and chopped
3	carrots, peeled and cut into thick sticks
2 ml	(*½ tsp*) oregano
15 ml	(*1 tbsp*) chopped fresh parsley
5 ml	(*1 tsp*) soy sauce
	salt and pepper
dash	paprika

Cut meat into cubes. Place in bowl and season with salt and pepper. Add shallots, wine and 15 ml (*1 tbsp*) olive oil; marinate 1 hour.

Preheat oven to 180°C (*350°F, gas mark 4*).

Heat peanut oil in large frying pan. Drain lamb, reserving marinade, and place meat in hot oil. Cook 7 to 8 minutes over high heat. Turn cubes over, season and continue cooking 2 to 3 minutes.

Sprinkle in flour and mix very well. Reduce heat to medium and continue cooking 5 minutes or until flour browns and starts to stick to bottom of pan. Stir occasionally to avoid burning.

Pour in beef stock and reserved marinade. Mix well and bring to boil. Mix in tomato purée and set frying pan aside.

Heat 5 ml (*1 tsp*) olive oil in small frying pan. Cook onion and garlic 3 to 4 minutes over high heat. Transfer onion and garlic to frying pan containing lamb. Add carrots, seasonings and soy sauce; mix well. Cover and bring to boil.

Place stew in oven, cover and cook 2 hours. Add beef stock during cooking if necessary.

Serve over egg noodles.

1 serving	*669 calories*	*15 g carbohydrate*
69 g protein	*37 g fat*	*2.5 g fibre*

Beef Sauté with Figs

serves 4

30 ml	(*2 tbsp*) peanut oil
450 g	(*1 lb*) rump steak, sliced on angle
12	figs, halved
1	apple, cored and sectioned with peel
12	water chestnuts, sliced
1	green pepper, thinly sliced
100 g	(*3½ oz*) canned chick peas, drained
25 ml	(*1½ tbsp*) cornflour
45 ml	(*3 tbsp*) cold water
300 ml	(*½ pt*) beef stock, heated
	salt and pepper
	few drops Pickapeppa sauce

Heat 15 ml (*1 tbsp*) oil in frying pan over high heat. Add meat and sear 2 minutes on both sides. Season well, remove meat from pan and set aside.

Add remaining oil to pan and heat. Cook figs, apple, water chestnuts, green pepper and chick peas 3 to 4 minutes over high heat. Be sure to season well during cooking.

Mix cornflour with water. Pour beef stock into frying pan, stir in diluted cornflour and add Pickapeppa sauce. Mix well and simmer 2 to 3 minutes.

Place meat in sauce, cook 30 seconds and serve over buttered noodles.

1 serving	478 calories	54 g carbohydrate
34 g protein	14 g fat	13.4 g fibre

Curried Meatballs

serves 4

450 g	(*1 lb*) lean minced beef
1 ml	(*¼ tsp*) chilli powder
30 ml	(*2 tbsp*) chopped fresh parsley
1	beaten egg
30 ml	(*2 tbsp*) vegetable oil
1½	large onions, finely chopped
1	celery stick, finely diced
1	red apple, cored, peeled and chopped
30 ml	(*2 tbsp*) curry powder
15 g	(*½ oz*) butter
30 ml	(*2 tbsp*) flour
400 ml	(*⅔ pt*) chicken stock, heated
	salt and pepper
	few drops hot pepper sauce

Place meat, chilli powder, half of parsley, egg, some salt and hot pepper sauce in food processor. Blend until meat forms ball. Shape mixture into small meatballs and set aside.

Heat oil in large frying pan. Cook onions, celery, apple and remaining parsley 6 to 7 minutes over medium heat.

Sprinkle in curry powder and mix well. Cook 5 to 6 minutes over low heat.

Add butter to pan and continue cooking 1 minute.

Place meatballs in pan and cook 5 to 6 minutes over medium heat, turning meatballs over often.

Sprinkle in flour, mix and continue cooking 2 to 3 minutes.

Pour in chicken stock and season very well. Bring to boil and cook 15 minutes over low heat.

Serve on rice.

1 serving	377 calories	18 g carbohydrate
29 g protein	21 g fat	2.8 g fibre

1. Cook onions, celery, apple and remaining parsley in hot oil for 6 to 7 minutes over medium heat.

2. Sprinkle in curry powder and mix well. Cook 5 to 6 minutes over low heat. Add butter and continue cooking 1 minute.

3. Place meatballs in pan and cook 5 to 6 minutes over medium heat, turning meatballs over often.

4. Sprinkle in flour, mix and continue cooking 2 to 3 minutes.

Green Meatballs With Spicy Tomato Sauce *serves 4*

350 g	(*¾ lb*) lean minced beef
350 g	(*¾ lb*) cooked chopped spinach
1	egg
45 g	(*1½ oz*) cooked chopped onions
15 ml	(*1 tbsp*) freshly chopped parsley
30 ml	(*2 tbsp*) vegetable oil
1	carrot, peeled and diced small
1	celery stick, diced small
30 ml	(*2 tbsp*) flour
800 g	(*1¾ lb*) canned tomatoes, drained and chopped
30 ml	(*2 tbsp*) tomato purée
300 ml	(*½ pt*) chicken stock, heated
	salt and pepper

Place beef, spinach, egg, onions and parsley in food processor. Season well and blend 3 minutes. When mixture forms ball, remove and shape meat into medium-size meatballs.

Heat oil in large frying pan over medium heat. Add meatballs (do not crowd pan) and cook 6 to 7 minutes, browning on all sides. Remove and set meatballs aside.

Add carrot and celery to pan; cook 6 minutes over medium heat. Mix in flour until well incorporated and continue cooking 2 minutes.

Mix in tomatoes, then tomato purée and chicken stock; mix again. Season and cook 3 minutes still over medium heat.

Place meatballs in sauce and cook 6 to 7 minutes over medium heat. Serve.

1 serving	328 calories	20 g carbohydrate
26 g protein	16 g fat	7.4 g fibre

Leftover Meatballs à la Lyonnaise

serves 4

15 ml	(*1 tbsp*) peanut oil
3	onions, thinly sliced
1	garlic clove, smashed and chopped
15 ml	(*1 tbsp*) chopped fresh parsley
2 ml	(*½ tsp*) celery seeds
5 ml	(*1 tsp*) cumin
15 g	(*½ oz*) butter
30 ml	(*2 tbsp*) flour
500 ml	(*17 fl oz*) chicken stock, heated
12	leftover cooked meatballs
30 g	(*1 oz*) grated mozzarella cheese
	salt and pepper

Heat oil in frying pan over high heat. Add onions, garlic and parsley; cover and cook 15 minutes over medium heat.

Add seasonings and butter; mix well. Stir in flour and cook 2 minutes.

Pour in chicken stock, mix well and bring to boil. Correct seasoning.

Place meatballs in sauce. Add cheese and simmer until reheated. Garnish servings with leftover cooked vegetables.

1 serving	336 calories	13 g carbohydrate
26 g protein	20 g fat	1.9 g fibre

Curried Beef Chuck Stew

serves 4

1.2 kg	(2½ lb) boneless beef chuck stewing meat, in 2.5-cm (1-in) cubes
1	onion, grated
1	green chilli pepper, chopped
2	garlic cloves, smashed and chopped
15 ml	(1 tbsp) coriander
15 ml	(1 tbsp) ginger
5 ml	(1 tsp) turmeric
2 ml	(½ tsp) cumin
15 ml	(1 tbsp) curry powder
300 ml	(½ pt) yogurt
30 ml	(2 tbsp) vegetable oil
1	onion, chopped
30 g	(1 oz) flour
1 litre	(1¾ pt) beef stock, heated
	salt and pepper

Place beef cubes, grated onion, chopped chilli pepper, garlic, coriander, ginger, turmeric, cumin, curry powder and yogurt in bowl. Mix together, season and chill 2 hours to marinate.

Preheat oven to 180°C (350°F, gas mark 4).

Heat oil in large frying pan over high heat. Add half of meat and sear about 5 to 6 minutes, browning on all sides. Season well and remove meat.

Add remaining meat to hot frying pan with chopped onion; repeat searing procedure.

Transfer all meat to ovenproof casserole. Mix in flour until well incorporated and cook 4 minutes over medium heat, stirring frequently. Pour in beef stock, correct seasoning and cover; cook 2 hours in oven or until meat is tender.

Serve with chutney or yogurt, if desired.

1 serving	663 calories	15 g carbohydrate
72 g protein	35 g fat	1.1 g fibre

Rice with Tarragon Mushrooms

serves 4

15 g	(*½ oz*) butter
2	shallots, chopped
1	garlic clove, smashed and chopped
½	celery stick, finely diced
15 ml	(*1 tbsp*) chopped lemon zest
200 g	(*7 oz*) long-grain rice, rinsed and drained
400 ml	(*⅔ pt*) chicken stock, heated
15 ml	(*1 tbsp*) peanut oil
225 g	(*½ lb*) fresh mushrooms, cleaned and halved
5 ml	(*1 tsp*) tarragon
	salt and pepper

Preheat oven to 180°C (*350°F, gas mark 4*).

Melt butter in ovenproof casserole over medium heat. Add shallots, garlic, celery and lemon zest; cook 3 minutes.

Stir in rice and season well. Continue cooking 2 to 3 minutes or until rice starts to stick to bottom of casserole.

Pour in chicken stock, mix and bring to boil. Correct seasoning, cover and cook 15 minutes in oven.

About 5 minutes before rice is cooked, heat oil in frying pan over high heat.

Add mushrooms and tarragon; season well. Sauté 2 to 3 minutes. Stir into rice in casserole and finish cooking 3 minutes in oven.

1 serving	*255 calories*	*43 g carbohydrate*
5 g protein	*7 g fat*	*1.7 g fibre*

Quick Curried Rice

serves 4

30 g	(*1 oz*) butter
½	celery stick, diced
1	medium onion, diced
25 ml	(*1½ oz*) curry powder (or to taste)
200 g	(*7 oz*) long-grain rice, rinsed and drained
400 ml	(*⅔ pt*) chicken stock, heated
	salt and pepper

Preheat oven to 180°C (*350°F, gas mark 4*).

Place butter, celery and onion in ovenproof casserole. Season with pepper and cook 3 minutes over medium heat.

Sprinkle in curry powder and mix well; continue cooking 4 to 5 minutes over low heat.

Add rice and mix well; season to taste. Cook 2 to 3 minutes to evaporate any water from rice and allow it to brown.

When rice starts to stick to bottom of casserole, pour in chicken stock. Stir and bring to boil over high heat.

Cover casserole and cook 18 minutes in oven.

1 serving	242 calories	43 g carbohydrate
4 g protein	6 g fat	0.7 g fibre

1. Cook celery and onion with butter in ovenproof casserole for 3 minutes over medium heat. Be sure to season well with pepper.

2. Add curry to taste and mix well; continue cooking 4 to 5 minutes over low heat.

3. Mix in rice and season to taste. Cook 2 to 3 minutes to allow any water to evaporate and to brown rice.

4. When rice starts to stick to bottom of casserole, add the hot chicken stock.

No Fail 18-Minute Rice

serves 4

30 g	(*1 oz*) butter
1	onion, chopped
1	celery stick, chopped
½	courgette, diced
200 g	(*7 oz*) long grain rice, rinsed
1 ml	(*¼ tsp*) celery salt
400 ml	(*⅔ pt*) light beef stock, heated
	salt and pepper

Preheat oven to 180°C (*350°F, gas mark 4*).

Melt butter in ovenproof casserole over medium heat. Add onion, celery and courgette; cover and cook 2 minutes.

Add rice, season and add celery salt. Cook 3 minutes, uncovered, or until rice starts to stick to bottom of casserole.

Pour in beef stock and bring to boil; correct seasoning. Cover and finish cooking 18 minutes in oven.

1 serving	218 calories	37 g carbohydrate
4 g protein	6 g fat	1.8 g fibre

Leftover Beef Chinese Style

serves 4

30 ml	(*2 tbsp*) peanut oil
450 g	(*1 lb*) rump steak, sliced on angle
½	yellow pepper
1	courgette, sliced
2	leaves Chinese cabbage, sliced
2	plum tomatoes, quartered
1	apple, cored and sectioned with peel
30 ml	(*2 tbsp*) chopped fresh ginger
15 ml	(*1 tbsp*) chopped fresh parsley
	salt and pepper

Heat oil in frying pan over high heat. Add meat and sear slices 2 minutes on each side. Season well, remove meat from pan and set aside.

Add all vegetables, apple, ginger and parsley to pan. Season and continue cooking 3 minutes over high heat.

Return meat to pan, mix and cook another 30 seconds. Serve immediately.

1 serving	289 calories	12 g carbohydrate
31 g protein	13 g fat	3.5 g fibre

Spinach Burgers with Mushroom Sauce   *serves 4*

600 g	(*1¼ lb*) lean minced beef
45 g	(*1½ oz*) cooked chopped onions
1	egg
15 ml	(*1 tbsp*) freshly chopped parsley
200 g	(*7 oz*) cooked chopped spinach
30 ml	(*2 tbsp*) olive oil
2	medium onions, sliced
225 g	(*½ lb*) fresh mushrooms, cleaned and sliced
400 ml	(*⅔ pt*) beef stock, heated
5 ml	(*1 tsp*) cornflour
30 ml	(*2 tbsp*) cold water
	few drops Worcestershire sauce
	salt and pepper

Place beef, cooked chopped onions, egg, parsley, spinach and Worcestershire sauce in food processor. Season well and blend 3 minutes. When mixture forms ball, remove and shape meat into 4 patties.

Heat oil in large frying pan over medium heat. Add patties and cook 8 to 10 minutes depending on thickness, turning over 2 to 3 times to avoid charring.

When cooked, remove from pan, set aside and keep hot.

Add sliced onions to frying pan and cook 6 minutes over medium heat. Add mushrooms and continue cooking 4 minutes.

Season and pour in beef stock; mix well. Mix cornflour with cold water; stir into sauce until well incorporated. Bring to boil, then serve over spinach burgers.

1 serving	386 calories	11 g carbohydrate
36 g protein	22 g fat	5.5 g fibre

1. Place beef, cooked chopped onions, egg, parsley, spinach and Worcestershire sauce in food processor. Season well.

2. Blend 3 minutes until mixture forms ball. Remove and shape into patties.

3. Add beef patties to hot oil and cook 8 to 10 minutes depending on thickness. Turn over 2 to 3 times to avoid charring.

4. With meat removed, add mushrooms to cooking onions in pan. Cook 4 minutes.

Minced Beef Rice Casserole

serves 4

15 ml	(*1 tbsp*) vegetable oil
½	medium onion, coarsely chopped
2	garlic cloves, smashed and chopped
½	green pepper, diced
½	celery stick, thinly sliced
1	leaf Chinese cabbage, thinly sliced
1 ml	(*¼ tsp*) basil
1 ml	(*¼ tsp*) chilli powder
225 g	(*½ lb*) lean minced beef
30 ml	(*2 tbsp*) chopped orange zest
300 ml	(*½ pt*) tomato sauce, heated
400 g	(*14 oz*) cooked rice
60 g	(*2 oz*) grated mozzarella cheese
pinch	thyme
pinch	ground ginger
	salt and pepper

Preheat oven to 200°C (*400°F, gas mark 6*).

Heat oil in frying pan over high heat.

Reduce heat to medium and cook onion and garlic 3 minutes.

Add green pepper, celery and cabbage; sprinkle in all seasonings. Mix well and continue cooking 5 minutes.

Correct seasoning and mix in minced beef; continue cooking 5 to 6 minutes.

Stir in orange zest and tomato sauce; season to taste. Bring to boil over high heat.

Mix in rice, correct seasoning and add cheese; mix again. Wrap frying pan handle in foil (or transfer to another utensil) and finish cooking 8 to 10 minutes in oven.

Decorate with orange slices and tomato wedges, if desired.

1 serving	*351 calories*	*34 g carbohydrate*
20 g protein	*15 g fat*	*2.0 g fibre*

Stuffed Beef Flank

serves 4

600 g	(*1¼ lb*) beef flank
30 ml	(*2 tbsp*) vegetable oil
225 g	(*½ lb*) fresh mushrooms, cleaned and finely chopped
30 ml	(*2 tbsp*) chopped lemon zest
2	spring onions, chopped
2 ml	(*½ tsp*) oregano
200 g	(*7 oz*) cooked rice
45 ml	(*3 tbsp*) steak sauce
1	onion, quartered and sectioned
300 ml	(*½ pt*) beer
300 ml	(*½ pt*) beef gravy
30 ml	(*2 tbsp*) tomato purée
	salt and pepper
	paprika to taste

Preheat oven to 180°C (*350°F, gas mark 4*).

Using sharp knife, split flank into two lengthways. Cut only ¾ of the way through thickness of meat so that flank can be opened into one large piece.

Season opened flank with pepper and paprika; then pound with meat bat to tenderize and flatten thin. Set aside.

Heat 15 ml (*1 tbsp*) oil in large frying pan. Add mushrooms, lemon zest and spring onions; season well.

Add oregano and mix well; cook 4 to 5 minutes over medium heat.

Stir in rice and continue cooking 4 to 5 minutes.

Pour mixture into food processor and blend well. Incorporate steak sauce by mixing for 2 to 3 minutes. Spread stuffing over beef flank. Roll and tie with kitchen string.

Heat remaining oil in frying pan over high heat. Add flank and sear well on all sides until brown. Season well.

Add onion and continue cooking 3 to 4 minutes. Remove meat from pan and set aside.

Pour beer into frying pan containing onion. Stir in beef gravy and tomato purée; correct seasoning.

Place meat in sauce. Cover and bring to boil. Place pan in oven and cook 1½ hours.

1 serving	384 calories	28 g carbohydrate
41 g protein	12 g fat	3.0 g fibre

Beef and Vegetable Stew

serves 4

1.8 kg	(*4 lb*) blade steak with bone
40 ml	(*2½ tbsp*) peanut oil
2	garlic cloves, smashed and chopped
2 ml	(*½ tsp*) basil
1 ml	(*¼ tsp*) oregano
1 ml	(*¼ tsp*) chilli powder
1	bay leaf
40 g	(*1¼ oz*) flour
750 ml	(*1¼ pt*) beef stock, heated
30 ml	(*2 tbsp*) tomato purée
2	large onions, cubed
1 ml	(*¼ tsp*) Worcestershire sauce
2	celery sticks, cubed
2	parsnips, peeled and cubed
2	large carrots, peeled and cubed
	salt and pepper
pinch	thyme

Preheat oven to 180°C (*350°F, gas mark 4*).

Bone meat and cut into cubes. Reserve bone for making your own homemade stock, if desired. Trim excess fat.

Heat 30 ml (*2 tbsp*) oil in large, deep frying pan over high heat. Add meat and sear on all sides.

Season meat well and add garlic and all seasonings; mix. Continue cooking 3 to 4 minutes over high heat.

Stir in flour and mix until well incorporated. Cook 5 to 6 minutes over low heat.

Pour in beef stock, stir and bring to boil. Mix in tomato purée and bring to boil again. Simmer 3 to 4 minutes over low heat.

Heat remaining oil in frying pan. Cook onions with Worcestershire sauce 2 to 3 minutes over high heat.

Add onions to meat mixture, cover and cook 1 hour in oven.

Add remaining vegetables to stew, mix, cover and cook 1 more hour in oven.

1 serving	892 calories	41 g carbohydrate
110 g protein	32 g fat	6.4 g fibre

1. When the oil is hot, add cubes of meat and begin searing.

2. All sides of the cubes must be browned before the meat is seasoned.

3. Add garlic and seasonings; continue cooking 3 to 4 minutes.

4. Sprinkle flour over meat; stir well to incorporate.

Hamburger Steaks in Sherry Sauce

serves 4

700 g	(1½ lb) lean minced beef
1	beaten egg
15 ml	(1 tbsp) chopped fresh parsley
1	onion, chopped and cooked
1 ml	(¼ tsp) chilli powder
25 ml	(1½ tbsp) olive oil
450 g	(1 lb) fresh mushrooms, cleaned and sliced
1 ml	(¼ tsp) tarragon
50 ml	(2 fl oz) sherry wine
400 ml	(⅔ pt) beef gravy, heated (commercial or homemade)
	salt and pepper

Blend meat, egg, parsley, onion, chilli powder, salt and pepper in food processor until mixture forms ball. Shape into hamburger steaks.

Brush both sides of meat with 5 ml (1 tsp) oil. Place frying pan over high heat; when hot, add steaks and cook 3 to 4 minutes.

Turn steaks over, reduce heat to medium and continue cooking another 3 to 4 minutes or longer, depending on size and your preference. Be sure to season well during cooking. When done, remove from pan, set aside and keep hot.

Heat remaining oil in frying pan. Add mushrooms and tarragon; cook 2 minutes over high heat.

Season, pour in sherry and cook 3 minutes over high heat.

Add beef gravy, mix well and finish cooking 2 to 3 minutes. Pour over steaks and serve.

1 serving	501 calories	13 g carbohydrate
47 g protein	29 g fat	3.7 g fibre

Pot Roast

serves 4–6

1.8 kg	(*4 lb*) topside of beef
2	garlic cloves, peeled and sliced in 3
25 ml	(*1½ tbsp*) dry mustard
45 g	(*1½ oz*) bacon fat
3	onions, diced large
350 g	(*¾ lb*) chopped tomatoes
600 ml	(*1 pt*) beef stock, heated
30 ml	(*2 tbsp*) tomato purée
30 ml	(*2 tbsp*) horseradish
1	bay leaf
	salt and pepper
pinch	thyme

Preheat oven to 150°C (*300°F, gas mark 2*).

Make slits in meat to insert garlic pieces. Spread dry mustard over meat and press with fingertips so that mustard adheres to meat. Pepper generously.

Heat bacon fat in ovenproof casserole over medium heat. Add beef and sear on all sides. Add onions and continue cooking 8 to 10 minutes over medium heat.

Season well, cover and cook 1 hour in oven. Turn beef over twice during cooking process.

Add tomatoes and remaining ingredients to casserole. Mix well, cover and finish cooking 1½ hours in oven.

When cooked, remove beef and set aside. Place casserole over medium heat and cook sauce about 8 minutes to thicken. Slice beef and serve.

1 serving	629 calories	11 g carbohydrate
90 g protein	25 g fat	1.7 g fibre

Delicious Blade Roast

serves 4

1.4 kg	(3 lb) blade roast, boned
2	garlic cloves, peeled and halved
15 g	(½ oz) bacon fat
3	onions, quartered
1	bay leaf
2 ml	(½ tsp) basil
400 ml	(⅔ pt) beer
	salt and pepper
pinch	thyme

Preheat oven to 180°C (*350°F, gas mark 4*).

Using small paring knife, cut incisions in meat and insert garlic pieces.

Place bacon fat in ovenproof casserole and place over high heat. When hot, add roast and sear until brown on both sides. Season well with salt and pepper after second side starts to brown.

Add onions and continue cooking 4 to 5 minutes.

Sprinkle in seasonings, season and pour in beer. Cover and cook 1 hour in oven.

Turn roast over and season again. Cover and continue cooking 1 hour.

Serve with vegetables.

1 serving	569 calories	13 g carbohydrate
82 g protein	21 g fat	1.7 g fibre

Corned Beef Brisket and Cabbage

serves 4–6

900 g	(*2 lb*) corned beef brisket
1	large cabbage, quartered
2	large carrots, pared and halved
5 ml	(*1 tsp*) sweet basil
1 ml	(*¼ tsp*) thyme
2	bay leaves
2	parsley sprigs
	few black peppercorns
	salt and freshly ground pepper

Place brisket in large saucepan and pour in enough water to cover meat by 5 cm (*2 in*). Cover with lid and bring to boil for 2 to 3 minutes.

Skim surface, cover again and cook 1 hour over medium heat.

Add vegetables, basil, thyme, bay leaves and peppercorns; season well. Cover and continue cooking 1 hour over medium heat.

Remove vegetables and transfer to bowl.

Cover saucepan and finish cooking 30 minutes or longer, depending on size.

Remove brisket from liquid, slice and serve with cooked vegetables and mustard.

1 serving	*614 calories*	*13 g carbohydrate*
37 g protein	*46 g fat*	*6.8 g fibre*

Beef and Kidney Pie

serves 2

30 ml	(*2 tbsp*) clarified butter
5 ml	(*1 tsp*) olive oil
450 g	(*lb*) top sirloin, trimmed of fat and cut into medium cubes
450 g	(*lb*) beef kidney, trimmed of fat and cut into medium cubes
2	small onions, cut into 6
2 ml	(*½ tsp*) basil
2 ml	(*½ tsp*) chilli powder
1	large carrot, peeled and cubed
2	small potatoes, peeled and cubed
30 g	(*1 oz*) flour
750 ml	(*1¼ pt*) beef stock, heated
	salt and pepper
pinch	thyme
dash	paprika
	few crushed chillies
	pastry dough (commercial or leftover)
	milk

Preheat oven to 180°C (*350°F, gas mark 4*).

Heat clarified butter and oil in frying pan. Add sirloin and cook 4 to 5 minutes over medium heat. Season well and turn beef to brown all sides. Remove cubes from pan and set aside.

Place beef kidney in hot frying pan. Sear 4 to 5 minutes over medium heat, turning pieces to brown all sides. Season well.

Return sirloin to frying pan with kidney. Add onions and all seasonings; mix well.

Add remaining vegetables and sprinkle in flour. Mix and cook 3 to 4 minutes over low heat.

Stir in beef stock and season well. Cook 2 to 3 minutes over medium heat.

Divide mixture between two individual baking dishes. Cover with rolled pastry dough and crimp edges against lip of dish.

Score 4 small holes along top of each pastry crust to allow steam to escape and finish by brushing dough with a bit of milk.

Cook 1 hour in oven.

1 serving	1312 calories	65 g carbohydrate
128 g protein	60 g fat	5.9 g fibre

1. Trim and cut meat and vegetables before beginning the recipe.

2. Both the sirloin and kidney should be seared in hot oil over medium heat. Be sure to turn pieces to brown on all sides.

3. Add onions and all seasonings to meat in pan; mix well.

4. Add remaining vegetables, sprinkle with flour and season well.

Beef Sirloin Strips on Pasta

serves 4

450 g	(*1 lb*) beef sirloin, cut in 5-mm (¼-*in*) thick strips
30 ml	(*2 tbsp*) vegetable oil
1	red pepper, thinly sliced
⅓	cucumber, peeled, seeded and cut in sticks
20	fresh mushrooms, cleaned and sliced
15 ml	(*1 tbsp*) freshly chopped ginger root
300 ml	(*½ pt*) beef stock, heated
5 ml	(*1 tsp*) cornflour
30 ml	(*2 tbsp*) cold water
525 g	(*18 oz*) cooked shell pasta, hot
	few drops teriyaki sauce
	salt and pepper

Place meat in bowl with teriyaki sauce to marinate 15 minutes.

Heat oil in large frying pan over high heat. Add meat and cook 1 minute on each side. Season well, remove from pan and set aside.

Add all vegetables and ginger to pan; season and cook 3 minutes over high heat, stirring once.

Pour in beef stock and cook 1 minute still over high heat. Mix cornflour with cold water; stir into mixture until well incorporated. Cook 1 more minute.

Return meat to pan and reheat 1 minute. Serve over hot pasta.

1 serving	434 calories	41 g carbohydrate
36 g protein	14 g fat	2.8 g fibre

Chicken Pot Pie

serves 4

2	**whole chicken breasts, skinned and boned**
2	**potatoes, peeled and cubed small**
2	**carrots, peeled and sliced 5 mm (¼ in) thick**
1	**onion, cut into 8**
1 ml	**(¼ tsp) tarragon**
15 ml	**(1 tbsp) chopped fresh parsley**
60 g	**(2 oz) butter**
750 ml	**(1¼ pt) cold water**
30 g	**(1 oz) flour**
dash	**paprika**
	salt and pepper
	few drops Worcestershire sauce
	ready-to-use pastry dough

Split chicken breasts into halves and cut each half into four pieces, for a total of 16 pieces.

Place chicken, potatoes, carrots, onion, tarragon, parsley, paprika and 15 g (½ oz) butter in deep frying pan. Season well and pour in cold water. Sprinkle in Worcestershire sauce, cover and bring to boil. Reduce heat to medium and cook chicken and vegetables until both are completely cooked. The meat should no longer be pink in the centre and the vegetables should be tender.

Using slotted spoon, remove vegetables and chicken and divide them into four individual-size baking dishes; set aside. Reserve cooking liquid in frying pan.

Heat remaining butter in saucepan. When bubbly, add flour and mix very well; cook 2 minutes, stirring frequently. Stir in reserved cooking liquid and mix thoroughly with whisk. Cook 4 to 5 minutes over medium heat to thicken sauce.

Preheat oven to 180°C (*350°F, gas mark 4*).

Pour sauce into each baking dish and cover with ready-to-use pastry dough. Crimp edges with fingers and score dough 3 times to allow steam to escape.

Place pies in oven and cook 30 minutes.

1 serving	*441 calories*	*33 g carbohydrate*
30 g protein	*21 g fat*	*3.3 g fibre*

Shepherd's Pie

serves 4

4	**potatoes, cooked in skins and still hot**
30 g	(*1 oz*) **butter**
175 ml	(*6 fl oz*) **milk, heated**
15 ml	(*1 tbsp*) **peanut oil**
3	**onions, finely chopped**
2	**spring onions, finely chopped**
2	**celery sticks, finely chopped**
1 ml	(*¼ tsp*) **chilli powder**
2 ml	(*½ tsp*) **basil**
450 g	(*1 lb*) **lean minced beef**
350 g	(*¾ lb*) **canned sweetcorn, drained**
30 ml	(*2 tbsp*) **melted butter**
	salt and pepper
pinch	**nutmeg**
pinch	**thyme**

Preheat oven to 180°C (*350°F, gas mark 4*).

Grease baking dish with butter and set aside.

Peel cooked potatoes, cut up and mash until smooth. Add 30 g (*1 oz*) butter and season with salt, pepper and nutmeg; mix well.

Incorporate hot milk to potatoes and set aside.

Heat oil in large, deep frying pan. Cook onions, spring onions and celery with all seasonings 3 to 4 minutes over high heat.

Mix well and add meat. Cook 4 to 5 minutes and season well.

Stir in corn and continue cooking 2 to 3 minutes.

Spread half of mashed potatoes in bottom of greased baking dish. Cover with meat mixture.

Spoon remaining potatoes in piping bag fitted with large star nozzle and cover meat mixture. Season well and sprinkle with melted butter.

Cook 20 minutes in oven.

1 serving	713 calories	77 g carbohydrate
36 g protein	29 g fat	6.3 g fibre

Chicken Livers with Mixed Vegetables

serves 4

15 ml	(*1 tbsp*) vegetable oil
600 g	(*1¼ lb*) chicken livers, well cleaned
15 ml	(*1 tbsp*) melted butter
3	spring onions, sliced
1	large courgette, sliced thick
1	red pepper, thinly sliced
6	water chestnuts, sliced
2 ml	(*½ tsp*) tarragon
5 ml	(*1 tsp*) chopped fresh parsley
400 ml	(*⅔ pt*) beef stock, heated
15 ml	(*1 tbsp*) cornflour
30 ml	(*2 tbsp*) cold water
	salt and pepper
pinch	thyme
pinch	paprika

Heat oil in frying pan over high heat. Add chicken livers when oil is very hot and cook 2 minutes.

Turn livers over, season and continue cooking 3 minutes over high heat.

Turn a second time, season again and continue cooking 3 minutes.

Remove livers and set aside.

Add melted butter to pan; then add all vegetables and water chestnuts. Season with salt and pepper and add all seasonings. Cook 4 to 5 minutes over high heat.

Pour in beef stock, stir and bring to boil.

Mix cornflour with water; stir into sauce and cook 1 minute over medium heat.

Place livers in sauce, correct seasoning, reheat 1 minute and serve.

1 serving	290 calories	9 g carbohydrate
32 g protein	14 g fat	2.1 g fibre

Sautéed Chicken Breast Medley

serves 4

30 g	(*1 oz*) butter
2	whole chicken breasts, skinned, split in 2 and boned
2	shallots, finely chopped
1	celery stick, diced
450 g	(*1 lb*) fresh mushrooms, cleaned and diced
1	green pepper, thinly sliced
1	red pepper, thinly sliced
15 ml	(*1 tbsp*) freshly chopped parsley
2 ml	(*½ tsp*) tarragon
400 ml	(*⅔ pt*) chicken stock, heated
5 ml	(*1 tsp*) cornflour
30 ml	(*2 tbsp*) cold water
	salt and pepper

Heat butter in large frying pan over medium heat. Add chicken and season well; cook 7 to 8 minutes.

Turn breasts over. Add shallots, celery, mushrooms, green pepper, red pepper, parsley and tarragon; season well. Continue cooking 7 to 8 minutes.

Transfer chicken breasts to serving platter; keep hot.

Pour chicken stock into frying pan and bring to boil. Mix cornflour with water; stir into sauce until well incorporated. Cook 1 minute.

Pour sauce and vegetables over chicken and serve.

1 serving	217 calories	10 g carbohydrate
24 g protein	9 g fat	3.9 g fibre

1. Add chicken breasts to hot butter and season well; cook 7 to 8 minutes over medium heat.

2. Turn breasts over — underside should be nicely browned.

3. Add vegetables and seasonings. Continue cooking 7 to 8 minutes.

4. With cooked chicken removed, add hot chicken stock to pan and bring to boil. Thicken sauce with diluted cornflour.

Chicken Vol-au-Vent

serves 4

2	whole chicken breasts, split into 2, skinned and diced large
40 g	(1¼ oz) butter
5 ml	(1 tsp) chopped fresh parsley
500 ml	(17 fl oz) chicken stock, heated
1 ml	(¼ tsp) tarragon
2	onions, cut into 6
225 g	(½ lb) fresh button mushrooms, cleaned and halved
150 g	(5 oz) frozen green peas
30 ml	(2 tbsp) flour
4	large cooked vol-au-vent shells
	juice ¼ lemon
	salt and pepper
pinch	thyme
pinch	nutmeg

Place chicken in deep frying pan. Add 15 g (½ oz) butter, parsley and lemon juice. Poach 2 minutes over very low heat.

Turn pieces over and season. Pour in chicken stock, add all seasonings and onions. Mix well and bring to boil.

Cover and cook 10 minutes over low heat.

Add mushrooms and peas. Season, cover and cook 8 minutes over medium heat.

Remove frying pan from heat. Using slotted spoon, remove chicken and vegetables; set aside. Reserve cooking liquid.

Melt remaining butter in saucepan. Add flour and mix well. Cook 2 minutes over medium heat.

Incorporate reserved cooking liquid from chicken into saucepan by mixing well with whisk. Season to taste and cook sauce 6 to 7 minutes over medium heat, stirring only once during cooking.

Place chicken and vegetables in sauce without adding the juice that may have collected. Cook 3 to 4 minutes.

Fill pastry shells with chicken mixture and serve.

1 serving	627 calories	42 g carbohydrate
36 g protein	35 g fat	7.9 g fibre

1. Place chicken in deep frying pan. Add 15 g (½ *oz*) butter, parsley and lemon juice. Poach 2 minutes over very low heat.

2. Turn pieces over and season. Pour in chicken stock and add all seasonings and onions. Mix well and bring to boil. Cover and cook 10 minutes over low heat.

3. Add mushrooms and peas. Season, cover and cook 8 minutes over medium heat.

4. Remove chicken and vegetables and set aside.

Chicken Wings Brière

serves 4

24	chicken wings
30 ml.	(*2 tbsp*) chopped fresh ginger
1	garlic clove, smashed and chopped
5 ml	(*1 tsp*) Worcestershire sauce
5 ml	(*1 tsp*) Pickapeppa sauce
30 ml	(*2 tbsp*) olive oil
60 ml	(*4 tbsp*) ketchup
	juice 1 lemon
	salt and pepper

Snip off tips from wings and discard. Blanch wings 8 to 10 minutes.

Mix together in bowl ginger, garlic, Worcestershire sauce and Pickapeppa sauce. Add lemon juice, oil and ketchup; mix again and season with pepper.

Drain blanched wings and place in bowl containing marinade; let stand 15 minutes.

Place wings in roasting tin and grill in preheated oven 3 to 4 minutes on each side, basting during cooking.

Season and serve.

1 serving	329 calories	5 g carbohydrate
39 g protein	17 g fat	0 g fibre

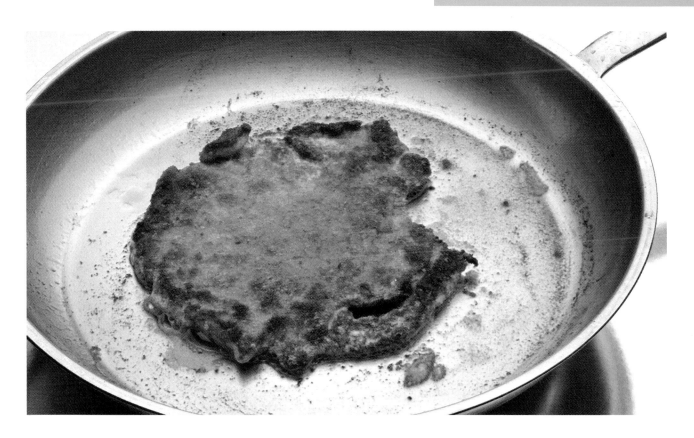

Breaded Chicken Breasts

serves 4

2	**whole chicken breasts, split into 2, skinned and boned**
150 g	**(5 oz) flour**
2	**beaten eggs**
125 g	**(4 oz) breadcrumbs**
30 ml	**(2 tbsp) peanut or vegetable oil**
15 g	**(½ oz) butter**
	salt and pepper

Place each chicken breast between 2 sheets of waxed paper; pound with meat bat until quite thin.

Season chicken with salt and pepper; dredge in flour. Dip in beaten eggs, and then coat with breadcrumbs.

Heat oil and butter in large frying pan. Add chicken and cook 3 to 4 minutes on each side over medium heat or until done.

Serve with your favourite sauce.

1 serving	465 calories	32 g carbohydrate
37 g protein	21 g fat	2.1 g fibre

Chicken Sautéed with Vinegar

serves 4

1.6 kg	(*3½ lb*) chicken, cleaned, cut into 8 pieces and skinned
30 ml	(*2 tbsp*) melted butter
2	garlic cloves, smashed and chopped
150 ml	(*¼ pt*) dry white wine
50 ml	(*2 fl oz*) wine vinegar
15 ml	(*1 tbsp*) tomato purée
400 ml	(*⅔ pt*) chicken stock, heated
15 ml	(*1 tbsp*) cornflour
45 ml	(*3 tbsp*) cold water
15 ml	(*1 tbsp*) freshly chopped parsley
	salt and pepper

Preheat oven to 180°C (*350°F, gas mark 4*).

Season chicken pieces. Heat butter in large frying pan over medium heat. Add chicken and brown on all sides. Season and add garlic; cook 3 minutes.

Pour in wine and vinegar; stir and continue cooking 4 to 5 minutes over high heat. Mix in tomato purée and chicken stock; season well.

Cover and cook chicken 18 to 20 minutes in oven, depending on size.

Remove cooked chicken from pan and set aside. Place frying pan over medium heat. Mix cornflour with cold water; stir into pan until well incorporated. Season and cook 3 minutes.

Return chicken to sauce and simmer 2 to 3 minutes over low heat. Sprinkle with parsley and serve.

1 serving	*592 calories*	*5 g carbohydrate*
98 g protein	*20 g fat*	*0.1 g fibre*

Chicken, Almonds and Raisins

serves 4

30 g	(*1 oz*) butter
1	large onion, chopped
1	garlic clove, smashed and chopped
150 ml	(*¼ pt*) dry white wine
150 ml	(*¼ pt*) chicken stock, heated
450 ml	(*¾ pt*) white sauce, heated
90 g	(*3 oz*) sultana raisins
75 g	(*2½ oz*) slivered almonds
350 g	(*¾ lb*) diced cooked chicken
1	egg yolk
50 ml	(*2 fl oz*) double cream
1 ml	(*¼ tsp*) cumin
15 ml	(*1 tbsp*) freshly chopped parsley
	salt and pepper

Heat butter in frying pan over medium heat. Add onion and garlic; cook 3 minutes.

Pour in wine and cook 3 minutes over high heat. Mix in chicken stock; continue cooking 3 minutes.

Stir in white sauce. Add raisins, almonds and chicken; mix well with wooden spoon and correct seasoning. Cook 3 minutes over low heat.

Mix egg yolk with cream and add cumin. Pour into chicken mixture and mix well. Simmer 3 minutes over very low heat. Do not allow sauce to boil!

Serve in hollowed out toasted rolls, if desired. Sprinkle with parsley.

1 serving	633 calories	20 g carbohydrate
37 g protein	45 g fat	0.5 g fibre

Chicken Salad in Cantaloupe Shells

serves 4

45 ml	(*3 tbsp*) mayonnaise
45 ml	(*3 tbsp*) plain yogurt
15 ml	(*1 tbsp*) curry powder
15 ml	(*1 tbsp*) freshly chopped parsley
1	cooked whole chicken breast, skinned and diced
2	small cantaloupe melons
	salt and pepper
	juice ½ lemon
	paprika

Place mayonnaise, yogurt, curry powder and parsley in small bow. Season and mix well. Add diced chicken and lemon juice; mix well.

Using zigzag cutting motion, split melons in half. Scoop out seeds and discard.

Fill shells with mounds of chicken mixture. Sprinkle with paprika and serve.

1 serving	236 calories	25 g carbohydrate
16 g protein	8 g fat	2.8 g fibre

Veal Croquettes

serves 4

30 g	(*1 oz*) butter
1	onion, finely chopped
450 g	(*1 lb*) lean minced veal
15 ml	(*1 tbsp*) curry powder
400 ml	(*⅔ pt*) thick white sauce*, heated
2	egg yolks
150 g	(*5 oz*) plain flour
2	beaten eggs
175 g	(*6 oz*) seasoned breadcrumbs
	salt and pepper
	peanut oil for frying

Place butter and onion in frying pan. Cook 4 to 5 minutes over low heat.

Add meat and season well. Sprinkle in curry powder and mix well with wooden spoon. Cook 7 to 8 minutes over high heat, stirring to break up lumps.

When meat is cooked, stir in white sauce and cook 2 minutes over medium-high heat.

Remove pan from heat and incorporate egg yolks. Return to burner and cook 2 minutes over medium heat, stirring constantly.

Transfer mixture to large dinner plate and smooth with spatula until flat. Let cool 30 minutes; then cover with cling film and refrigerate a minimum of 4 hours before using.

Preheat plenty of peanut oil in deep-fryer at 190°C (*375°F*).

Shape cold croquette mixture into cylindrical-type rolls. Roll each in flour, coat lightly with beaten egg and finish by rolling in breadcrumbs.

Deep-fry croquettes until golden brown.

Serve with your favourite sauce.

* See Poached Salmon with Egg Sauce, page 324.

1 serving	717 calories	54 g carbohydrate
42 g protein	37 g fat	1.8 g fibre

221

Veal Burgers

serves 4

700 g	(*1½ lb*) lean minced veal
1	beaten egg
30 ml	(*2 tbsp*) vegetable oil
1	large green pepper, thinly sliced
2	apples, cored and thinly sliced, with peel
15 g	(*½ oz*) butter
1	large onion, halved and thinly sliced
4	cooked potatoes, peeled and cut into 5-mm (*¼-in*) slices
pinch	paprika
	few drops Worcestershire sauce
	salt and pepper

Place meat, egg, paprika and Worcestershire sauce in food processor. Season and blend until meat forms ball. Shape into 4 burgers.

Heat oil in large frying pan over medium heat. Add burgers and cook 3 to 4 minutes. Turn over, season and continue cooking 3 to 4 minutes depending on size and preference.

Remove meat from pan, set aside and keep hot.

Add green pepper and apples to pan; season well. Cook 3 minutes over medium heat.

Meanwhile, melt butter in another frying pan. Add onion and potatoes; season well. Cook 3 to 4 minutes over medium heat.

Serve green pepper and apples over burgers. Accompany with potatoes on the side or on separate plates.

1 serving	626 calories	45 g carbohydrate
44 g protein	30 g fat	5.4 g fibre

Veal Stew

serves 2

900 g	(*2 lb*) veal shoulder, cubed and trimmed of fat
1	celery stick, cubed
1	onion, quartered
1	large potato, peeled and cubed
3	parsley sprigs
2 ml	(*½ tsp*) tarragon
1	bay leaf
30 g	(*1 oz*) butter
30 ml	(*2 tbsp*) flour
30 ml	(*2 tbsp*) double cream
	salt and pepper
dash	paprika

Place veal in saucepan and cover with cold water. Bring to boil and continue cooking 3 minutes.

Drain meat, rinse under cold water and place in clean saucepan.

Add celery, onion, potato, salt and pepper. Add seasonings and bay leaf; pour in enough cold water to cover.

Cover saucepan and bring to boil. Cook 1 hour 15 minutes over medium-low heat.

Remove vegetables from saucepan and set aside. Continue cooking veal until tender. Remove with slotted spoon and reserve liquid.

Melt butter in separate saucepan. Add flour and mix well. Cook 2 minutes over low heat, stirring constantly.

Pour in cooking liquid from veal; mix well with whisk. Stir in cream and season to taste.

Place vegetables and veal in sauce, stir and simmer 1 minute or until reheated.

1 serving	1049 calories	27 g carbohydrate
98 g protein	61 g fat	2.8 g fibre

Crêpes Stuffed with Veal

serves 4

150 g	(5 oz) plain flour
3	large eggs
250 ml	(8 fl oz) milk
50 ml	(2 fl oz) tepid water
45 ml	(3 tbsp) melted butter, warm
15 ml	(1 tbsp) chopped fresh parsley
30 g	(1 oz) butter
1	onion, chopped
1	celery stick, diced small
225 g	(½ lb) fresh mushrooms, cleaned and sliced
2 ml	(½ tsp) tarragon
1 ml	(¼ tsp) celery seeds
350 g	(¾ lb) lean minced veal
600 ml	(1 pt) cheesy white sauce*
90 g	(3 oz) grated mozzarella cheese
	salt and white pepper
pinch	paprika

Place flour and pinch of salt in large bowl. Whisk in eggs until smooth. Whisk in milk and water; then strain batter through sieve into clean bowl.

Mix in melted butter, parsley and paprika; season. Cover with sheet of cling film touching surface and chill 1 hour. Prepare crêpes using crêpe batter.

Preheat oven to 200°C (400°F, gas mark 6).

Melt 30 g (1 oz) butter in frying pan over medium heat. Cook onion and celery 4 minutes. Add mushrooms and seasonings; mix well. Cook 3 to 4 minutes.

Mix in meat and correct seasoning; brown meat 3 minutes. Cover and cook another 3 minutes.

Pour in cheesy white sauce, cook another 2 minutes and remove pan from heat. Stuff crêpes with mixture and place in baking dish. Top with leftover stuffing and cheese. Melt in oven 7 to 8 minutes.

* See Broccoli with Old-Fashioned Cheddar Sauce, page 376.

1 serving	845 calories	48 g carbohydrate
44 g protein	53 g fat	3.5 g fibre

1. It is necessary to use plain flour for the crêpe batter.

2. After flour and pinch of salt have been placed in a bowl, add eggs. Blend together with whisk until smooth and lump-free.

3. After liquids have been incorporated, pour batter through wire sieve into clean bowl.

4. Making crêpes is easiest with a special pan. If not available, use a short-rimmed frying pan.

Zesty Sliced Pork

serves 4

30 ml	(*2 tbsp*) peanut oil
3	pork cutlets, fat trimmed and cut into strips 1 cm (*½ in*) wide
1	carrot, peeled and sliced
6	large fresh mushrooms, cleaned and sliced
15 ml	(*1 tbsp*) chopped fresh ginger
2	stalks short bok choy, sliced thick
15 ml	(*1 tbsp*) soy sauce
	salt and pepper

Heat oil in frying pan over high heat. Add meat and carrot; cook 3 minutes.

Turn meat strips over, season and continue cooking 3 minutes.

Add mushrooms and ginger; continue cooking 2 minutes.

Correct seasoning and add bok choy; sprinkle in soy sauce, mix and cook 2 minutes.

Serve immediately.

1 serving	282 calories	4 g carbohydrate
26 g protein	18 g fat	1.9 g fibre

Braised Pork Shoulder with Vegetables *serves 4*

15 ml	(*1 tbsp*) peanut oil
1.4 kg	(*3 lb*) pork shoulder, boned
2	garlic cloves, peeled and halved
2	onions, halved
250 ml	(*8 fl oz*) dry white wine
800 g	(*1¾ lb*) canned tomatoes
5 ml	(*1 tsp*) basil
1 ml	(*¼ tsp*) thyme
2 ml	(*½ tsp*) oregano
1	bay leaf
½	turnip, cut into large cubes
30 ml	(*2 tbsp*) cornflour
60 ml	(*4 tbsp*) cold water
	salt and pepper
	few drops Worcestershire sauce
	few drops Pickapeppa sauce

Heat oil in large saucepan. Meanwhile, make several incisions in pork with small knife and insert garlic pieces.

Sear meat 8 minutes over medium-high heat. Be sure to turn meat to brown all sides and season at the end of cooking.

Add onions and continue cooking 7 to 8 minutes over medium heat.

Pour in wine and cook 3 more minutes.

Add tomatoes with juice, add all seasonings including bay leaf and cover. Cook 1¼ hours over low heat, stirring occasionally.

Add turnip, season and continue cooking, covered, 1¼ hours or longer depending on size of pork shoulder.

Remove meat from saucepan and set aside.

Mix cornflour with water; stir into sauce. Add Worcestershire sauce and Pickapeppa sauce and bring to boil. Cook 2 to 3 minutes.

Slice meat and serve with vegetables and sauce. Garnish with green peas.

1 serving	*709 calories*	*22 g carbohydrate*
72 g protein	*37 g fat*	*3.4 g fibre*

Feta-Stuffed Aubergine Shells

serves 2

1	large aubergine
15 ml	(*1 tbsp*) olive oil
15 ml	(*1 tbsp*) peanut oil
½	onion, chopped
225 g	(*½ lb*) lean minced beef
½	red pepper, chopped
2 ml	(*½ tsp*) sweet basil
2 ml	(*½ tsp*) chilli powder
90 g	(*3 oz*) feta cheese, crumbled
4	slices mozzarella cheese, about 2.5 cm (*1 in*) wide
	salt and pepper

Preheat oven to 200°C (*400°F, gas mark 6*).

Slice aubergine into two equal halves lengthways. Score flesh in a crisscross pattern and brush with olive oil. Place in baking dish and cook 30 minutes in oven.

Using spoon, scoop out most of the cooked flesh while still leaving sturdy shell; set aside.

Heat peanut oil in large frying pan. Add onion, beef and red pepper; season well.

Add basil and chilli powder to pan and mix well. Cook 5 to 6 minutes over medium heat.

Chop aubergine flesh and add to pan. Continue cooking 3 to 4 minutes.

Add feta cheese and cook 2 minutes or until melted.

Spoon filling into aubergine shells and top with slices of mozzarella. Grill until melted and serve at once.

1 serving	703 calories	14 g carbohydrate
47 g protein	51 g fat	3.5 g fibre

Pork Cutlets in Mustard Sauce

serves 4

30 ml	(*2 tbsp*) vegetable oil
4	pork cutlets, fat trimmed
450 g	(*1 lb*) fresh mushrooms, cleaned and sliced
1	apple, cored, peeled and sliced thick
400 ml	(*⅔ pt*) chicken stock, heated
15 ml	(*1 tbsp*) cornflour
30 ml	(*2 tbsp*) cold water
15 ml	(*1 tbsp*) Dijon mustard
	salt and pepper

Heat half of oil in frying pan. When hot, add pork cutlets and cook 3 to 4 minutes over medium-high heat.

Turn cutlets over, season well and continue cooking 3 to 4 minutes, depending on size.

Remove cutlets from frying pan and keep hot.

Add remaining oil, mushrooms and apple to pan. Season and cook 3 minutes over high heat.

Stir in chicken stock and bring to boil. Mix cornflour with water; stir into sauce and cook 3 to 4 minutes over low heat.

Remove pan from heat and stir in mustard. Place pork in sauce and serve.

1 serving	*394 calories*	*13 g carbohydrate*
36 g protein	*22 g fat*	*3.8 g fibre*

Spicy Sausages with Aubergine

serves 4

45 ml	(*3 tbsp*) peanut oil
1	aubergine, peeled and diced
1	onion, diced
2	garlic cloves, smashed and chopped
3	spring onions, chopped
600 g	(*1¼ lb*) hot spicy sausages
	salt and pepper
	chopped fresh parsley

Heat 30 ml (*2 tbsp*) oil in large frying pan. When hot, add aubergine, onion, garlic and spring onions; season well. Cover and cook 20 minutes over medium heat, stirring frequently.

Mix in sausages and add remaining oil. Partly cover and continue cooking 15 minutes.

Reduce heat to low and finish cooking 7 to 8 minutes. Sprinkle with parsley and serve.

1 serving	501 calories	8 g carbohydrate
25 g protein	41 g fat	1.9 g fibre

Garlicky Sweet Sausages

serves 4

30 ml	(*2 tbsp*) peanut oil
3	potatoes, peeled, halved and thinly sliced
600 g	(*1¼ lb*) sweet sausages
2	garlic cloves, smashed and chopped
1	onion, thinly sliced
200 ml	(*⅓ pt*) chicken stock, heated
	salt and pepper

Heat half of oil in large frying pan over high heat. Add potatoes and season; cook, partly covered, 15 minutes. Be sure to stir frequently.

Add sausages and remaining oil; season well. Partly cover and continue cooking 10 to 12 minutes over medium heat. Turn sausages over twice during cooking.

Stir in garlic and onion. Cook, partly covered, 10 minutes, stirring several times.

Pour in chicken stock and bring to boil. Correct seasoning and cook 5 minutes, uncovered, over low heat. Serve.

1 serving	537 calories	25 g carbohydrate
26 g protein	37 g fat	2.6 g fibre

Hot Sausages in Tomato Sauce

serves 4

15 ml	(*1 tbsp*) olive oil
1	onion, chopped
1	celery stick, diced
½	small hot pepper, chopped
2	garlic cloves, smashed and chopped
800 g	(*1¾ lb*) canned tomatoes, drained and chopped
2 ml	(*½ tsp*) oregano
15 ml	(*1 tbsp*) chopped fresh parsley
150 ml	(*¼ pt*) canned tomato purée
150 ml	(*¼ pt*) beef stock, heated
15 ml	(*1 tbsp*) peanut oil
600 g	(*1¼ lb*) hot spicy sausages, blanched 7 minutes
	salt and pepper
pinch	sugar

Heat olive oil in large, deep frying pan. When hot, add onion, celery, hot pepper and garlic; cook 5 to 6 minutes over medium heat.

Stir in tomatoes and season. Add sugar, oregano, parsley, tomato purée and beef stock. Stir well and bring to boil. Cook 20 minutes over medium heat.

Heat peanut oil in frying pan. When hot, add sausages and cook 15 minutes over medium heat, turning pieces over frequently.

Serve with tomato sauce.

1 serving	538 calories	22 g carbohydrate
27 g protein	38 g fat	3.1 g fibre

Sweet Sausages with Tomatoes

serves 4

30 ml	(*2 tbsp*) peanut oil
600 g	(*1¼ lb*) sweet sausages
2 ml	(*½ tsp*) sweet basil
1	onion, halved and sliced
6	plum tomatoes, quartered
1	small hot yellow pepper, chopped
1	large apple, cored, peeled and thinly sliced
400 ml	(*⅔ pt*) beef stock, heated
15 ml	(*1 tbsp*) cornflour
45 ml	(*3 tbsp*) cold water
	salt and pepper
	few drops soy sauce

Heat oil in large, deep frying pan over high heat. When hot, add sausages and reduce heat to medium. Cook, partly covered, 10 minutes, turning pieces over 2 or 3 times during cooking.

Sprinkle in basil and season well. Add vegetables and apple; continue cooking, partly covered, another 10 minutes.

Remove sausages from pan and set aside.

Increase heat to high and cook vegetables another 2 minutes.

Stir in beef stock, season and bring to boil.

Mix cornflour with water; stir into sauce. Sprinkle in soy sauce and finish cooking 2 minutes.

Serve immediately with sausages.

1 serving	526 calories	20 g carbohydrate
26 g protein	38 g fat	4.0 g fibre

Chilli Con Carne

serves 4

30 ml	(*2 tbsp*) vegetable oil
2	onions, chopped
2	garlic cloves, smashed and chopped
1	yellow pepper, chopped
700 g	(*1½ lb*) lean minced beef
2 ml	(*½ tsp*) caraway seeds
2 ml	(*½ tsp*) celery seeds
550 g	(*19 oz*) canned red kidney beans, drained
375 g	(*13 oz*) stewed tomatoes
300 ml	(*½ pt*) beef stock, heated
60 ml	(*4 tbsp*) tomato purée
pinch	cayenne
pinch	paprika
	few crushed red peppers
	salt and pepper
pinch	sugar

Preheat oven to 180°C (*350°F, gas mark 4*).

Heat oil in large, deep frying pan. Add onions, garlic and yellow pepper; cook 7 to 8 minutes over medium heat.

Stir in meat and season. Add all seasonings and mix very well. Cook 5 to 6 minutes over medium heat.

Stir in kidney beans and continue cooking 4 to 5 minutes.

Add tomatoes and sugar; cook 2 to 3 minutes. Stir in beef stock and tomato purée; correct seasoning. Bring to boil.

Cover pan and cook 45 minutes in oven. Serve chilli with fresh bread, if desired.

1 serving	547 calories	36 g carbohydrate
49 g protein	23 g fat	10.8 g fibre

1. Heat oil in large, deep frying pan. Cook onions, garlic and yellow pepper 7 to 8 minutes over medium heat.

2. Stir in meat and season. Add all seasonings and mix very well. Cook 5 to 6 minutes over medium heat.

3. Stir in kidney beans and continue cooking 4 to 5 minutes.

4. Add tomatoes and sugar; cook 2 to 3 minutes.

Stuffed Green Peppers

serves 4

15 ml	(*1 tbsp*) vegetable oil
3	figs, finely chopped
1	onion, finely chopped
1	celery stick, finely chopped
200 g	(*7 oz*) cooked rice
225 g	(*1/2 lb*) canned sweetcorn
2 ml	(*1/2 tsp*) tarragon
2	green peppers, halved across width, seeded and blanched 6 minutes
15 ml	(*1 tbsp*) olive oil
2	shallots, chopped
225 g	(*1/2 lb*) fresh mushrooms, cleaned and sliced
800 g	(*1 3/4 lb*) canned tomatoes, drained and chopped
5 ml	(*1 tsp*) tomato purée
125 ml	(*4 fl oz*) chicken stock, heated
	salt and pepper
pinch	sugar

Preheat oven to 180°C (*350°F, gas mark 4*).

Heat vegetable oil in frying pan. Add figs, onion and celery; season well. Cook 4 to 5 minutes over medium heat.

Stir in rice and corn. Correct seasoning, add tarragon and mix well. Cook 4 to 5 minutes.

Pour mixture into food processor and blend for 2 minutes; set aside.

Place blanched peppers in ovenproof baking dish and fill with stuffing; set aside.

Heat olive oil in frying pan. Add shallots and mushrooms; cook 3 to 4 minutes over high heat.

Add tomatoes, sugar, tomato purée and chicken stock; mix well. Bring to boil. Season and continue cooking 2 to 3 minutes over medium heat.

Pour sauce over stuffed peppers and cook, uncovered, 45 minutes in oven.

Serve with your favourite grated cheese.

1 serving	318 calories	48 g carbohydrate
9 g protein	10 g fat	8.6 g fibre

Stuffed Cabbage Leaves in Sauce   *serves 4*

8	**large curly cabbage leaves, well washed and dried**
30 ml	(*2 tbsp*) **peanut oil**
1	**green pepper, finely chopped**
2	**spring onions, finely chopped**
225 g	(*½ lb*) **fresh mushrooms, cleaned and finely chopped**
½	**onion, finely chopped**
2	**garlic cloves, chopped**
1 ml	(*¼ tsp*) **chilli powder**
2 ml	(*½ tsp*) **sweet basil**
1 ml	(*¼ tsp*) **thyme**
15 ml	(*1 tbsp*) **chopped fresh parsley**
450 g	(*1 lb*) **lean minced beef**
30 ml	(*2 tbsp*) **tomato purée**
50 ml	(*2 fl oz*) **chicken stock, heated**
90 g	(*3 oz*) **feta cheese, chopped**
30 g	(*1 oz*) **butter**
400 ml	(*⅔ pt*) **canned tomato sauce, heated**
	salt and pepper

Preheat oven to 180°C (*350°F, gas mark* 4).

Remove tough stems from bottom of cabbage leaves. Place leaves in salted boiling water. Cover and cook 4 to 5 minutes.

Drain leaves and place each on separate piece of absorbent kitchen paper. Pat dry with another piece of paper. Transfer to serving platter and set aside. Heat oil in large, deep frying pan over high heat. Add green pepper, spring onions, mushrooms, onion and garlic; season well. Sprinkle in seasonings and parsley; mix well. Cook 8 minutes, covered, over medium heat.

Stir in beef and season; continue cooking, covered, 7 to 8 minutes. Add tomato purée and chicken stock; mix well. Cook 4 to 5 minutes, uncovered.

Stir in cheese and continue cooking 2 minutes.

Spoon stuffing on each cabbage leaf. Fold sides over to meet and roll. Melt butter in frying pan. Place stuffed rolls in pan and cook 6 to 7 minutes on each side over high heat. Transfer to baking dish and pour in tomato sauce. Cover with foil and prick wrap with knife for steam vents.

Bake 1 hour in oven. If desired, garnish portions with vegetables.

1 serving	*499 calories*	*21 g carbohydrate*
34 g protein	*31 g fat*	*6.4 g fibre*

Hearty Gruyère Burgers with Ham and Mushrooms   *serves 2*

225 g	(½ lb) lean minced beef
30 ml	(*2 tbsp*) cooked chopped onion
½	beaten egg
15 ml	(*1 tbsp*) freshly chopped parsley
5 ml	(*1 tsp*) butter
1	shallot, chopped
4	large fresh mushrooms, cleaned and chopped
15 ml	(*1 tbsp*) double cream
15 ml	(*1 tbsp*) vegetable oil
2	thick slices toasted bread, trimmed of crust
2	slices Black Forest ham
30 g	(*1 oz*) grated Gruyère cheese
	few drops Worcestershire sauce
	salt and pepper

Place beef, onion, egg, half of parsley and Worcestershire sauce in food processor. Season well and blend 2 minutes. When mixture forms ball, remove and shape meat into 2 patties. Set aside.

Heat butter in small frying pan. Add shallot and cook 2 minutes over medium heat. Add mushrooms and remaining parsley; season well. Cook 3 to 4 minutes.

Stir in cream and cook 1 more minute. Set aside.

Heat oil in large frying pan over medium heat. Add patties and cook 8 to 10 minutes, depending on thickness, turning over 2 to 3 times to avoid charring.

When burgers are done, place on toasted bread and top with mushroom mixture. Add slice of ham and finish with grated cheese. Grill 3 minutes in oven to melt, and serve.

1 serving	477 calories	15 g carbohydrate
39 g protein	29 g fat	2.2 g fibre

Vegetable Beef Stew

serves 4

30 ml	(*2 tbsp*) vegetable oil
700 g	(*1½ lb*) blade steak, trimmed of fat and cut in 2.5-cm (*1-in*) cubes
2	onions, quartered
1	garlic clove, smashed and chopped
50 g	(*1¾ oz*) flour
1.2 litres	(*2¼ pt*) beef stock, heated
2 ml	(*½ tsp*) basil
1	bay leaf
30 ml	(*2 tbsp*) tomato purée
1	celery stick, diced large
2	carrots, peeled and cubed
2	potatoes, peeled and cubed
½	turnip, peeled and cubed
	salt and pepper
pinch	thyme

Preheat oven to 180°C (*350°F, gas mark 4*).

Heat oil in large ovenproof casserole. Add cubes of meat and sear 5 to 6 minutes, browning on all sides over high heat.

Season meat well and add onions and garlic; cook 4 to 5 minutes. Season again, cover and cook 1 hour in oven.

Mix in flour until well incorporated. Cook 3 minutes on stove over medium heat. Season well.

Pour in beef stock and add all seasonings including bay leaf; mix well. Cook 5 to 6 minutes over medium heat. Mix in tomato purée.

Cover and cook 30 minutes in oven.

Add all vegetables to casserole. Cover and finish cooking stew 45 minutes in oven. Serve.

1 serving	*515 calories*	*32 g carbohydrate*
45 g protein	*23 g fat*	*4.4 g fibre*

Pol's Favourite Meat Loaf

serves 4-6

15 g	(½ oz) butter
1	onion, chopped
2	garlic cloves, chopped
15 ml	(1 tbsp) chopped fresh parsley
2	spring onions, sliced
700 g	(1½ lb) lean minced beef
225 g	(½ lb) lean minced veal
50 ml	(2 fl oz) double cream
1	egg yolk
3	slices white bread, crusts trimmed
150 ml	(¼ pt) milk
2 ml	(½ tsp) caraway seeds
1 ml	(¼ tsp) nutmeg
1 ml	(¼ tsp) thyme
2 ml	(½ tsp) savory
1	egg white, lightly beaten
3	long sticks celery, peeled
3	bay leaves
	salt and pepper
	paprika to taste
	few crushed red peppers

Preheat oven to 180°C (*350°F, gas mark 4*).

Melt butter in large frying pan. Add onion, garlic, parsley and spring onions; cook 3 to 4 minutes over low heat. Place meat in mixing bowl and season well. Add cooked onion mixture and mix well. Pour in cream and mix until incorporated. Add egg yolk and mix again.

Place bread in small bowl and pour in milk. Let stand several minutes; then squeeze out excess milk from bread and place pieces in bowl containing meat. Incorporate well, add all seasonings and mix until well combined.

Add egg white and incorporate thoroughly. Press half of meat mixture into 14 x 24-cm (5½ x 9½-in) loaf tin. Arrange celery sticks on meat (trim to size if necessary) and press in slightly.

Cover with remaining meat and press firmly to take shape of mould. Lay bay leaves on top. Cover with sheet of perforated foil and place mould in roasting tin containing about 2.5 cm (*1 in*) hot water. Cook 1 hour 15 minutes in oven. Remove foil at halfway point.

Serve meat loaf with condiments or a sauce such as onion sauce.

1 serving	403 calories	11 g carbohydrate
38 g protein	23 g fat	1.4 g fibre

1. Place meat in mixing bowl and season well. Add cooked onion mixture and mix well.

2. After cream has been incorporated, add egg yolk and mix again.

3. Place pieces of soaked bread in bowl containing meat and incorporate well.

4. To make meat loaf, fill mould with half of meat mixture. Arrange peeled celery sticks on meat and press in slightly.

Baked Red Cabbage

serves 4

1	head red cabbage, cut into 6 pieces
30 g	(*1 oz*) bacon fat
1	garlic clove, smashed and chopped
15 ml	(*1 tbsp*) wine vinegar
4	thick rashers back bacon, rolled in cornmeal and grilled
	salt and pepper

Preheat oven to 200°C (*400°F, gas mark 6*).

Parboil cabbage in salted boiling water for 45 minutes, covered.

Drain well and set aside.

Heat bacon fat in large, deep frying pan over high heat. Add garlic and cabbage; season generously. Cook 6 to 7 minutes.

Cover pan and finish cooking in oven for 45 minutes.

Sprinkle cabbage with wine vinegar and let stand several minutes. Serve with grilled back bacon.

1 serving	190 calories	14 g carbohydrate
11 g protein	10 g fat	8.5 g fibre

WINING AND DINING ON LAND

Main course recipes for every-day dining, unexpected company and formal entertaining

Coq au Vin

serves 4

45 ml	(*3 tbsp*) melted butter
2.3 kg	(*5 lb*) capon, cleaned, cut into 8 pieces and skinned
2	medium onions, in small wedges
3	garlic cloves, smashed and chopped
15 ml	(*1 tbsp*) chopped fresh chives
15 ml	(*1 tbsp*) chopped fresh parsley
500 ml	(*17 fl oz*) dry red wine
500 ml	(*17 fl oz*) light beef gravy, heated
1	bay leaf
225 g	(*½ lb*) fresh mushrooms, cleaned and halved
	salt and pepper

Preheat oven to 180°C (*350°F, gas mark 4*).

Heat 15 ml (*1 tbsp*) butter in large ovenproof casserole. Add half of chicken and brown on all sides for 5 to 6 minutes over medium-high heat. Remove chicken and set aside.

Add another 15 ml (*1 tbsp*) butter and repeat for remaining chicken. Add onions, garlic, chives and parsley to casserole; cook 2 minutes.

Return first half of chicken to casserole and pour in wine; bring to boil.

Mix in gravy and season well. Drop in bay leaf, cover casserole and cook 45 minutes in oven.

About 10 minutes before chicken is done, quickly sauté mushrooms in remaining 15 ml (*1 tbsp*) of butter. Add to casserole and resume cooking.

Serve with rice, potatoes or other vegetable.

1 serving	978 calories	15 g carbohydrate
90 g protein	62 g fat	2.7 g fibre

Quick Baked Chicken with Vegetables

serves 4

30 g	(*1 oz*) butter
2	whole chicken breasts, skinned, split into 2 and boned
½	celery stick, diced
2	large tomatoes, diced large
½	cucumber, peeled, seeded and diced
1	shallot, chopped
2 ml	(*½ tsp*) herbes de Provence
	salt and pepper

Preheat oven to 180°C (*350°F, gas mark 4*).

Heat butter in large ovenproof frying pan over medium heat. Add chicken and brown 3 minutes on each side, seasoning well when turning over.

Add remaining ingredients, being sure to season well. Continue cooking 2 minutes.

Cover pan and finish cooking 10 to 12 minutes in oven.

Serve with fresh asparagus, if desired.

Hunter Chicken

serves 4

1.6 kg	(*3½ lb*) chicken, cleaned, cut into 8 pieces and skinned
30 g	(*1 oz*) butter
3	shallots, finely chopped
450 g	(*1 lb*) fresh mushrooms, cleaned and halved
300 ml	(*½ pt*) dry white wine
375 ml	(*13 fl oz*) beef stock, heated
30 ml	(*2 tbsp*) tomato purée
15 ml	(*1 tbsp*) cornflour
45 ml	(*3 tbsp*) cold water
5 ml	(*1 tsp*) chervil
5 ml	(*1 tsp*) parsley
5 ml	(*1 tsp*) tarragon
	salt and pepper

Season chicken pieces. Heat butter in frying pan over medium heat. Add chicken and cook 18 to 20 minutes, turning chicken over twice.

Remove cooked chicken and set aside but keep hot.

Add shallots and mushrooms to frying pan; season and cook 4 minutes over medium heat.

Pour in wine and cook 3 minutes over high heat. Add beef stock and tomato purée; mix well.

Mix cornflour with cold water and stir into sauce until well incorporated. Season and add chervil, parsley and tarragon; continue cooking 4 to 5 minutes.

Place chicken in sauce and simmer 3 minutes over low heat before serving.

1 serving	653 calories	12 g carbohydrate
104 g protein	21 g fat	4.0 g fibre

Chicken Sauté Madeira

serves 4

1.6 kg	(*3½ lb*) chicken, cleaned, cut into 8 pieces and skinned
30 g	(*1 oz*) butter
2	shallots, finely chopped
125 ml	(*4 fl oz*) Madeira wine
600 ml	(*1 pt*) white sauce (not too thick), heated
15 ml	(*1 tbsp*) freshly chopped parsley
	salt and pepper

Season chicken pieces well. Heat butter in large frying pan over medium heat. Add chicken and cook 18 to 20 minutes turning pieces over twice.

Add shallots, mix well and cook another 2 minutes. Pour in wine and cook 1 minute.

Add white sauce, mix well and cook 3 to 4 minutes over low heat. Sprinkle with parsley and serve.

1 serving	784 calories	12 g carbohydrate
103 g protein	36 g fat	0.3 g fibre

Chicken Kiev

serves 4

2	whole chicken breasts, skinned, split into 2 and boned
60 g	(*2 oz*) frozen garlic butter*
75 g	(*2½ oz*) seasoned flour
2	beaten eggs
125 g	(*4 oz*) breadcrumbs
30 ml	(*2 tbsp*) peanut oil

Preheat oven to 180°C (*350°F, gas mark 4*).

Using small knife, cut small pockets into flesh of breasts. Be careful that knife does not run through to other side. Insert slivers of frozen garlic butter and pat meat back into shape.

Dredge chicken in flour, dip in beaten eggs and coat thoroughly with breadcrumbs. Use your fingertips to press crumbs into meat.

Heat oil in large frying pan over medium-high heat. When hot, add chicken and brown 3 minutes on each side.

Transfer to ovenproof platter and finish cooking 10 to 12 minutes in oven.

Serve with slices of cantaloupe melon for a pretty presentation.

* See Escargots with Garlic Butter, page 66.

1 serving	478 calories	27 g carbohydrate
34 g protein	26 g fat	0.8 g fibre

Breaded Chicken Pawpaw

serves 4

1	ripe pawpaw, peeled and sliced
2	small whole chicken breasts, skinned, split into 2 and boned
75 g	(*2½ oz*) seasoned flour
2	beaten eggs
50 ml	(*2 fl oz*) seasoned milk
125 g	(*4 oz*) seasoned breadcrumbs
30 ml	(*2 tbsp*) sunflower oil
	juice ¼ lemon

Preheat oven to 190°C (*375°F, gas mark 5*).

Place slices of fruit in small bowl and marinate in lemon juice while preparing chicken.

Place chicken breasts between sheets of greaseproof paper and pound each to an even 1 cm (*½ in*) thickness.

Dredge in flour and shake off excess. Mix eggs with milk and dip chicken; coat thoroughly with breadcrumbs.

Heat oil in large ovenproof frying pan over high heat. When hot, add chicken and cook 3 minutes on each side.

Transfer to oven and finish cooking another 4 minutes or adjust time depending on original size of breasts.

Serve with lemony pawpaw slices.

1 serving	410 calories	36 g carbohydrate
35 g protein	14 g fat	1.2 g fibre

Vermouth Chicken with Green Grapes

serves 4

30 g	(*1 oz*) butter
30 ml	(*2 tbsp*) chopped onion
2	whole chicken breasts, skinned and split into 2 pieces
2 ml	(*½ tsp*) tarragon
150 g	(*5 oz*) seedless green grapes
1	green pepper, thinly sliced
30 ml	(*2 tbsp*) dry vermouth
300 ml	(*½ pt*) chicken stock, heated
15 ml	(*1 tbsp*) cornflour
45 ml	(*3 tbsp*) cold water
	few drops Tabasco sauce
	salt and pepper

Heat butter in large frying pan. Add onion and Tabasco sauce; cover and cook 3 minutes over low heat.

Set chicken breasts in pan and season well. Sprinkle in tarragon, cover and cook 16 to 18 minutes over medium-low heat. Turn chicken over once halfway through cooking time.

Add grapes and green pepper to pan; cook another 4 minutes.

When chicken is cooked, remove from pan and set aside.

Increase heat to high and add vermouth to pan; cook 2 minutes.

Mix in chicken stock and continue cooking 2 minutes; correct seasoning. Mix cornflour with water; stir into sauce.

Return chicken to pan and simmer 2 to 3 minutes to reheat.

Serve with rice, potatoes or other vegctable.

1 serving	229 calories	10 g carbohydrate
27 g protein	9 g fat	0.7 g fibre

Chicken in Creamy Red Wine Sauce *serves 4*

1.6 kg	(3½ lb) chicken, cleaned, cut into 8 pieces and skinned
15 g	(½ oz) butter
15 ml	(1 tbsp) oil
2	shallots, finely chopped
1	onion, quartered
450 g	(1 lb) fresh mushrooms, cleaned and halved
500 ml	(17 fl oz) dry red wine
125 ml	(4 fl oz) double cream
5 ml	(1 tsp) cornflour
45 ml	(3 tbsp) cold water
15 ml	(1 tbsp) freshly chopped parsley
	salt and pepper
	Tabasco sauce

Season chicken pieces. Heat butter and oil in frying pan over medium heat. Add chicken and cook 15 minutes, turning pieces over once.

Add shallots, onion, mushrooms and season well. Cook another 6 to 7 minutes, then remove chicken from pan and keep hot.

Add wine to frying pan and bring to boil; cook 5 to 6 minutes. Mix in cream and reduce heat to medium; cook 4 to 5 minutes.

Mix cornflour with cold water and stir into sauce until well incorporated. Cook 1 minute over low heat. Season with Tabasco to taste and sprinkle with parsley; serve over chicken.

Boneless Chicken with Deglazed Lemon Sauce *serves 4*

30 g	(*1 oz*) butter
2	whole chicken breasts, skinned, split into 2 and boned
50 ml	(*2 fl oz*) chicken stock, heated
15 ml	(*1 tbsp*) chopped fresh parsley
	salt and pepper
	juice 1 lemon

Preheat oven to 180°C (*350°F, gas mark 4*).

Heat butter in large ovenproof frying pan over medium heat. Add chicken breasts and brown 3 minutes. Turn chicken over, season and brown another 3 minutes.

Transfer pan to oven and cook 10 to 12 minutes.

When chicken is cooked, remove from pan and set aside.

Place frying pan over high heat; add lemon juice and cook 1 minute.

Pour in chicken stock and add parsley; mix and cook another 2 minutes. Season.

Pour sauce over chicken and serve with a vegetable such as asparagus.

1 serving	166 calories	1 g carbohydrate
27 g protein	6 g fat	0.1 g fibre

Chicken Breasts à la Diable

serves 4

2	whole chicken breasts, skinned, split in 2 and boned
45 ml	(*3 tbsp*) melted butter
30 ml	(*2 tbsp*) Dijon mustard
15 ml	(*1 tbsp*) water
45 ml	(*3 tbsp*) breadcrumbs
	salt and pepper

Preheat oven to 190°C (*375°F, gas mark* 5).

Place chicken breasts in roasting tin and season well. Baste with melted butter and place chicken in middle of oven. Change oven setting to grill and cook 8 to 10 minutes, turning breasts over at halfway mark.

Mix mustard with water. Brush over chicken breasts and sprinkle each with breadcrumbs. Baste with a little more melted butter. Return to oven and continue cooking 3 to 4 minutes. Serve.

1 serving	*245 calories*	*4 g carbohydrate*
28 g protein	*13 g fat*	*0.2 g fibre*

Chicken Legs Supreme

serves 4

30 ml	(*2 tbsp*) melted butter
4	medium-size chicken legs, skinned and cut into 2 pieces
2	shallots, chopped
½	aubergine, peeled and diced
30 g	(*1 oz*) flour
250 ml	(*8 fl oz*) dry red wine
300 ml	(*½ pt*) beef stock, heated
1 ml	(*¼ tsp*) thyme
2 ml	(*½ tsp*) marjoram
15 ml	(*1 tbsp*) grated orange zest
	salt and pepper
	few drops Tabasco sauce

Preheat oven to 180°C (*350°F, gas mark 4*).

Place melted butter in large frying pan over medium heat. When hot, add chicken pieces and shallots; season well. Cook 6 minutes, turning chicken over at 3-minute mark.

Add aubergine and mix well. Cover and cook 10 minutes.

Mix in flour and cook 2 minutes, uncovered, over medium heat.

Pour in wine, mix well, and add beef stock. Mix again. Sprinkle in seasonings, orange zest and Tabasco sauce. Bring to boil.

Cover pan and cook in oven 30 minutes. To keep frying pan handle cool, wrap in foil.

Correct seasoning and serve.

1 serving	258 calories	6 g carbohydrate
27 g protein	14 g fat	0.6 g fibre

Chicken Breasts Florence on Rice

serves 4

30 g	(*1 oz*) butter
2	whole chicken breasts, skinned, split into 2 and boned
1	green pepper, sliced
225 g	(*½ lb*) fresh mushrooms, cleaned and sliced
1	celery stick, sliced thick
400 ml	(*⅔ pt*) chicken stock, heated
30 ml	(*2 tbsp*) teriyaki sauce
15 ml	(*1 tbsp*) cornflour
45 ml	(*3 tbsp*) cold water
	salt and pepper
	lemon wedges

Heat butter in large frying pan over medium heat. Add chicken and cook 4 minutes. Turn over and season well; cook another 4 minutes.

Continue cooking 7 minutes or according to size of breasts, turning chicken over once. Be sure to season several more times.

When chicken is cooked, transfer to plate and keep hot in oven.

Add green pepper, mushrooms and celery to hot frying pan. Cook 3 to 4 minutes over medium heat.

Season, pour in chicken stock and teriyaki sauce; bring to boil. Cook 4 to 5 minutes over medium heat.

Mix cornflour with water; stir into sauce and cook 1 more minute.

Place chicken in sauce and let simmer 2 minutes to reheat.

Serve on a bed of white rice and garnish with lemon wedges.

1 serving	229 calories	8 g carbohydrate
29 g protein	9 g fat	1.9 g fibre

255

Sautéed Veal Cutlets with Wild Mushroom Sauce   *serves 4*

4	**5-mm (¼-*in*) thick veal cutlets, trimmed of fat**
150 g	**(5 oz) lightly seasoned flour**
30 g	**(1 oz) butter**
125 g	**(4 oz) fresh oyster mushrooms, cleaned and halved**
3	**spring onions, chopped**
15 ml	**(1 *tbsp*) chopped fresh parsley**
125 ml	**(4 fl oz) light beef consommé, heated**
	juice ½ lemon
	salt and pepper

Dredge cutlets in flour and shake off excess. Heat butter in frying pan over medium-high heat. Add meat and sauté 3 minutes.

Turn cutlets over, season and sauté about 2 minutes, depending on size. Remove meat and keep hot in oven.

Add mushrooms, spring onions and parsley to pan; cook 3 to 4 minutes over high heat.

Pour in consommé and bring to boil. Sprinkle in lemon juice, correct seasoning and serve at once with veal. Accompany with grilled tomato slices.

1 serving	*325 calories*	*16 g carbohydrate*
27 g protein	*17 g fat*	*1.9 g fibre*

Springtime Veal Escalopes

serves 4

900 g	(*2 lb*) veal escalopes*, cut into 5-cm (*2-in*) squares
30 g	(*1 oz*) butter
2	red peppers, cut into thick wedges
125 g	(*¼ lb*) fresh mushrooms, cleaned and sliced
2	shallots, chopped
	salt and pepper
	few drops lemon juice

Sauté veal** in hot butter over high heat for 1 minute. Turn pieces over, season lightly and cook 1 more minute. Remove from pan and set aside.

With veal set aside, add red peppers, mushrooms and shallots to hot pan. Cook 3 to 4 minutes over medium-high heat.

Season well, sprinkle in lemon juice and serve immediately with veal. Add more lemon juice if desired. Accompany with noodles.

* Escalopes are pounded pieces of veal cutlet usually about 5 mm (*¼ in*) thick.
** Cook veal in several batches (dividing butter) to avoid overcrowding and allow for proper searing.

1 serving	470 calories	3 g carbohydrate
47 g protein	30 g fat	1.1 g fibre

Sausage-Stuffed Veal Escalopes

serves 4

30 g	(*1 oz*) butter
12	fresh mushrooms, cleaned and chopped
2	shallots, chopped
15 ml	(*1 tbsp*) chopped fresh parsley
125 g	(*4 oz*) sausagemeat
50 ml	(*2 fl oz*) double cream
4	large veal escalopes
	salt and pepper

Preheat oven to 180°C (*350°F, gas mark 4*).

Heat half of butter in frying pan over medium heat. Add mushrooms, shallots and parsley; cook 3 minutes.

Mix in sausagemeat and reduce heat to low; cook another 4 to 5 minutes.

Pour in cream, increase heat to high and season well. Cook 3 to 4 minutes to reduce cream.

Transfer contents of pan to food processor and purée. Set stuffing aside to cool.

Spread cooled stuffing over opened, flat escalopes. Roll lengthways, tuck in ends and tie with kitchen string.

Heat remaining butter in frying pan. Add veal and sear 2 to 3 minutes over medium-high heat, browning all sides. Season well.

Transfer to ovenproof casserole, cover and cook 10 to 12 minutes in oven.

Serve with potatoes and your choice of sauce.

1 serving	454 calories	3 g carbohydrate
34 g protein	34 g fat	1.6 g fibre

1. Cook mushrooms, shallots and parsley 3 minutes in hot butter.

2. Mix in sausagemeat and cook 4 to 5 minutes over low heat.

3. Pour in cream, increase heat to high and season well. Reduce cream for 3 to 4 minutes.

4. After stuffing has been puréed and cooled, spread over entire surface of escalope.

Royal Veal Fillet

serves 4

15 ml	(*1 tbsp*) vegetable oil
2	veal fillets *, 450 g (*1 lb*) each, fat trimmed
½	celery stick, diced
1	medium onion, diced small
1	carrot, peeled and diced
1	shallot, chopped
15 ml	(*1 tbsp*) chopped fresh chives
2 ml	(*½ tsp*) oregano
2 ml	(*½ tsp*) basil
125 ml	(*4 fl oz*) dry white wine
300 ml	(*½ pt*) light beef consommé, heated
15 ml	(*1 tbsp*) cornflour
45 ml	(*3 tbsp*) cold water
	salt and pepper

Preheat oven to 190°C (*375°F, gas mark 5*).

Heat oil in large ovenproof frying pan over medium-high heat. When hot, add veal and sear on all sides until nicely browned.

Reduce heat to medium. Add all vegetables, shallot, chives and seasonings; cook another 2 minutes.

Season well and pour in wine; cook 2 minutes.

Mix in consommé and place frying pan in oven; cook 16 minutes, uncovered.

Remove meat from pan and set aside.

Place frying pan over low heat. Mix cornflour with water and stir into sauce; cook 30 seconds or until thickened slightly.

Slice veal and serve with sauce. Accompany with fresh carrots and peas.

* Veal fillet may be difficult to find in your local supermarket. Try your butcher, who should be able to provide you with this special and exceptionally tender cut.

1 serving	423 calories	7 g carbohydrate
47 g protein	23 g fat	1.2 g fibre

Braised Veal Roast Sunday Dinner

serves 4

1.4 kg	(*3 lb*) veal roast, tied
150 g	(*5 oz*) seasoned flour
30 ml	(*2 tbsp*) oil
2	onions, cut into 4 or 6
2	carrots, peeled and diced large
2	small celery sticks, diced large
15 ml	(*1 tbsp*) chopped fresh parsley
2 ml	(*½ tsp*) oregano
1 ml	(*¼ tsp*) celery salt
250 ml	(*8 fl oz*) dry white wine
250 ml	(*8 fl oz*) chicken stock, heated
15 ml	(*1 tbsp*) cornflour
45 ml	(*3 tbsp*) cold water
	salt and pepper
pinch	thyme
dash	crushed chillies

Preheat oven to 180°C (*350°F, gas mark 4*). Dredge meat in flour.

Heat oil in large ovenproof casserole. When hot, add meat and sear on all sides over medium-high heat until nicely browned.

Add vegetables and season well. Continue cooking 2 minutes.

Sprinkle in parsley, oregano, celery salt, thyme and crushed chillies; mix well.

Pour in wine and cook 3 to 4 minutes over high heat. Add chicken stock and bring to boil. Cover casserole and cook 1 hour in oven.

Remove veal and transfer to serving platter; set aside.

Mix cornflour with cold water; stir into sauce remaining in casserole and cook 1 to 2 minutes to thicken.

Slice meat and serve with sauce and vegetables. Accompany with slices of French bread.

1 serving	743 calories	25 g carbohydrate
73 g protein	39 g fat	3.2 g fibre

Vegetable-Stuffed Veal Shoulder

serves 4

1.4 kg	(*3 lb*) boned veal shoulder roast*
30 g	(*1 oz*) butter
1	onion, finely chopped
2	garlic cloves, chopped
2 ml	(*½ tsp*) tarragon
2 ml	(*½ tsp*) thyme
1 ml	(*¼ tsp*) sage
17 ml	(*3½ tsp*) chopped fresh parsley
3	slices white bread, crusts trimmed
50 ml	(*2 fl oz*) single cream
12	large fresh mushrooms, cleaned and chopped
30 ml	(*2 tbsp*) olive oil
2	onions, cut into 6
2 ml	(*½ tsp*) rosemary
1	red pepper, diced large
2	courgettes, thickly sliced on angle
250 ml	(*8 fl oz*) dry white wine
250 ml	(*8 fl oz*) chicken stock, heated
	salt and pepper

Heat butter in small saucepan. Add chopped onion, garlic, tarragon, 1 ml (*¼ tsp*) each of thyme and sage, and 2 ml (*½ tsp*) parsley; cook 2 minutes over medium heat. Meanwhile, soak bread in cream in small bowl. Add mushrooms to saucepan and season well. Reduce heat to low, cover and cook 6 minutes. Remove cover and continue cooking 4 to 6 minutes. Mash bread and squeeze out excess cream. Incorporate bread to stuffing in saucepan and set aside to cool slightly.

Preheat oven to 180°C (*350°F, gas mark 4*). Spread vegetable stuffing over opened meat. Close and secure loosely with kitchen string. Heat oil in large ovenproof casserole over high heat. Add meat and sear on all sides. Add onions, rosemary and remaining parsley and thyme. Continue cooking 2 to 3 minutes over medium heat. Mix in red pepper and courgettes; season well. Cook 2 more minutes. Pour in wine and cook 4 to 5 minutes over high heat. Pour in chicken stock, mix and bring to boil. Cover casserole and cook 1 hour in oven.

To serve, slice meat and serve with red pepper and courgettes.

* Have your butcher prepare roast for stuffing by cutting it open and flattening it in one large piece.

1 serving	865 calories	29 g carbohydrate
77 g protein	49 g fat	6.8 g fibre

Roast Veal Sirloin

serves 4

1.2 kg	(2½ *lb*) veal sirloin roast, tied
15 g	(½ *oz*) butter
2	onions, cut into 4
	salt and pepper
	chopped fresh parsley

Preheat oven to 220°C (*425°F, gas mark 7*). Season meat generously with pepper.

Heat butter in roasting tin over medium-high heat. When hot, add meat and sear 8 to 10 minutes on all sides. Season lightly as meat is seared.

Add onions to tin and mix; cook another 2 minutes.

Transfer tin to oven and roast meat 40 minutes.

Serve with onions and meat juices. Accompany with Brussels sprouts and sprinkle with parsley.

1 serving	*561 calories*	*6 g carbohydrate*
60 g protein	*33 g fat*	*1.3 g fibre*

Stuffed Pork Fillet in Vegetable Gravy

serves 4

15 g	(½ oz) butter
½	stick celery, chopped
2	spring onions, chopped
125 g	(¼ lb) fresh mushrooms, cleaned and chopped
2 ml	(½ tsp) oregano
2 ml	(½ tsp) basil
90 g	(3 oz) cooked rice
2	pork fillets, trimmed of fat
15 ml	(1 tbsp) oil
2	leeks, cleaned * and sliced
2	spring onions, sliced
1	garlic clove, smashed and chopped
2 ml	(½ tsp) herbes de Provence
125 ml	(4 fl oz) dry red wine
375 ml	(13 fl oz) light beef gravy, heated
5 ml	(1 tsp) chopped fresh parsley
	salt and pepper

Preheat oven to 180°C (*350°F, gas mark 4*).

Begin by preparing stuffing. Heat butter in frying pan; cook celery, chopped spring onions, mushrooms, oregano and basil 5 to 6 minutes over medium heat. Mix in rice and continue cooking 2 minutes; correct seasoning. Transfer to food processor and blend stuffing; set aside to cool.

Without cutting all the way through, split fillets into 2 lengthways to make one large piece. Open each filet, place between 2 sheets of greaseproof paper and pound to double width. Spread stuffing over flattened fillets and roll. Secure with kitchen string.

Heat oil in large ovenproof frying pan. Sear fillets 6 to 8 minutes over medium-high heat, browning all sides. Add leeks, sliced spring onions, garlic and herbes de Provence; season well and cook another 2 to 3 minutes. Pour in wine and gravy; mix, cover and cook in oven 35 minutes or according to size of fillets. To serve, remove string, slice meat and accompany with sauce. Sprinkle with parsley.

* To clean leeks properly, see technique, page 375.

1 serving	616 calories	18 g carbohydrate
64 g protein	32 g fat	2.3 g fibre

Pork Fillet Braised in Vegetable Broth *serves 4*

15 ml	(*1 tbsp*) vegetable oil
2	450 g (*1 lb*) pork fillets, trimmed of fat
1	celery stick, diced
2	carrots, peeled and diced
1	courgette, sliced 1 cm (*½ in*) thick
1	garlic clove, smashed and chopped
15 ml	(*1 tbsp*) oregano
50 ml	(*2 oz*) dry white wine
375 ml	(*13 fl oz*) light chicken stock, heated
15 ml	(*1 tbsp*) cornflour
45 ml	(*3 tbsp*) cold water
	salt and pepper

Preheat oven to 180°C (*350°F, gas mark 4*).

Heat oil in large ovenproof frying pan over medium-high heat. When very hot, add fillets and sear on all sides.

Add vegetables, garlic and oregano; increase heat to high and mix well. Cook 2 minutes.

Pour in wine and cook another 2 minutes.

Pour in chicken stock and season well. Cover frying pan and cook 30 to 35 minutes in oven.

When cooked, remove meat from broth and set aside. Mix cornflour with water; stir into broth and cook 1 minute to thicken.

Slice meat and serve with vegetable broth.

1 serving	510 calories	9 g carbohydrate
60 g protein	26 g fat	2.5 g fibre

Traditional Pork Chops and Apples

serves 4

30 ml	(*2 tbsp*) vegetable oil
4	2-cm (*3/4-in*) thick boneless pork chops, trimmed of fat
1	onion, chopped
1	celery stick, sliced
3	apples, cored, peeled, halved and sliced 1 cm (*1/2 in*) thick
2 ml	(*1/2 tsp*) cinnamon
250 ml	(*8 fl oz*) chicken stock, heated
	salt and pepper
pinch	ground cloves

Heat oil in large frying pan over medium heat. When hot, add chops and cook 5 to 6 minutes. Turn pork over, season well and continue cooking 5 to 6 minutes or adjust time depending on size of chops. Remove from pan and keep warm.

Add onion and celery to pan; cook 3 to 4 minutes over medium heat.

Add apples, seasonings and continue cooking 5 minutes. Pour in chicken stock and correct seasoning; cook 3 more minutes.

Pour apples and sauce over pork chops and serve.

1 serving	470 calories	18 g carbohydrate
23 g protein	34 g fat	2.6 g fibre

Boneless Pork Chops with Pickle Sauce   *serves 4*

15 g	(*½ oz*) butter
1	shallot, finely chopped
2	spring onions, cut in 2.5-cm (*1-in*) lengths
1	red pepper, cut into julienne
2	large dill pickles, cut into julienne
45 ml	(*3 tbsp*) red wine vinegar
50 ml	(*2 fl oz*) dry white wine
375 ml	(*13 fl oz*) light beef gravy, heated
15 ml	(*1 tbsp*) vegetable oil
4	2-cm (*¾-in*) thick boneless pork chops
	salt and pepper

Begin by preparing pickle sauce. Heat butter in saucepan over medium heat. Add shallot, vegetables and pickles; sauté 2 minutes.

Stir in vinegar and wine; cook 2 minutes over high heat.

Mix in gravy and season well. Reduce heat to low and simmer sauce 4 to 6 minutes.

Meanwhile, prepare pork by heating oil in large frying pan*. When hot, add meat and sear 3 minutes over high heat.

Turn chops over, season well and reduce heat to medium. Cook another 3 minutes. Turn over a third time and finish cooking 2 minutes or longer, depending on thickness.

Arrange pork chops on dinner plates and spoon sauce over. Jacket potatoes go nicely with this recipe.

* If pan is not large enough to hold 4 chops without crowding, then use two pans or cook meat in batches.

1 serving	383 calories	7 g carbohydrate	**267**
37 g protein	23 g fat	1.4 g fibre	

Old-Fashioned Pork Stew with Vegetables   *serves 4*

30 g	(*1 oz*) bacon fat
1.4 kg	(*3 lb*) pork shoulder, trimmed of fat and cut into 2.5-cm (*1-in*) cubes
1	garlic clove, smashed and chopped
1	onion, chopped
15 ml	(*1 tbsp*) soy sauce
30 g	(*1 oz*) flour
600 ml	(*1 pt*) beef stock, heated
15 ml	(*1 tbsp*) tomato purée
1	bay leaf
2 ml	(*½ tsp*) rosemary
15 g	(*½ oz*) butter
2	carrots, peeled and diced large
2	onions, quartered
2	potatoes, peeled and diced large
5 ml	(*1 tsp*) brown sugar
	salt and pepper

Preheat oven to 180°C (*350°F, gas mark 4*).

Heat half of bacon fat in large ovenproof casserole over medium-high heat. When hot, add half of pork and sear 8 to 10 minutes on all sides over high heat. Remove pork and set aside.

Heat remaining bacon fat in casserole and sear rest of pork.

With both batches of pork in casserole, add garlic and chopped onion. Mix well and season; cook 3 minutes over medium-high heat.

Sprinkle in soy sauce and mix well. Add flour and stir with wooden spoon until incorporated; cook 3 more minutes over medium heat.

Pour in beef stock, mixing well; then add tomato purée, bay leaf and rosemary; bring to boil.

Cover casserole and cook stew 1 hour in oven.

Before end of cooking, melt butter in frying pan over medium heat. Add vegetables and brown sugar; sauté about 5 minutes.

Add vegetables to stew, mix well, and resume cooking for 1 hour or until meat is tender.

1 serving	845 calories	34 g carbohydrate
85 g protein	41 g fat	4.3 g fibre

Pork Chops 'n Peppers

serves 4

30 ml	(*2 tbsp*) vegetable oil
4	2-cm (*¾-in*) thick boneless pork chops, trimmed of fat
3	spring onions, chopped
1	celery stick, sliced
15 ml	(*1 tbsp*) freshly chopped ginger root
1	green pepper, diced large
1	red pepper, diced large
375 ml	(*13 fl oz*) chicken stock, heated
15 ml	(*1 tbsp*) cornflour
45 ml	(*3 tbsp*) cold water
	salt and pepper
	few drops Tabasco sauce

Heat oil in large frying pan over medium heat. When hot, add chops and cook 4 to 5 minutes. Turn pork over, season well and continue cooking 4 to 5 minutes or adjust time depending on size. Remove from pan and keep hot.

Add spring onions, celery and ginger; cook 3 minutes over medium heat. Add both peppers, season and cook another 2 minutes.

Pour in chicken stock, correct seasoning and cook 3 minutes. Mix cornflour with cold water; stir into sauce until well incorporated. Add Tabasco sauce and bring to boil; cook 1 more minute. Serve over pork.

1 serving	*430 calories*	*7 g carbohydrate*
24 g protein	*34 g fat*	*0.9 g fibre*

Kidney Sauté in Red Wine Sauce

serves 4

2	calf kidneys, well cleaned
45 g	(*1½ tbsp*) butter
225 g	(*½ lb*) fresh mushrooms, cleaned and quartered
2	shallots, chopped
50 ml	(*2 fl oz*) dry red wine
250 ml	(*8 fl oz*) beef stock, heated
15 ml	(*1 tbsp*) cornflour
30 ml	(*2 tbsp*) cold water
45 ml	(*3 tbsp*) double cream
	salt and pepper

Trim fat from kidneys and discard. Slice kidneys 5 mm (¼ *in*) thick.

Heat 15 g (½ *oz*) butter in large frying pan. When melted, increase heat to high and add half of kidneys; cook 2 minutes.

Turn kidneys over, season and cook another 2 minutes. Remove from pan and set aside. Add another 15 g (½ *oz*) butter to hot pan and cook rest of kidneys following same procedure.

With all kidneys set aside, place remaining 15 g (½ *oz*) butter in pan. Add mushrooms and shallots; cook 4 minutes over high heat.

Add red wine; cook another 3 minutes.

Pour in beef stock and season well. Mix cornflour with water; stir into sauce and cook 3 to 4 minutes over medium heat.

Mix in cream and cook 2 more minutes.

Place kidneys in sauce and simmer 2 minutes to reheat. Serve with croutons, if desired.

1 serving	212 calories	5 g carbohydrate
12 g protein	16 g fat	1.6 g fibre

1. Choose very fresh calf kidneys for this recipe and be sure to clean them thoroughly.

2. Trim fat from kidneys and discard. Slice 5 mm (¼ *in*) thick.

3. It is best to cook kidneys in two batches. Overcrowding the pan will cause the fat to boil instead of sauté.

4. After all kidneys have been sautéed and set aside, add rest of butter to pan and cook mushrooms and shallots 4 minutes over high heat.

Leg of Lamb Lorence

serves 4

1.6 kg	(*3½ lb*) leg of lamb, boned by butcher
2	garlic cloves, peeled and cut into 3
30 ml	(*2 tbsp*) melted butter
5 ml	(*1 tsp*) basil
2 ml	(*½ tsp*) oregano
3	small onions, quartered
2	celery sticks, diced
30 g	(*1 oz*) flour
500 ml	(*17 fl oz*) light beef stock, heated
15 ml	(*1 tbsp*) tomato purée
pinch	thyme
	pepper

Preheat oven to 220°C (*425°F, gas mark 7*). Allow 16 minutes per 450 g (*1 lb*).

Remove the fell (thin covering) from lamb if not already done by butcher. Stud meat with slivers of garlic and brush with melted butter.

Place lamb in roasting tin, mix seasonings together and rub over meat. Place in oven and cook about 1 hour for "pink" meat. Adjust time if desired.

About halfway through cooking time, surround lamb with onions and celery; resume cooking.

When lamb is cooked, remove from roasting tin and transfer to serving platter; keep hot in oven.

Place roasting tin on stove over medium heat and cook juices 4 minutes.

Mix in flour with wooden spoon. Reduce heat to low and cook 5 to 6 minutes or until flour is lightly browned.

Pour in beef stock and stir in tomato purée; whisk well. Season with pepper only and bring to boil. Continue cooking 5 to 6 minutes over medium heat.

Pour sauce through sieve into bowl and prepare to serve with lamb.

Accompany with a variety of vegetables.

1 serving	794 calories	12 g carbohydrate
65 g protein	54 g fat	1.7 g fibre

Double Loin of Lamb 5th Avenue

serves 4

1.4 kg	(*3 lb*) **double loin of lamb** *
2 ml	(*½ tsp*) **oregano**
1 ml	(*¼ tsp*) **thyme**
1 ml	(*¼ tsp*) **savory**
30 ml	(*2 tbsp*) **melted butter**
125 ml	(*4 fl oz*) **dry white wine**
½	**onion, finely chopped**
15 ml	(*1 tbsp*) **chopped fresh parsley**
300 ml	(*½ pt*) **beef stock, heated**
	salt and pepper

Preheat oven to 230°C (*450°F, gas mark 8*).

Lay lamb on cutting board and sprinkle with oregano, thyme and savory; pepper well. Roll and tie loins.

Place meat with bones in roasting tin and baste with melted butter. Pour wine over meat. Sear 12 minutes in oven.

Reduce heat to 180°C (*350°F, gas mark 4*) and continue cooking about 25 minutes for "pink" lamb. Adjust time if you prefer medium.

When meat is done, remove from tin and set aside. Cover with foil to keep hot.

With bones still in tin, add onion and parsley; cook 3 minutes over high heat.

Pour in beef stock and bring to boil. Continue cooking 3 to 4 minutes over medium-high heat.

Slice lamb and serve with onion sauce. Accompany with fresh asparagus.

* Have your butcher bone the loins and remove most of the fat. Bring the bones home too!

1 serving	741 calories	2 g carbohydrate
64 g protein	53 g fat	0.4 g fibre

Lamb Chops with Grilled Aubergine Rounds serves 4

45 ml	(*3 tbsp*) olive oil
45 ml	(*3 tbsp*) teriyaki sauce
1	garlic clove, smashed and chopped
2 ml	(*½ tsp*) rosemary
1	aubergine, cut into rounds 1 cm (*½ in*) thick
8	lamb chops, trimmed of fat
	juice ½ lemon
	salt and freshly ground pepper

Preheat oven to 200°C (*400°F, gas mark 6*).

Mix oil with teriyaki sauce, garlic, rosemary, lemon juice and pepper. Brush over aubergine rounds and lamb chops.

Place aubergine in roasting tin and change oven setting to grill. Place tin in oven 15 cm (*6 in*) from top element. With oven door ajar, cook aubergine 5 to 6 minutes each side.

Meanwhile, cook basted lamb chops in hot frying pan over high heat for 3 to 4 minutes on each side, depending on thickness. Remember to season when turning over meat.

1 serving	317 calories	4 g carbohydrate
28 g protein	21 g fat	0.7 g fibre

Sautéed Lamb Chops with Wine Sauce *serves 4*

8	**loin lamb chops**
45 ml	**(3 tbsp) olive oil**
1	**medium onion, thinly sliced**
50 ml	**(2 fl oz) dry white wine**
400 ml	**(²/₃ pt) beef stock, heated**
5 ml	**(1 tsp) tomato purée**
15 ml	**(1 tbsp) cornflour**
45 ml	**(3 tbsp) cold water**
15 ml	**(1 tbsp) Dijon mustard**
15 ml	**(1 tbsp) freshly chopped chives**
	salt and pepper

Preheat oven to 190°C (*375°F, gas mark 5*).

Trim fat from lamb chops and scrape about 2.5 cm (*1 in*) of bone clean. Place between 2 sheets of greaseproof paper and flatten with meat bat.

Heat 30 ml (*2 tbsp*) oil in large frying pan over medium heat. Add chops and cook 3 minutes. Turn lamb over, season and continue cooking 2 minutes. Transfer to oven and continue cooking 6 to 7 minutes or adjust time depending on size and preference. Remove chops from pan, set aside and keep warm.

Add remaining oil to pan and heat on stove over medium heat. Add onion and cook 3 minutes over high heat. Add wine and continue cooking 2 minutes.

Pour in beef stock and mix in tomato purée; bring to boil. Mix cornflour with cold water; stir into sauce until well incorporated. Cook 2 more minutes over medium heat.

Remove pan from heat and stir in mustard and chives. Return chops to pan and simmer 2 minutes over low heat. Serve.

1 serving	*532 calories*	*5 g carbohydrate*
56 g protein	*32 g fat*	*0.3 g fibre*

Lamb Shoulder Stew

serves 4

30 ml	(*2 tbsp*) oil	
1.6 kg	(*3½ lb*) lamb shoulder, trimmed of fat and cubed	
2	onions, chopped	
1	garlic clove, smashed and chopped	
15 ml	(*1 tbsp*) chopped fresh ginger	
30 g	(*1 oz*) flour	
750 ml	(*1¼ pt*) light chicken stock, heated	
1	bay leaf	
1	small head cauliflower, in florets	
1	small courgette, diced	
	salt and pepper	

Heat oil in large casserole. When hot, add meat and sear 5 to 6 minutes, turning to brown all sides.

Add onions, garlic and ginger; mix well and continue cooking 5 minutes.

Mix in flour and cook 1 minute over medium-low heat.

Pour in chicken stock, add bay leaf and season well. Bring to boil.

Partly cover casserole and cook 1 hour over low heat.

Add vegetables and continue cooking for 30 minutes.

1 serving	831 calories	17 g carbohydrate
67 g protein	55 g fat	3.9 g fibre

Curried Blade Steak Stew

serves 4

30 g	(*1 oz*) bacon fat
1.6 kg	(*3½ lb*) blade steak, trimmed of fat and cut into 2.5-cm (*1-in*) cubes
2	onions, finely chopped
45 ml	(*3 tbsp*) curry powder
15 ml	(*1 tbsp*) cumin powder
30 g	(*1 oz*) flour
750 ml	(*1¼ pt*) beef stock, heated
30 ml	(*2 tbsp*) tomato purée
1	bay leaf
5 ml	(*1 tsp*) rosemary powder
	salt and pepper

Preheat oven to 180°C (*350°F, gas mark 4*).

Heat half of bacon fat in large frying pan. When hot, add half of meat and sear on all sides over high heat.

Remove meat when nicely browned and set aside. Add remaining fat and repeat procedure for rest of meat.

Transfer all seared meat to ovenproof casserole and season well.

Add onions to frying pan in which meat was seared. Sauté 3 to 4 minutes over high heat and transfer to casserole.

Sprinkle curry powder and cumin over meat; mix well and add flour. Mix with wooden spoon until completely incorporated.

Place casserole over medium heat and cook until flour begins sticking to bottom of casserole. Stir once or twice.

Pour in beef stock, mix well, and add tomato purée and remaining seasonings. Mix and cover casserole. Cook stew 2½ hours in oven.

Serve on bed of egg noodles.

1 serving	621 calories	12 g carbohydrate
87 g protein	25 g fat	1.4 g fibre

Country-Style Beef Bourguignon

serves 4

30 ml	(*2 tbsp*) light oil
1.8 kg	(*4 lb*) boneless blade roast, trimmed of fat
4	blanched garlic cloves
1	bay leaf
1 ml	(*¼ tsp*) thyme
2 ml	(*½ tsp*) basil
15 ml	(*1 tbsp*) chopped fresh parsley
3	onions, cut into wedges
60 g	(*2 oz*) flour
500 ml	(*17 fl oz*) dry red wine
250 ml	(*8 fl oz*) beef stock, heated
15 ml	(*1 tbsp*) cornflour
45 ml	(*3 tbsp*) cold water
	salt and pepper

Preheat oven to 180°C (*350°F, gas mark 4*).

Heat oil in large ovenproof casserole over high heat. Add roast and sear 8 to 10 minutes, browning all sides.

Add garlic, bay leaf, thyme, basil and parsley; season well. Add onions and continue cooking 4 to 5 minutes over high heat.

Add flour, incorporating a little at a time, while turning over meat. Continue cooking another 4 to 5 minutes over medium heat.

Season meat well and pour in wine and beef stock; bring to boil. Cover and cook 3 hours in oven. Turn roast over several times during cooking.

Transfer cooked meat to serving platter and prepare to slice. If sauce is too thin, thicken with cornflour diluted in cold water. Be sure to mix in well.

Accompany this dish with potatoes or grilled tomato halves.

1 serving	720 calories	19 g carbohydrate
98 g protein	28 g fat	2.1 g fibre

1. Sear meat in hot oil for 8 to 10 minutes, browning all sides. Avoid turning roast too often or meat will not be properly seared.

2. Add garlic, bay leaf, thyme, basil and parsley; season well. Add onions and continue cooking 4 to 5 minutes over high heat.

3. Add flour, incorporating it a little at a time, while turning over meat. The flour will thicken the sauce during cooking. Continue cooking another 4 to 5 minutes over medium heat to remove raw taste of flour.

4. Season meat well and pour in wine and beef stock; bring to boil and prepare to finish cooking in oven.

Classic Steak au Poivre

serves 4

60 ml	(*4 tbsp*) black peppercorns
4	225-g (*8-oz*) strip loin steaks, trimmed of fat
15 ml	(*1 tbsp*) olive oil
2	shallots, finely chopped
50 ml	(*2 fl oz*) brandy
250 ml	(*8 fl oz*) dry red wine
375 ml	(*13 fl oz*) beef stock, heated
50 ml	(*2 fl oz*) double cream
5 ml	(*1 tsp*) cornflour
30 ml	(*2 tbsp*) cold water
	salt

Gather peppercorns on cutting board and crush using bottom of heavy frying pan. Press pepper into flesh of steaks on both sides.

Heat half of olive oil in large frying pan over high heat. When oil is very hot, add 2 steaks and sear 3 minutes. Turn steaks over, season generously and reduce heat to medium-high; sear second side 3 to 4 minutes.

Turn steaks over again and finish cooking 3 to 4 minutes or according to taste. Transfer to platter and keep hot in oven while procedure is repeated for remaining steaks.

Add second batch of steaks to platter in oven. Leave frying pan on stove and add shallots; cook 1 minute.

Increase heat to high and pour in brandy. Flambé and continue cooking 2 minutes.

Pour in wine, cook another 2 minutes, then mix in beef stock. Continue cooking 3 minutes. Stir in cream and cook 2 minutes.

Mix cornflour with cold water; stir into sauce until well incorporated. Cook 1 minute then ladle over steaks and serve.

1 serving	451 calories	2 g carbohydrate
59 g protein	23 g fat	0.1 g fibre

Braised Cross-Rib Roast Americana

serves 4

30 g	(*1 oz*) bacon fat
2.3 kg	(*5 lb*) cross-rib roast, tied
2	celery sticks, cut into 4
2	carrots, peeled and cut into 4
4	onions, quartered
1	garlic clove, peeled
3	parsley sprigs
2	bay leaves
2 ml	(*½ tsp*) thyme
5 ml	(*1 tsp*) chervil
2 ml	(*½ tsp*) basil
300 ml	(*½ pt*) dry white wine
750 ml	(*1¼ pt*) light beef gravy, heated
15 ml	(*1 tbsp*) chopped fresh parsley
	salt and pepper

Preheat oven to 160°C (*325°F, gas mark 3*).

Heat bacon fat in large ovenproof casserole. When hot, add meat and sear on all sides over high heat.

Season meat and add all vegetables, garlic, parsley sprigs, bay leaves and seasonings. Cook 2 minutes over medium-high heat.

Pour in wine, increase heat to high and cook another 2 minutes.

Stir in gravy, season well and bring to boil.

Cover casserole and cook 3 hours in oven. Halfway through cooking time, turn over meat.

Remove meat from casserole and slice to serve. Accompany with sauce and, if desired, honey-glazed carrots. Sprinkle portions with chopped parsley.

1 serving	962 calories	9 g carbohydrate
119 g protein	50 g fat	0 g fibre

Tournedos with Pepper Sauce

serves 4

15 ml	(*1 tbsp*) oil
1	green pepper, diced
225 g	(*½ lb*) fresh mushrooms, cleaned and diced
2 ml	(*½ tsp*) oregano
2 ml	(*½ tsp*) chopped fresh chives
1	garlic clove, smashed and chopped
1	tomato, diced
125 ml	(*4 fl oz*) chicken stock, heated
15 ml	(*1 tbsp*) tomato purée
4	175-g (*6-oz*) tournedos
	salt and pepper

Heat half of oil in frying pan over high heat. Add diced green pepper and cook 1 minute.

Add mushrooms, oregano, chives and garlic; continue cooking 2 minutes.

Add tomato, chicken stock and tomato purée; season well. Mix and cook 6 to 8 minutes over medium-low heat.

Meanwhile, brush remaining oil over both sides of meat. Cook in hot frying pan over high heat for 3 minutes.

Turn tournedos over, season well and continue cooking 2 minutes for rare meat. Serve with sauce. Accompany with potatoes, if desired.

1 serving	*305 calories*	*6 g carbohydrate*
41 g protein	*13 g fat*	*2.2 g fibre*

1. Heat half of oil in frying pan over high heat and cook green pepper for 1 minute.

2. Add mushrooms, oregano, chives and garlic; continue cooking 2 minutes.

3. Add tomato, and then...

4. Add chicken stock and tomato purée; season well and mix. Cook 6 to 8 minutes over medium-low heat while you are preparing the tournedos.

Strip Loin Steaks with Texas Garlic Sauce serves 4

7	garlic cloves
1	egg yolk
125 ml	(4 fl oz) olive oil
15 ml	(1 tbsp) vegetable oil
4	225-g (8-oz) strip loin steaks, trimmed of fat
	salt and pepper

Peel garlic cloves and place them in small saucepan. Pour in 300 ml (½ pt) water and bring to boil. Continue cooking 4 to 5 minutes.

Drain cloves well, place in mortar and mash. Add egg yolk and incorporate using pestle.

Incorporate olive oil in thin stream, whisking constantly. Continue mixing until sauce is very thick. Pour through wire sieve and set aside.

Heat half of vegetable oil in large, heavy-bottomed frying pan over high heat. When oil starts to smoke, add 2 steaks and sear 3 minutes without touching.

Turn steaks over and season generously. Reduce heat to medium-high and sear second side 3 to 4 minutes for rare meat. For medium-rare, turn steaks a third time and cook another 3 to 4 minutes over medium heat.

Remove steaks from pan and keep hot in oven while cooking other 2 steaks.

To serve, ladle garlic sauce over one end of steaks and accompany with steamed mangetouts.

1 serving	653 calories	2 g carbohydrate
51 g protein	49 g fat	0 g fibre

Strip Loin Steaks Louise

serves 4

30 ml	(*2 tbsp*) vegetable oil
4	225-g (*8-oz*) strip loin steaks, trimmed of fat
15 g	(*½ oz*) butter
225 g	(*½ lb*) fresh oyster mushrooms, cleaned and sliced in half
2	spring onions, sliced on angle
1	green pepper, halved and sliced on angle
200 ml	(*⅓ pt*) prepared demi-glace roast gravy mix
dash	Worcestershire sauce
	salt and pepper

Mix 15 ml (*1 tbsp*) oil with Worcestershire sauce and baste over steaks; pepper well.

Cook steaks in 2 batches to avoid crowding the pan. If preferred, use 2 pans.

In a large, heavy-bottomed frying pan, heat half of remaining oil over high heat. When oil starts to smoke, add 2 steaks and sear them 3 minutes without touching.

Turn steaks over and season generously. Reduce heat to medium-high and sear second side 3 to 4 minutes for rare meat. For medium-rare, turn steaks over a third time and cook another 3 to 4 minutes over medium heat.

When steaks are done to taste, remove from pan and keep hot in oven. Add remaining oil and repeat procedure for other 2 steaks.

Meanwhile, heat butter in another frying pan over medium-high heat. Add vegetables and cook 4 to 5 minutes.

Season well and pour in demi-glace gravy; mix well and bring to quick boil.

Serve vegetables with steaks.

1 serving	475 calories	6 g carbohydrate
52 g protein	27 g fat	2.1 g fibre

Double Strip Loin Steak

serves 4

900-g	(*2-lb*) piece strip loin steak
30 ml	(*2 tbsp*) oil
15 ml	(*1 tbsp*) teriyaki sauce
2 ml	(*½ tsp*) herbes de Provence
30 ml	(*2 tbsp*) green peppercorns, crushed
	salt and pepper

Place meat on dinner plate. Mix oil with teriyaki sauce and pour over steak. Spread herbs and crushed peppercorns on top.

Using tongs, turn over meat to coat both sides with mixture; marinate 30 minutes.

Preheat oven to 220°C (*425°F, gas mark 7*).

Place meat in hot heavy-bottomed frying pan and sear about 3 minutes on each side over high heat. Sear a little longer for medium-cooked meat. Be sure to season well when turning over meat.

Transfer to oven and finish cooking 10 to 12 minutes.

Slice as shown in technique and serve with vegetables such as fresh French beans and potatoes. Accompany with sauce, if desired.

1 serving	411 calories	1 g carbohydrate
50 g protein	23 g fat	0 g fibre

1. Most likely your local supermarket will not carry this cut of meat. Just ask your butcher to cut a 900-g (*2-lb*) piece of strip loin steak for you.

2. Cover meat with marinade ingredients.

3. Turn steak over so that both sides are coated; let stand 30 minutes.

4. After searing and cooking meat, slice as shown here and serve.

Strip Steaks with Choron Sauce

serves 4

350 g	(*3/4 lb*) unsalted butter
15 ml	(*1 tbsp*) chopped fresh parsley
15 ml	(*1 tbsp*) chopped shallot
15 ml	(*1 tbsp*) coarsely ground pepper
45 ml	(*3 tbsp*) red wine vinegar
30 ml	(*2 tbsp*) dry red wine
2	egg yolks
15 ml	(*1 tbsp*) tomato purée
15 ml	(*1 tbsp*) vegetable oil
4	225-g (*8-oz*) strip loin steaks, trimmed of fat
	salt and pepper

Place butter in stainless-steel bowl set over saucepan half-filled with hot water. Without touching bowl, melt over low heat.

Skim whitish foam from surface and discard. Set bowl aside.

Place parsley, shallot, ground pepper, vinegar and wine in clean saucepan. Cook over medium heat until liquid has evaporated. Transfer to clean stainless-steel bowl, add egg yolks and whisk well.

Set bowl over saucepan with hot water. Over very low heat, gradually add 1/4 of clarified butter, whisking constantly.

Whisk in tomato purée. Add rest of butter using above technique; then strain sauce through wire sieve. Season and set aside.

Cook meat in 2 batches. Heat oil in large, heavy-bottomed frying pan over high heat. When smoking, add meat and sear 3 minutes. Turn over, season and sear 3 to 4 minutes over medium-high for rare meat. Repeat procedure. Serve with sauce.

1 serving	1058 calories	1 g carbohydrate
52 g protein	94 g fat	0.1 g fibre

1. When butter has melted in bowl, skim off whitish foam and discard.

2. Place parsley, shallot, coarsely ground pepper, wine vinegar and wine in saucepan. Cook over medium heat until all the liquid has evaporated.

3. With parsley mixture transferred to bowl, add egg yolks and mix well with whisk.

4. Butter must be incorporated very slowly in a thin stream while whisking constantly. Start by incorporating ¼ of the butter. Then mix in tomato purée. Continue adding rest of butter using the same technique.

Sirloin Tip Roast au Jus

serves 4

60 ml	(4 tbsp) dry mustard
1.4 kg	(3 lb) sirloin tip roast, tied
2	garlic cloves, peeled and halved
30 ml	(2 tbsp) melted butter
3	onions, cut into 6
300 ml	(½ pt) beef stock, heated
5 ml	(1 tsp) chopped fresh parsley
	salt and pepper

Preheat oven to 180°C (350°F, gas mark 4). Allow 30 minutes per 450 g (1 lb) for medium-done meat.

Mix mustard with just enough cold water to make paste; using back of small spoon, mix until smooth and lump-free.

Make several incisions in meat and stud with garlic slivers. Rub meat lightly with salt and cover with mustard paste.

Heat butter in roasting tin over medium heat. Place meat in tin and roast 1½ hours in oven or until meat is done to taste.

When cooked, remove meat from tin and set aside.

Add onions to tin and cook 4 minutes over medium-high heat. Pour in beef stock and mix in parsley; season and continue cooking 3 minutes.

Carve roast and serve with the gravy. Accompany with fresh French beans.

1 serving	554 calories	9 g carbohydrate
80 g protein	22 g fat	1.7 g fibre

Rump Roast

serves 4

1.4 kg	(*3 lb*) rump roast
2	garlic cloves, peeled and cut into 3
5 ml	(*1 tsp*) rosemary
1	onion, quartered
15 ml	(*1 tbsp*) chopped fresh parsley
	thin slices pork fat
	salt and freshly ground pepper

Preheat oven to 180°C (*350°F, gas mark 4*). Allow 30 minutes per 450 g (*1 lb*) for medium-done meat.

Make incisions in meat and stud with garlic slivers. Cover roast with slices of pork fat and secure with kitchen string.

Place roast in small roasting tin and cook 1 hour in oven.

Season well and sprinkle with rosemary; continue cooking another 30 minutes or until meat is done to taste.

When cooked, remove meat from tin and discard fat. Return meat to tin with drippings and let stand 15 minutes; then remove from tin and set aside on cutting board.

Place roasting tin over high heat and add onion; cook 2 minutes.

Season well with pepper and continue cooking 3 to 4 minutes. Strain sauce and serve with roast and onions. Sprinkle with parsley.

1 serving	*508 calories*	*3 g carbohydrate*
79 g protein	*20 g fat*	*0.6 g fibre*

Tournedos with Hunter Sauce

serves 4

15 g	(½ oz) butter
3	spring onions, diced
225 g	(½ lb) fresh mushrooms, cleaned and diced
1	garlic clove, smashed and chopped
1	shallot, chopped
2	tomatoes, diced large
2 ml	(½ tsp) oregano
125 ml	(4 fl oz) dry white wine
250 ml	(8 fl oz) light beef gravy, heated
4	200-g (7-oz) tournedos
5 ml	(1 tsp) oil
	salt and pepper

Heat butter in large frying pan over medium-high heat. Add spring onions, mushrooms, garlic and shallot; cook 3 to 4 minutes.

Add tomatoes and oregano; season well. Mix and cook 3 to 4 minutes over high heat.

Pour in wine and continue cooking 2 to 3 minutes.

Correct seasoning and incorporate beef gravy. Simmer over low heat until tournedos are ready.

Brush tournedos on both sides with oil. Cook in hot frying pan over high heat for 3 minutes. Turn tournedos over, season and continue cooking 3 to 4 minutes for rare meat.

Serve with hunter sauce.

1 serving	359 calories	7 g carbohydrate
49 g protein	15 g fat	1.5 g fibre

1. Heat butter in large frying pan over medium-high heat. Add spring onions, mushrooms, garlic and shallot; cook 3 to 4 minutes.

2. Add tomatoes and oregano; season well. Mix and cook 3 to 4 minutes over high heat.

3. Pour in wine and continue cooking 2 to 3 minutes.

4. Correct seasoning and incorporate beef gravy. Simmer sauce over low heat.

Flank Steak à la Provençale

serves 4

1	large flank steak, trimmed of fat
30 ml	(*2 tbsp*) vegetable oil
60 ml	(*4 tbsp*) teriyaki sauce
3	blanched garlic cloves, mashed
15 ml	(*1 tbsp*) olive oil
3	onions, cut into wedges
3	tomatoes, peeled and cut into wedges
30 ml	(*2 tbsp*) tomato purée
2 ml	(*½ tsp*) oregano
	salt and pepper
pinch	thyme

Score meat on both sides and place in shallow baking dish. Mix vegetable oil with teriyaki sauce and half of garlic; pour over meat and marinate 1½ hours in refrigerator. Turn meat occasionally to baste both sides.

When ready to cook meat, heat olive oil in frying pan. Cook onions with remaining garlic 3 to 4 minutes over medium heat.

Mix well and cover; continue cooking 6 to 7 minutes over low heat.

Add tomatoes, tomato purée and seasonings to mixture; continue cooking 8 to 10 minutes over low heat. Do not cover.

Meanwhile, coat heavy frying pan, preferably cast-iron, with thin film of oil. Heat pan and add flank steak; sear 6 minutes over high heat.

Turn steak over, season generously and cook another 6 minutes, depending on thickness. Meat should be cooked rare to keep it tender.

Slice meat quite thinly on angle and serve with tomatoes.

1 serving	*634 calories*	*18 g carbohydrate*
82 g protein	*26 g fat*	*3.1 g fibre*

WINING AND DINING BY SEA

Tantalizing seafood entrées

Glorious Fish Salad

serves 4

60 g	(2 oz) stuffed green olives
16	canned miniature corn cobs, halved
2	hard-boiled eggs, sliced
125 g	(4 oz) cooked French beans
170 g	(6 oz) cooked mangetouts
½	red pepper, thinly sliced
1	cooked potato, peeled and sliced
350 g	(¾ lb) leftover cooked fish, flaked into bite-size pieces
15 ml	(1 tbsp) Dijon mustard
30 ml	(2 tbsp) wine vinegar
15 ml	(1 tbsp) lemon juice
90 ml	(6 tbsp) olive oil
	salt and pepper

Place olives, corn, eggs, beans, mangetouts, red pepper and potato in mixing bowl; season well.

Add fish, toss gently and season again. Set aside.

Place mustard in second bowl. Season and add vinegar, lemon juice and oil. Mix very well with whisk. Correct seasoning.

Pour dressing over salad ingredients, toss to coat evenly and serve on crisp lettuce leaves. Decorate platter with fruit.

1 serving	469 calories	25 g carbohydrate
27 g protein	32 g fat	6.6 g fibre

Elegant Curried Halibut Steaks

serves 2

1	halibut steak, cut into 2
30 ml	(*2 tbsp*) curry powder
1	carrot, peeled and sliced
1	sprig dill
5 ml	(*1 tsp*) butter
¹/₂	onion, sliced
125 g	(*¹/₄ lb*) fresh mushrooms, cleaned and sliced
30 ml	(*2 tbsp*) flour
30 ml	(*2 tbsp*) double cream
	salt and pepper

Place fish in buttered baking dish and sprinkle with half of curry powder. Add carrot and dill; pour in enough cold water to cover and season. Bring to boil over medium heat.

Turn fish over and let simmer about 5 to 6 minutes or until middle bone can be removed easily. Then remove fish and set aside, reserving 400 ml (²/₃ *pt*) of cooking liquid.

Melt butter in saucepan. Add onion, cover and cook 3 to 4 minutes over medium heat.

Add mushrooms; continue cooking 3 to 4 minutes.

Sprinkle in remaining curry powder and mix well. Cook 1 minute, uncovered.

Incorporate flour and cook 1 more minute.

Pour in reserved cooking liquid from fish and mix very well. Add cream and continue cooking sauce 7 to 8 minutes, stirring 2 or 3 times.

Arrange fish on plates and spoon sauce over. Surprise your guests by garnishing with purple grapes.

1 serving	390 calories	16 g carbohydrate
41 g protein	18 g fat	3.4 g fibre

Poached Halibut Pernod

serves 2

1	large halibut steak, cut into 2 across width
15 ml	(*1 tbsp*) chopped fresh parsley
15 ml	(*1 tbsp*) Pernod
1	shallot, chopped
	salt and pepper
	juice ½ lemon

Butter a frying pan and add fish; season with salt and pepper. Sprinkle in parsley, lemon juice, Pernod and shallot.

Cover with greaseproof paper touching surface and cook 4 to 5 minutes over medium heat.

Turn fish over; cover and continue cooking 4 to 5 minutes. When bone can be removed easily, fish is cooked.

Serve with vegetables.

1 serving	262 calories	5 g carbohydrate
38 g protein	10 g fat	0.1 g fibre

Halibut Steak with Garlic Butter

serves 2

225 g	(½ *lb*) unsalted butter, softened
15 ml	(*1 tbsp*) chopped fresh parsley
1	shallot, chopped
2	garlic cloves, smashed and chopped
1	large halibut steak, cut into 2
	pepper
	lemon juice
	Tabasco sauce

Mix butter with parsley; then add shallot and garlic. Using wooden spoon, mix until well blended. Season with pepper, lemon juice and Tabasco sauce. Mix again until thoroughly incorporated.

Butter baking dish with some of garlic butter. Add fish and spread more garlic butter on top. Pepper well.

Place in preheated oven and grill 7 minutes.

Turn fish over, spread with more garlic butter and continue grilling 7 to 8 minutes. Adjust time depending on size.

Serve with potatoes and onions.

1 serving	413 calories	0 g carbohydrate
38 g protein	29 g fat	0 g fibre

Golden Sautéed Halibut with Almonds   *serves 4*

30 g	(*1 oz*) butter
5 ml	(*1 tsp*) oil
2	large halibuts steaks, cut into 2 across width
30 ml	(*2 tbsp*) slivered almonds
	flour
	salt and pepper

Place 15 g (½ *oz*) butter and oil in frying pan over medium heat.

Meanwhile, dredge fish in flour and season well. Add to hot pan and cook 3 minutes.

Turn fish over, season and increase heat to medium-high. Cook another 4 minutes or according to size. When bone can be removed easily, fish is done.

Transfer fish to hot serving platter and set aside.

Add remaining butter to still hot frying pan. Sauté almonds 2 minutes over medium-high heat.

Pour almonds and pan juices over fish and serve. Accompany with spinach, if desired.

1 serving	*368 calories*	*7 g carbohydrate*
40 g protein	*20 g fat*	*0.4 g fibre*

Pan-Fried Sole and Squash

serves 4

4	large sole fillets
30 g	(*1 oz*) butter
15 ml	(*1 tbsp*) oil
1	shallot, chopped
2	yellow summer squash, sliced
	flour
	salt and pepper
	juice 1 lemon

Dredge fish in flour and season with salt and pepper.

Place butter and oil in frying pan over medium-high heat. When hot, add fish and cook 3 minutes.

Turn fillets over; continue cooking 3 minutes. Remove fish and set aside.

Quickly add shallot and squash to pan; sprinkle with lemon juice. Sauté 2 minutes and serve at once with fish.

1 serving	231 calories	14 g carbohydrate
19 g protein	11 g fat	2.8 g fibre

Breaded Sole Fillets Sesame

serves 4

4	sole fillets
30 ml	(*2 tbsp*) sesame seeds
125 g	(*4 oz*) breadcrumbs
2	beaten eggs
15 ml	(*1 tbsp*) vegetable oil
15 g	(*½ oz*) butter
	seasoned flour
	salt and pepper
	lemon slices

Dredge fish in flour. Mix sesame seeds with breadcrumbs and spread on plate.

Dip floured fish in beaten egg and coat with breadcrumbs, pressing lightly with fingertips.

Heat oil and butter in large frying pan. Add fish and cook fillets 2 minutes over medium-high heat.

Turn fillets over, season and continue cooking 2 to 3 minutes. Adjust time according to size of fillets.

Accompany with lemon slices and, if desired, serve with squash.

1 serving	317 calories	26 g carbohydrate
24 g protein	13 g fat	0.8 g fibre

Rolled Sole Fillets with Light Creamy Sauce   *serves 4*

4	**large sole fillets**
1	**carrot, peeled and sliced on angle**
12	**large fresh mushrooms, cleaned and sliced**
1	**celery stick, sliced**
1	**shallot, sliced**
2	**fresh lovage leaves**
250 ml	**(8 fl oz) dry white wine**
125 ml	**(4 fl oz) water**
15 ml	**(1 tbsp) chopped fresh parsley**
30 g	**(1 oz) butter**
30 g	**(1 oz) flour**
30 ml	**(2 tbsp) double cream (optional)**
	salt and pepper

Lay fillets flat on cutting board, roll each and secure with toothpicks. Place in frying pan.

Add carrot, mushrooms, celery, shallot, fresh lovage, wine, water and parsley; season well. Cover with greaseproof paper touching surface and bring to boil over medium heat.

As soon as liquid starts to boil, turn fish rolls over. Reduce heat to low, cover with greaseproof paper and cook 2 to 3 minutes.

Remove fish rolls from pan and set aside.

Continue cooking liquid in pan 5 minutes over high heat, uncovered.

Meanwhile, melt butter in saucepan over low heat. Mix in flour until well incorporated and continue cooking 1 minute.

Gradually incorporate cooking liquid with vegetables while mixing. Cook sauce 2 to 3 minutes over low heat.

Incorporate cream, if desired, and place fish (with toothpicks removed) in sauce. Simmer 2 minutes to reheat sole. Serve.

1 serving	*202 calories*	*10 g carbohydrate*
18 g protein	*10 g fat*	*2.8 g fibre*

Sole Fillets with Garlic Butter and Mushrooms   *serves 2*

2	sole fillets
15 g	(½ oz) butter
125 g	(¼ lb) fresh mushrooms, cleaned and sliced
15 g	(½ oz) garlic butter
15 ml	(1 tbsp) chopped fresh parsley
	seasoned flour
	salt and pepper

Dredge fish in flour. Melt regular butter in frying pan. Add fish and cook 2 minutes over medium-high heat.

Turn fillets over, season and continue cooking 1 to 2 minutes, depending on size. Transfer cooked fish to hot serving platter.

Return frying pan to stove top and add mushrooms and garlic butter. Sprinkle in parsley and cook 3 to 4 minutes over medium-high heat.

Serve mushrooms with fish.

1 serving	225 calories	9 g carbohydrate
18 g protein	13 g fat	2.0 g fibre

Pike Fillets Forestière

serves 4

15 g	(½ oz) butter
15 ml	(1 tbsp) vegetable oil
4	pike fillets
1	shallot, chopped
125 g	(¼ lb) fresh mushrooms, cleaned and diced
2	cooked potatoes, peeled and diced
1	lemon, peeled, flesh diced
	salt and pepper

Heat butter and oil in large frying pan over medium-high heat. Add fish (skin side down) and cook 2 minutes.

Turn fillets over, season and continue cooking 2 minutes; adjust time depending on size. Transfer fish to hot platter; set aside.

Return frying pan to stove top. Add shallot and vegetables; season well. Cook 3 to 4 minutes over medium-high heat.

Stir in diced lemon and cook 1 minute. Spoon over fillets and accompany with baby carrots, if desired.

1 serving	244 calories	17 g carbohydrate
26 g protein	8 g fat	3.2 g fibre

Turbot with Capers and Mushrooms

serves 2

2	turbot fillets
30 g	(*1 oz*) butter
5 ml	(*1 tsp*) oil
15 ml	(*1 tbsp*) capers
1	apple, cored, peeled and sliced
12	large fresh mushrooms, cleaned and sliced
5 ml	(*1 tsp*) chopped fresh parsley
	seasoned flour
	salt and pepper

Dredge fish in flour. Heat butter and oil in frying pan over medium-high heat. Add fish and cook 2 minutes.

Turn fillets over, season and continue cooking 2 minutes; adjust time depending on size. Remove fish to hot platter and set aside.

Add capers, apple and mushrooms to frying pan. Sauté 3 minutes over medium-high heat.

Sprinkle with parsley and serve over fish.

1 serving	340 calories	23 g carbohydrate
26 g protein	16 g fat	5.5 g fibre

Haddock Sauté with Tomatoes

serves 2

275 g	(*10 oz*) haddock fillet, cut into 2.5-cm (*1-in*) pieces
15 ml	(*1 tbsp*) vegetable oil
30 ml	(*2 tbsp*) chopped onion
45 g	(*1½ oz*) sliced celery
1	garlic clove, smashed and chopped
200 g	(*7 oz*) coarsely chopped tomatoes
5 ml	(*1 tsp*) oregano
	salt and pepper
	seasoned flour

Dredge fish in flour. Heat oil in frying pan over medium-high heat. Add fish, onion, celery and garlic; cook 3 minutes.

Turn pieces of fish over, season and continue cooking 3 to 4 minutes.

Stir in tomatoes and oregano; season. Cook 3 to 4 minutes over medium-low heat.

Serve over pasta.

1 serving	*216 calories*	*13 g carbohydrate*
23 g protein	*8 g fat*	*2.6 g fibre*

Perch Fillets with Tomato Fondue

serves 2

45 ml	(*3 tbsp*) olive oil
15 ml	(*1 tbsp*) chopped shallot
45 g	(*1½ oz*) chopped red onion
3	blanched garlic cloves, chopped
15 ml	(*1 tbsp*) chopped fresh lovage
15 ml	(*1 tbsp*) chopped fresh parsley
800 g	(*1¾ lb*) canned tomatoes, drained and chopped
30 ml	(*2 tbsp*) tomato purée
30 ml	(*2 tbsp*) teriyaki sauce
15 ml	(*1 tbsp*) chopped fresh ginger
2	perch fillets
	salt and pepper
	juice ½ lemon

Begin by preparing tomato fondue. Place 15 ml (*1 tbsp*) oil and shallot in frying pan. Add red onion, 1 chopped garlic clove, lovage and parsley; cook 4 to 5 minutes over medium heat.

Stir in tomatoes and season well. Bring to boil and continue cooking 10 minutes over medium heat.

Mix in tomato purée, correct seasoning and mix again. Cook another 3 to 4 minutes.

Meanwhile, place teriyaki sauce, lemon juice, remaining garlic and ginger in small bowl. Add remaining olive oil and mix well.

Brush mixture over both sides of fillets and place in metal fish grill. Cook fish about 7 minutes, turning fish grill over 2 to 3 times and basting occasionally. You can use any of the following: barbecue preheated at medium-high, preheated oven grill or preheated stove-top grill.

When fish is done, serve with tomato fondue, which may be reheated slightly if necessary.

1 serving	435 calories	25 g carbohydrate
23 g protein	27 g fat	4.0 g fibre

1. A metal fish grill is a worthwhile investment and makes some recipes much easier to prepare. It keeps fish from sticking to the cooking surface.

2. Sauté shallot, red onion, part of garlic, fresh lovage and parsley in oil for 4 to 5 minutes over medium heat.

3. Stir in tomatoes and season well. Bring to boil and continue cooking 10 minutes over medium heat.

4. Mix in tomato purée, correct seasoning and mix again. Cook another 3 to 4 minutes.

Poached Cod in Milk

serves 4

2	350-g (*12-oz*) cod fillets, cut into 2
2	shallots, chopped
15 ml	(*1 tbsp*) chopped fresh parsley
1 litre	(*1¾ pt*) hot milk
	salt and pepper

Place fish in buttered baking dish or frying pan. Add shallots and parsley; season well.

Pour in milk and cook over low heat for 4 to 5 minutes. Do not allow liquid to boil.

Turn fish over and continue simmering 4 to 5 minutes, depending on size. Monitor heat.

Serve with a vegetable.

1 serving	*207 calories*	*0 g carbohydrate*
36 g protein	*7 g fat*	*0 g fibre*

Cucumber Sautéed Cod Fillets

serves 2

1	350-g (*12-oz*) cod fillet, cut into 2 pieces
15 g	(*½ oz*) butter
5 ml	(*1 tsp*) vegetable oil
½	cucumber, peeled, seeded and sliced
1	garlic clove, smashed and chopped
1	sprig dill, chopped
	seasoned flour
	salt and pepper
	juice ½ lemon

Dredge fish in flour. Heat butter and oil in large frying pan over medium-high heat. Add cod and cook 3 minutes over medium heat.

Turn fish over; season well. Add cucumber, garlic and dill. Continue cooking 3 minutes; adjust time depending on size.

Remove fish and transfer to hot serving platter. Continue cooking cucumber 2 minutes over high heat.

Sprinkle lemon juice over cucumber and serve with fish.

1 serving	*355 calories*	*17 g carbohydrate*
38 g protein	*15 g fat*	*0.9 g fibre*

Herb-Stuffed Red Mullet

serves 2

1	**medium red mullet, cleaned**
3	**large parsley sprigs**
1	**spring onion, cut into 3**
1	**sprig tarragon**
5 ml	(*1 tsp*) **herbes de Provence**
	salt and pepper
	oil

Preheat oven to 220°C (*425°F, gas mark 7*).

Slash outside skin of fish several times and season cavity well.

Place parsley, spring onion, tarragon and herbes de Provence inside fish. Set, untied, in oiled roasting tin.

Season outside of fish and brush with oil. Cook in oven 15 minutes or according to size. The fish is cooked when backbone turns white.

Remove from tin, cut off head and tail and fillet fish to serve.

1 serving	*196 calories*	*1 g carbohydrate*
30 g protein	*8 g fat*	*0.8 g fibre*

Grilled Mullet and Green Pepper
serves 4

30 ml	(*2 tbsp*) oil
1	garlic clove, smashed and chopped
5 ml	(*1 tsp*) teriyaki sauce
4	red mullet fillets, skin side scored
1	green pepper, quartered
	juice ½ lemon
	salt and pepper

Pour oil in bowl. Add lemon juice, garlic, teriyaki sauce and pepper. Mix well.

Brush mixture over both sides of fillets and marinate 1 hour.

Place fish and green pepper in baking dish; brush green pepper with leftover marinade. Grill 10 to 12 minutes in preheated oven; adjust time depending on size of fillets.

Serve at once.

1 serving	232 calories	2 g carbohydrate
29 g protein	12 g fat	0.2 g fibre

Sautéed Red Mullet Fillets

serves 2

1	large red mullet fillet, cut into 2 pieces
15 g	(½ oz) butter
125 g	(¼ lb) fresh mushrooms, cleaned and sliced
1	courgette, sliced
1	small onion, sliced
1	carrot, peeled and thinly sliced
1	sprig dill, chopped
	seasoned flour
	salt and pepper
	juice ½ lemon

Score skin side of fillets and dredge fish in flour.

Heat butter in frying pan over medium heat. Add fish (skin side down) and season; cook 3 to 4 minutes, partly covered.

Turn fish over and add all vegetables and dill; season well. Continue cooking 3 to 4 minutes.

Turn fish over once more and finish cooking 2 minutes. Transfer fish to hot serving platter.

Cook vegetables another 5 minutes, covered. Sprinkle with lemon juice and serve with red mullet.

1 serving	380 calories	33 g carbohydrate
35 g protein	12 g fat	6.8 g fibre

Baked Bluefish

serves 4

800-g	(*1³/₄-lb*) piece bluefish, boned and butterflied
5	large parsley sprigs
1	spring onion, cut in 2 lengthways
2 ml	(*¹/₂ tsp*) herbes de Provence
1	small celery stick
15 ml	(*1 tbsp*) olive oil
	salt and pepper
	juice 1 lemon

Preheat oven to 220°C (*425°F, gas mark 7*).

Oil baking dish and set aside.

With fish opened, place parsley, spring onion, herbes de Provence and celery on flesh and season well. Close fish but do not tie.

Place in baking dish and sprinkle fish with oil and lemon juice. Bake 14 minutes in oven. Serve.

1 serving	*234 calories*	*3 g carbohydrate*
33 g protein	*10 g fat*	*0.7 g fibre*

Creamy Salmon Casserole

serves 4

15 g	(*½ oz*) butter
4	small onions, quartered
15 ml	(*1 tbsp*) chopped fresh dill
225 g	(*½ lb*) fresh mushrooms, cleaned and quartered
50 ml	(*2 fl oz*) dry white wine
375 ml	(*13 fl oz*) white sauce, heated
750 ml	(*1¼ pt*) leftover cooked salmon, flaked
60 g	(*2 oz*) grated cheese of your choice
	salt and pepper

Place butter, onions and dill in saucepan. Cook, partly covered, 3 to 4 minutes over low heat.

Add mushrooms and continue cooking 3 to 4 minutes, partly covered, over medium heat.

Pour in wine; cook 2 to 3 minutes, uncovered, over high heat.

Mix in white sauce and cook another 3 to 4 minutes over low heat; season well.

Add salmon, mix and transfer contents to baking dish; sprinkle top with cheese. Grill 4 to 5 minutes in preheated oven until lightly browned and bubbly; then serve.

1 serving	449 calories	17 g carbohydrate
39 g protein	25 g fat	2.8 g fibre

1. Place butter, onions and dill in saucepan. Cook, partly covered, 3 to 4 minutes over low heat.

2. Add mushrooms and continue cooking 3 to 4 minutes, partly covered, over medium heat.

3. Increase heat to high and pour in wine; cook 2 to 3 minutes, uncovered.

4. Mix in white sauce and cook another 3 to 4 minutes over low heat; season well.

Dill-Seasoned Salmon Steaks

serves 4

15 ml	(*1 tbsp*) oil
4	salmon steaks, 2 cm (*3/4 in*) thick
15 g	(*1/2 oz*) butter
2	shallots, finely chopped
1	large sprig dill or fennel, finely chopped
	salt and pepper
	juice 1/2 lemon

Preheat oven to 200°C (*400°F, gas mark 6*).

Heat oil in large frying pan over medium-high heat. When hot, add salmon and cook 2 minutes.

Turn fish over, season well and continue cooking 2 minutes. Transfer pan to oven and finish cooking 12 to 14 minutes. Turn salmon over at halfway point.

Remove fish from pan and keep hot.

Wipe pan clean and add butter. Place on stove top over medium heat. Add shallots and dill and cook about 2 minutes.

Sprinkle in lemon juice and pour sauce over salmon. Serve with potatoes and a fresh green vegetable.

1 serving	330 calories	1 g carbohydrate
41 g protein	18 g fat	0 g fibre

Italian Baked Salmon

serves 4

15 ml	(*1 tbsp*) olive oil
4	salmon steaks, 2 cm (¾ *in*) thick
1	shallot, chopped
1	garlic clove, smashed and chopped
800 g	(*1¾ lb*) canned tomatoes, drained and chopped
5 ml	(*1 tsp*) oregano
	salt and pepper
	lemon juice

Preheat oven to 200°C (*400°F, gas mark 6*).

Heat oil in large frying pan over medium-high heat. Add salmon and cook 2 minutes. Turn fish over, season and continue cooking 2 minutes.

Add shallot and garlic; cook 1 more minute.

Add tomatoes and oregano; correct seasoning. Transfer pan to oven and bake for 12 to 14 minutes. At halfway mark, turn salmon over.

Transfer fish to hot serving platter; set aside.

Return frying pan to stove top over high heat. Sprinkle in lemon juice, cook 1 minute and serve over salmon.

1 serving	339 calories	9 g carbohydrate
42 g protein	15 g fat	1.7 g fibre

Salmon Trout Teriyaki

serves 2

2	**salmon trout fillets**
2	**spring onions, sliced on angle**
15 g	(*½ oz*) **butter**
15 ml	(*1 tbsp*) **teriyaki sauce**
2 ml	(*½ tsp*) **herbes de Provence**
	juice 1 lime
	salt and pepper

Place fish in buttered baking dish. Cover with spring onions and remaining ingredients.

Grill fish 6 minutes in preheated oven.

Serve with a little tomato fondue *, if desired.

* See Perch Fillets with Tomato Fondue, page 308.

1 serving	*432 calories*	*5 g carbohydrate*
22 g protein	*36 g fat*	*0.8 g fibre*

Salmon Trout with Mixed Vegetables

serves 2

1	large salmon trout fillet
15 ml	(*1 tbsp*) olive oil
1	blanched garlic clove, chopped
5 ml	(*1 tsp*) fennel seeds
5 ml	(*1 tsp*) teriyaki sauce
15 ml	(*1 tbsp*) peanut oil
1	spring onion, sliced on angle
½	yellow summer squash, cut into sticks
½	green pepper, cut into sticks
½	courgette, cut into sticks
8	fresh mushrooms, cleaned and sliced
	juice ½ lime
	few drops Tabasco sauce
	salt and pepper
	juice 1 lemon

Skin fish (if not already done) by slipping knife between flesh and skin. Cut fish into pieces about 1 cm (½ *in*) thick on an angle.

Place pieces in bowl and add olive oil, garlic, fennel seeds, teriyaki sauce, lime juice and Tabasco sauce; season well. Marinate 15 minutes.

Heat peanut oil in frying pan over high heat. Add fish and sauté 3 minutes.

Remove fish and set aside.

Add all vegetables to frying pan, season and cook 4 to 5 minutes over high heat.

Return fish to pan with vegetables; sprinkle with lemon juice. Simmer 1 minute before serving.

1 serving	569 calories	16 g carbohydrate
25 g protein	45 g fat	5.1 g fibre

Informal Salmon Stir-Fry

serves 4

4	125-g (*4-oz*) salmon fillets
15 ml	(*1 tbsp*) oil
225 g	(*½ lb*) mangetouts, topped and tailed
175 g	(*6 oz*) bean sprouts, washed
1	courgette, cut into sticks
30 ml	(*2 tbsp*) chopped fresh ginger
	lemon juice
	soy sauce
	salt and pepper

Preheat oven to 200°C (*400°F, gas mark 6*).

Place fish on platter and sprinkle with lemon juice and soy sauce; marinate 10 minutes.

Heat oil in large frying pan over medium heat. Add fish and cook 3 minutes. Turn fillets over, season and continue cooking 6 to 7 minutes in oven.

Transfer fish to hot serving platter.

Add vegetables and ginger to frying pan; sprinkle with a little more soy sauce. Cook 3 to 4 minutes over high heat.

Season vegetables with pepper only and serve with fish.

1 serving	359 calories	11 g carbohydrate
45 g protein	15 g fat	5.2 g fibre

Fresh Salmon Amandine

serves 2

2	salmon steaks, about 1 cm (*½ in*) thick
15 ml	(*1 tbsp*) oil
15 g	(*½ oz*) butter
15 ml	(*1 tbsp*) chopped fresh parsley
15 ml	(*1 tbsp*) slivered almonds
	flour
	salt and pepper
	juice ½ lemon

Preheat oven to 200°C (*400°F, gas mark 6*).

Dredge salmon in flour, season and set aside.

Heat oil in frying pan over medium-high heat. Add fish and cook 3 minutes. Turn steaks over, reduce heat to medium and cook another 3 minutes.

Wrap pan handle in foil and transfer to oven; continue cooking 4 to 5 minutes.

Remove fish and transfer to hot serving platter. Set aside.

Add butter, parsley and almonds to frying pan that contained fish; cook 2 minutes over medium heat.

Sprinkle in lemon juice, mix and immediately pour over fish. Serve with spinach.

1 serving	*446 calories*	*12 g carbohydrate*
41 g protein	*26 g fat*	*0.7 g fibre*

Poached Salmon with Egg Sauce

serves 4

WHITE SAUCE: *

45 g	*(1½ oz)* **butter**
30 g	*(1 oz)* **flour**
500 ml	*(17 fl oz)* **milk**
pinch	**nutmeg**
pinch	**cloves**
	white pepper

Melt butter in saucepan. When butter starts to bubble, add flour. Mix well, using wooden spoon, and cook 2 minutes over low heat.

Slowly pour in milk while mixing with wooden spoon. Add nutmeg, cloves and pepper. Cook sauce 12 minutes over low heat, stirring 4 times.

* This is a versatile white sauce that can be used in other recipes. For a thinner sauce, simply increase the quantity of milk by 250 ml (*8 fl oz*).

POACHED SALMON:

4	**salmon steaks, 2 cm** *(¾ in)* **thick**
2	**shallots, sliced**
2	**sprigs dill**
2	**small carrots, peeled and sliced**
2	**hard-boiled eggs, chopped**
	juice 1 lemon
	salt and pepper

Place salmon in buttered ovenproof baking dish or large frying pan. Add shallots, dill, carrots and lemon juice; season.

Pour in enough cold water to cover fish and bring to boil over medium-high heat. Do not cover fish.

Reduce heat to low and turn fish over; simmer 3 to 4 minutes. When middle bone can be removed easily, fish is cooked.

Carefully remove fish from cooking liquid and transfer to serving plates.

Mix chopped eggs with white sauce and spoon over salmon. Serve.

1 serving	481 calories	15 g carbohydrate
49 g protein	25 g fat	0.8 g fibre

1. Begin by melting butter in saucepan.

2. When butter starts to bubble, add flour.

3. Cook flour/butter mixture 2 minutes over low heat while mixing with wooden spoon. It is important to cook the flour long enough to eliminate its raw taste.

4. Pour in the milk; when incorporated with the cooked flour, it will begin thickening as it is cooked over low heat.

Poached Salmon Hollandaise

serves 4

HOLLANDAISE:

1	shallot, finely chopped
45 ml	(*3 tbsp*) dry white wine
15 ml	(*1 tbsp*) freshly chopped fennel
2	eggs yolks
250 ml	(*8 fl oz*) clarified butter
	salt and pepper
	lemon juice

Place shallot, wine and fennel in stainless steel bowl. Set over medium heat and cook 2 minutes. Remove and let cool.

Have ready saucepan half-filled with hot water set over low heat. Add egg yolks to mixture in stainless steel bowl and whisk well. Place bowl over saucepan.

Gradually incorporate clarified butter in thin stream while mixing constantly with whisk. When mixture becomes thick, season and add lemon juice to taste. Remove bowl from saucepan and set aside.

SALMON:

1.5 litres	(*2¾ pt*) fish stock, heated
4	salmon fillets
	few drops lemon juice

Pour fish stock into medium-sized roasting tin and bring to boil over high heat. Reduce heat to low and add fillets. Simmer 10 to 12 minutes or adjust time depending on size. Turn fish over once.

Using slotted utensil, remove cooked fillets and accompany with hollandaise sauce. Sprinkle fish with lemon juice.

1 serving	756 calories	2 g carbohydrate
43 g protein	64 g fat	0 g fibre

Grilled Salmon Steaks

serves 2

2	salmon steaks, about 1 cm (½ *in*) thick
2	shallots, chopped
2	slices lemon
2	parsley sprigs
5 ml	(*1 tsp*) olive oil
	few drops lemon juice
	salt and pepper

Preheat oven to 200°C (*400°F, gas mark 6*).

Butter small roasting tin. Place salmon steaks in tin and sprinkle with shallots.

Place slice of lemon on each steak and top with remaining ingredients.

Change oven setting to grill and cook 7 minutes or adjust time according to size.

Serve with potatoes, if desired.

1 serving	273 calories	0 g carbohydrate
39 g protein	13 g fat	0.3 g fibre

Sautéed Salmon with Peppers and Onion   *serves 4*

4	**salmon fillets**
150 g	**(5 oz) seasoned flour**
30 ml	**(2 tbsp) vegetable oil**
1	**green pepper, thinly sliced**
1	**red pepper, thinly sliced**
1	**medium onion, thinly sliced**
15 ml	**(1 tbsp) freshly chopped parsley**
	salt and pepper

Preheat oven to 190°C (*375°F, gas mark 5*).

Season salmon and dredge in flour. Heat oil in large frying pan over medium heat. Add fish and cook 4 minutes on each side.

Transfer pan to oven and finish cooking fish 6 to 7 minutes or adjust time depending on thickness. When cooked, remove fish from pan to serving platter and keep warm.

Add both peppers and onion to frying pan; cook 4 to 5 minutes over high heat.

Season well and serve vegetables with fish. Sprinkle with parsley.

1 serving	454 calories	30 g carbohydrate
43 g protein	18 g fat	1.9 g fibre

Baked Breaded Salmon Fillets

serves 4

4	**125-g (*4-oz*) salmon fillets, skinned**
2	**beaten eggs**
15 ml	**(*1 tbsp*) oil**
15 g	**(*½ oz*) butter**
1	**cucumber, peeled, seeded and sliced**
½	**red pepper, cut into julienne**
1	**yellow pepper, cut into julienne**
	seasoned flour
	seasoned breadcrumbs
	salt and pepper
	grated zest 1 lemon

Preheat oven to 200°C (*400°F, gas mark 6*).

Dredge fish in flour, dip in beaten egg and thoroughly coat with breadcrumbs.

Heat oil in large frying pan. Add fish and cook 2 minutes over medium heat. Turn fish over, season and continue cooking 2 minutes.

Transfer to oven and continue cooking fish 10 to 12 minutes.

Before fish is done, place butter and vegetables in saucepan. Add lemon zest, cover and cook 5 minutes.

Season and serve with fish.

1 serving	*424 calories*	*20 g carbohydrate*
41 g protein	*20 g fat*	*1.2 g fibre*

Fresh Salmon with Vinaigrette

serves 4

525 g	(*18 oz*) **fresh cooked flaked salmon**
15 ml	(*1 tbsp*) **freshly chopped parsley**
15 ml	(*1 tbsp*) **freshly chopped chives**
1	**celery stick, thinly sliced**
1	**yellow pepper, thinly sliced**
1	**large carrot, peeled and grated**
60 ml	(*4 tbsp*) **olive oil**
	juice 1 lemon
	salt and pepper

Place salmon in bowl. Add parsley, chives, celery, yellow pepper and carrot; mix well.

Add remaining ingredients and mix again. Correct seasoning and, if desired, serve on lettuce leaves.

1 serving	*259 calories*	*4 g carbohydrate*
20 g protein	*19 g fat*	*1.0 g fibre*

Mixed Pasta With Salmon

serves 4

30 g	(*1 oz*) butter
225 g	(*¹/₂ lb*) fresh mushrooms, cleaned and sliced
1	shallot, chopped
40 g	(*1¹/₄ oz*) flour
¹/₂	green pepper, diced
¹/₂	yellow pepper, diced
500 ml	(*17 fl oz*) hot milk
350 g	(*³/₄ lb*) flaked cooked salmon
3	portions cooked linguini, hot
1¹/₂	portions cooked rotini, hot
	salt and pepper
	nutmeg and paprika

Heat butter in frying pan over medium heat. Add mushrooms and shallot; cook 3 to 4 minutes.

Mix in flour until well incorporated and cook 1 minute over low heat.

Stir in both peppers and incorporate half of milk; mix very well. Add remaining milk and season well. Add nutmeg and paprika. Cook 7 minutes over medium heat, stirring occasionally.

Stir in salmon and simmer 2 to 3 minutes. Pour sauce over mixed pasta and serve.

1 serving	624 calories	89 g carbohydrate
31 g protein	16 g fat	2.1 g fibre

Coquilles Saint-Jacques Bretonne

serves 4

45 g	(*1½ oz*) butter
2	shallots, chopped
150 g	(*5 oz*) chopped red onion
45 ml	(*3 tbsp*) chopped fresh parsley
3	blanched garlic cloves, chopped
45 ml	(*3 tbsp*) dry white wine
700 g	(*1½ lb*) scallops, chopped
30 g	(*1 oz*) dried crusty bread, finely diced
2 ml	(*½ tsp*) tarragon
	salt and pepper

Place 30 g (*1 oz*) butter in frying pan. Add shallots, onion, parsley and garlic; cover and cook 10 minutes over low heat.

Pour in wine and cook 3 minutes over high heat.

Stir in scallops and breadcrumbs; add remaining butter. Season and add tarragon. Cook 5 to 6 minutes over medium heat.

Divide mixture into 4 scallop shells set on baking sheet.

Press mixture lightly with back of a spoon.

Place on middle rack of preheated oven; grill 8 minutes until nicely browned. Serve.

1 serving	308 calories	16 g carbohydrate
34 g protein	12 g fat	0.8 g fibre

1. Place 30 ml (*2 tbsp*) butter in frying pan. Add shallots, onion, parsley and garlic; cover and cook 10 minutes over low heat.

2. After wine has been reduced, add scallops, breadcrumbs and remaining butter. Season and add tarragon.

3. Cook 5 to 6 minutes over medium heat to evaporate liquid and dry out mixture.

4. Divide mixture into 4 scallop shells — use natural shells or dishes, if preferred. Prepare to grill.

Grilled Mussel Coquilles

serves 4

30 g	(*1 oz*) butter
2	blanched garlic cloves, chopped
225 g	(*½ lb*) fresh mushrooms, cleaned and chopped
1	shallot, chopped
15 ml	(*1 tbsp*) chopped fresh parsley
225 g	(*½ lb*) cooked chopped mussels
30 g	(*1 oz*) dried crusty bread, finely diced
250 ml	(*8 fl oz*) tomato fondue*
	salt and pepper
	fine breadcrumbs
	melted butter

Place butter in frying pan. Add garlic, mushrooms, shallot and parsley; season well. Cook 5 minutes over medium heat.

Mix in chopped mussels and diced crusty bread; continue cooking 2 to 3 minutes.

Pour in tomato fondue, mix well, and cook another 2 minutes. Correct seasoning.

Divide mixture into 4 scallop shells and sprinkle with fine breadcrumbs; moisten with a bit of melted butter.

Grill 2 minutes in preheated oven. Serve with fresh sliced bread.

* See Perch Fillets with Tomato Fondue, page 308.

1 serving	302 calories	21 g carbohydrate
14 g protein	18 g fat	2.5 g fibre

Mussels in the Shell with Wine Sauce   *serves 4*

4 kg	(*9 lb*) fresh mussels, scrubbed and bearded
2	shallots, finely chopped
30 ml	(*2 tbsp*) chopped fresh parsley
50 ml	(*2 fl oz*) dry white wine
1	slice lemon
250 ml	(*8 fl oz*) single cream, heated
	salt and pepper

Place mussels in large saucepan, being sure to discard any opened shells. Add shallots, parsley, wine and lemon slice. Season with pepper but do not salt.

Cover and cook over medium-high heat until mussels open. Stir once during cooking.

Remove mussels one at a time and transfer to large serving bowl.

Discard lemon slice and return saucepan to stove over high heat; reduce liquid 3 to 4 minutes.

Pour in cream, stir well and cook another 3 to 4 minutes. Correct seasoning and pour sauce over mussels.

1 serving	385 calories	18 g carbohydrate
49 g protein	13 g fat	0.2 g fibre

Mussels in Tomato Sauce over Pasta

serves 4

15 ml	(*1 tbsp*) oil
45 ml	(*3 tbsp*) chopped red onion
3	blanched garlic cloves, chopped
30 ml	(*2 tbsp*) chopped fresh parsley
2 ml	(*½ tsp*) tarragon
1.2 kg	(*2½ lb*) canned stewed tomatoes, drained and chopped
1	sprig fresh oregano, chopped
45 ml	(*3 tbsp*) tomato purée
350 g	(*¾ lb*) shelled cooked mussels
4	portions cooked pasta, hot
	salt and pepper
pinch	sugar

Place oil, onion, garlic, parsley and tarragon in frying pan. Cook 3 minutes over medium heat.

Add tomatoes and fresh oregano; season well. Mix and continue cooking 10 minutes.

Stir in tomato purée and sugar; cook 4 to 5 minutes over low heat.

Mix in mussels and simmer 1 minute over very low heat. Serve at once over hot pasta. If desired, decorate plates with empty mussel shells.

1 serving	387 calories	58 g carbohydrate
23 g protein	7 g fat	3.1 g fibre

1. Cook oil with onion, garlic, parsley and tarragon 3 minutes over medium heat.

2. Add tomatoes and fresh oregano; season well. Mix and continue cooking 10 minutes.

3. Stir in tomato purée and sugar; cook 4 to 5 minutes over low heat.

4. Mix in mussels and simmer 1 minute over very low heat before serving.

Quick Prawn Sauté with Tomatoes

serves 4

24	**medium-large prawns**
15 ml	(*1 tbsp*) **vegetable oil**
15 ml	(*1 tbsp*) **chopped fresh parsley**
5 ml	(*1 tsp*) **herbes de Provence**
2	**garlic cloves, smashed and chopped**
2	**spring onions, chopped**
50 ml	(*2 fl oz*) **dry white wine**
1.2 kg	(*2½ lb*) **canned tomatoes, drained and chopped**
	salt and pepper
	few drops Tabasco sauce

Peel prawns, leaving tails intact. Slit backs and remove veins; wash and set aside.

Heat oil in large frying pan over high heat. When hot, add prawns and cook 2 minutes.

Turn prawns over, season and continue cooking 1 minute.

Add parsley, herbes de Provence, garlic and spring onions; cook 2 minutes. Using tongs, remove prawns and set aside.

With frying pan still over high heat, pour in wine and continue cooking 3 minutes.

Mix in tomatoes, season well and sprinkle in Tabasco sauce. Cook 8 to 10 minutes over high heat, stirring several times.

Place prawns in tomatoes, reheat 1 minute and serve.

1 serving	266 calories	14 g carbohydrate
39 g protein	6 g fat	3.1 g fibre

1. Peel prawns, leaving tails intact. Slit backs using small paring knife and remove veins. Wash prawns in cold water.

2. Begin sautéing prawns in hot oil over high heat for 2 minutes. Then turn over, season and cook 1 more minute.

3. Add parsley, herbes de Provence, garlic and spring onions; cook 2 minutes.

4. Using tongs, remove prawns before they become overcooked and set aside.

Pepper Prawns

serves 4

32	**medium-large prawns**
5 ml	(*1 tsp*) **herbes de Provence**
15 ml	(*1 tbsp*) **ground pepper**
5 ml	(*1 tsp*) **paprika**
15 ml	(*1 tbsp*) **teriyaki sauce**
50 ml	(*2 fl oz*) **dry white wine**
	juice 1 lemon

Without peeling, place prawns in saucepan. Add herbes de Provence, ground pepper, paprika and lemon juice.

Sprinkle in teriyaki sauce and mix well. Pour in wine, cover and bring to boil over high heat.

As soon as water starts to boil, remove saucepan from heat and drain prawns. Serve at once (on newspaper if desired) with seafood sauce.

1 serving	230 calories	4 g carbohydrate
49 g protein	2 g fat	0 g fibre

Grilled Butterflied Prawns

serves 4

24	large prawns
150 g	(5 oz) finely chopped cooked red onion
15 ml	(1 tbsp) chopped fresh parsley
2	blanched garlic cloves, chopped
45 g	(1½ oz) butter, softened
	few drops Worcestershire sauce
	salt and pepper

Take unpeeled prawns and cut down along backs to open butterfly-style; remove veins. Arrange on ovenproof platter.

Mix remaining ingredients together in food processor.

Spread mixture over opened prawns and grill 4 to 5 minutes, depending on size, in preheated oven.

Serve with vegetables.

1 serving	263 calories	4 g carbohydrate
37 g protein	11 g fat	0.6 g fibre

Fresh Prawns with Garlic Purée

serves 4

16-18	garlic cloves, peeled
30 ml	(*2 tbsp*) olive oil
24	medium-large prawns
3	slices lemon
125 ml	(*4 fl oz*) dry white wine
5 ml	(*1 tsp*) butter
2 ml	(*½ tsp*) herbes de Provence
5 ml	(*1 tsp*) cornflour
30 ml	(*2 tbsp*) cold water
125 ml	(*4 fl oz*) single cream, heated
	few drops lemon juice
	salt and pepper
	few drops hot pepper sauce

Place garlic cloves in small saucepan with enough water to cover. Bring to boil over high heat; continue cooking 8 to 10 minutes over medium heat.

Drain and transfer cloves to mortar; mash with pestle. Transfer purée to fine sieve and force through into bowl. If preferred, use food processor.

Incorporate oil to garlic purée while whisking constantly. Sprinkle with lemon juice, season, mix and set aside.

Place unpeeled prawns and lemon slices in clean saucepan. Add wine, butter, herbes de Provence and hot pepper sauce. Bring to boil over high heat.

Stir prawns and continue cooking 1 minute. Remove casserole from stove and let stand several minutes before removing prawns with tongs.

Leaving saucepan on stove, reduce cooking liquid 2 minutes over high heat.

Mix cornflour with cold water; stir into liquid. Pour in cream, season and bring to boil. Continue cooking 2 minutes over medium heat.

Peel prawns, leaving tails intact and serve with sauce. Accompany with garlic purée for dipping.

1 serving	293 calories	7 g carbohydrate
37 g protein	13 g fat	0 g fibre

1. Place garlic cloves in small saucepan with enough water to cover. Bring to boil over high heat; continue cooking 8 to 10 minutes over medium heat.

2. Transfer drained cloves to mortar and mash with pestle.

3. Transfer garlic purée to fine sieve and force through into bowl.

4. Cook unpeeled prawns with lemon slices, wine, butter, herbes de Provence and hot pepper sauce.

King Crab Legs

serves 4

4	**large king crab legs**
125 g	**(*4 oz*) garlic butter**
	breadcrumbs
	pepper

Preheat oven to 200°C (*400°F, gas mark 6*).

Cut crab legs in half across width; split open lengthways.

Spread garlic butter over meat and sprinkle with breadcrumbs; place on ovenproof platter. Pepper well.

Change oven setting to grill and place crab legs in oven; grill 5 to 6 minutes.

1 serving	*408 calories*	*9 g carbohydrate*
30 g protein	*28 g fat*	*0.2 g fibre*

GLORIOUS GREENS

*The good things of
the earth in an explosion
of vibrant colors*

Tangy Coleslaw

serves 4–6

1	medium cabbage, quartered
2	carrots, peeled and grated
15 ml	(*1 tbsp*) freshly chopped parsley
45 ml	(*3 tbsp*) cider vinegar, heated to boiling point
60 ml	(*4 tbsp*) mayonnaise
30 ml	(*2 tbsp*) horseradish
60 ml	(*4 tbsp*) double cream
	salt and pepper
	juice 1 lemon

Place pieces of cabbage in large saucepan filled with boiling water. Blanch 4 to 5 minutes over high heat. Drain cabbage and set aside to cool.

Thinly slice cabbage and place in large bowl. Add carrots and parsley; mix well. Season with salt and pepper.

Pour hot vinegar over shredded cabbage and continue mixing. Set aside.

Place mayonnaise and horseradish in small bowl; blend together. Lightly whip cream and add to bowl with lemon juice, salt and pepper to taste; mix all together.

Spoon over cabbage and mix well until incorporated. Marinate 1 hour at room temperature before serving.

1 serving	138 calories	10 g carbohydrate
2 g protein	10 g fat	3.4 g fibre

1. Place cabbage pieces in plenty of boiling water. Blanch 4 to 5 minutes over high heat.

2. Place thinly sliced cabbage in large bowl. Add carrots and parsley; mix well. Season with salt and pepper.

3. Pour hot vinegar over shredded cabbage and continue mixing. Set aside.

4. Spoon dressing over cabbage and mix well.

347

Mixed Sweet Pepper Salad

serves 4

30 ml	(*2 tbsp*) olive oil
3	rashers back bacon, cut into strips
1	small aubergine, peeled and cut into julienne
1	green pepper, cut into julienne
2	red peppers, cut into julienne
2	shallots, chopped
1	garlic clove, smashed and chopped
	salt and pepper
	vinaigrette to taste
	chopped fresh parsley

Heat half of oil in frying pan over high heat. Add bacon and cook 2 to 3 minutes, mixing once during cooking.

Stir in aubergine and cook 4 to 5 minutes over medium heat.

Add remaining vegetables, shallots and garlic; sprinkle in remaining oil. Season, cover and cook 7 to 8 minutes over medium heat. Stir once or twice.

Transfer mixture to serving bowl and toss in vinaigrette to taste. Sprinkle with chopped parsley and other garnishes, if desired, before serving.

1 serving	229 calories	5 g carbohydrate
5 g protein	21 g fat	1.3 g fibre

Vegetarian Platter

serves 4

4	**baking potatoes**
2	**carrots, pared and sliced on angle**
1	**courgette, cut into sticks**
225 g	**(¹/₂ lb) French beans, pared**
4	**onions, cut into 4**
1	**green pepper, cut into 4**
	salt and pepper

Prick potatoes with fork several times and wrap in foil. Bake in preheated oven at 220°C (*425°F, gas mark 7*) for 1 hour or until done.

Before potatoes are cooked, place all vegetables in basket of steamer in order in which they are listed. Steam vegetables, removing them as they become cooked, and transfer to bowl of cold water.

When all vegetables are cooked, return to steamer to reheat.

Arrange vegetables and baked potatoes on serving platter and serve with your favourite toppings, such as soured cream, cheese sauce, melted butter, etc.

1 serving	*345 calories*	*75 g carbohydrate*
9 g protein	*1 g fat*	*9.4 g fibre*

Caesar Salad Variation

serves 4

2 to 3	**garlic cloves, smashed and chopped**
15 ml	**(*1 tbsp*) Dijon mustard**
1	**egg yolk**
4 to 5	**anchovy fillets, drained and finely chopped**
45 ml	**(*3 tbsp*) wine vinegar**
125 ml	**(*4 fl oz*) olive oil**
2	**large heads romaine lettuce, washed and dried***
	salt and pepper
	juice 1 lemon
	crumbled cooked bacon
	garlic croutons
	grated Parmesan cheese

Place garlic, mustard and egg yolk in bowl; season well. Add lemon juice, anchovies and vinegar; whisk together.

Incorporate oil in thin stream while whisking constantly. Correct seasoning.

Tear lettuce leaves into small pieces and place in salad bowl. Sprinkle in bacon and croutons. Pour in vinaigrette and toss. Sprinkle with cheese and serve.

* Washing and drying the lettuce properly is essential. If it is not thoroughly dried, the vinaigrette will not adhere properly and the salad will taste watery.

1 serving	408 calories	12 g carbohydrate
9 g protein	36 g fat	1.5 g fibre

1. Place garlic, mustard and egg yolk in bowl; season well.

2. Add lemon juice, anchovies and vinegar; whisk together.

3. Incorporate oil in thin stream while whisking constantly. Correct seasoning.

4. The vinaigrette should be quite thick.

Julienne Vegetable Salad

serves 4

1	celery stick
1	large carrot, peeled
1	green pepper
1	red pepper
½	courgette
1	aubergine
1	apple, cored and peeled
15 ml	(*1 tbsp*) chopped fresh parsley
15 ml	(*1 tbsp*) Dijon mustard
1	egg yolk
5 ml	(*1 tsp*) curry powder
45 ml	(*3 tbsp*) wine vinegar
90 ml	(*6 tbsp*) olive oil
	salt and pepper
dash	paprika
	lettuce leaves, washed and dried

Cut all vegetables (leave skin on aubergine) and apple into julienne sticks. It is easier if you square the ends and sides of each vegetable before starting. Try to cut the julienne sticks a uniform size.

Place celery and carrot in salted boiling water. Cover and cook 3 minutes over medium heat.

Add remaining vegetables, season and cover. Continue cooking 2 minutes.

Drain vegetables and rinse under cold water. Drain again and transfer to bowl. Add apple and set aside.

Mix together parsley, mustard, egg yolk, curry powder, paprika, vinegar, salt and pepper in small bowl.

Incorporate oil in thin stream while whisking constantly. If oil is added too quickly, it will be more difficult to incorporate.

Season dressing to taste and pour over salad ingredients. Toss well until evenly coated.

Arrange lettuce leaves on serving platter and add salad. If desired, decorate with hard-boiled egg yolk forced through wire sieve.

1 serving	275 calories	15 g carbohydrate
2 g protein	23 g fat	3.2 g fibre

Cold Beetroot Salad

serves 4

6	small fresh beetroots
15 ml	(*1 tbsp*) chopped fresh parsley
2	shallots, chopped
2	sweet pickled gherkins, chopped
15 ml	(*1 tbsp*) Dijon mustard
30 ml	(*2 tbsp*) wine vinegar
45 ml	(*3 tbsp*) olive oil
	salt and pepper

Cut off tops of beetroots and discard. Wash beetroots thoroughly in plenty of cold water, using brush if necessary. Cook in salted boiling water until tender.

When cooked, drain well and set aside until cool enough to handle. Peel and slice beetroots 5 mm (¼ in) thick.

Place slices in bowl. Season, add parsley, shallots and gherkins; set aside.

In smaller bowl, mix together mustard and vinegar. Add olive oil and whisk until incorporated.

Pour vinaigrette over beetroots, toss and correct seasoning.

Serve on lettuce or spinach leaves.

1 serving	139 calories	9 g carbohydrate
1 g protein	11 g fat	2.5 g fibre

The Great Purple Salad

serves 4

6 to 8	cooked beetroots, peeled and sliced
2	spring onions, sliced
15 ml	(*1 tbsp*) chopped fresh parsley
4	slices corned beef, cut into strips
15 ml	(*1 tbsp*) strong mustard
30 ml	(*2 tbsp*) wine vinegar
45 ml	(*3 tbsp*) olive oil
	salt and pepper
	romaine lettuce leaves, washed and dried

Place beetroots, onions, parsley and corned beef in bowl. Toss together and season; toss again and set aside.

Place mustard, vinegar, salt and pepper in small bowl; mix together.

Whisk in oil, correct seasoning and pour over salad. Toss until evenly coated.

Decoratively arrange lettuce leaves in glass or attractive serving bowl. Spoon salad on top and serve.

1 serving	193 calories	9 g carbohydrate
10 g protein	13 g fat	3.5 g fibre

Jeffrey's Salad

serves 4

225 g	(*½ lb*) **French beans, pared and cooked**
4	**cooked beetroots, peeled and sliced**
2	**fresh plum tomatoes, sliced**
3	**anchovy fillets, chopped**
12	**stuffed green olives**
2	**cooked potatoes, peeled and sliced**
30 ml	(*2 tbsp*) **capers**
15 ml	(*1 tbsp*) **Dijon mustard**
5 ml	(*1 tsp*) **tarragon**
1	**garlic clove, smashed and chopped**
45 ml	(*3 tbsp*) **tarragon wine vinegar**
125 ml	(*4 fl oz*) **olive oil**
15 ml	(*1 tbsp*) **lemon juice**
2	**hard-boiled eggs, sliced**
	salt and pepper

Place beans, beetroots, tomatoes, anchovies, olives, potatoes and capers in large bowl. Toss together and season well.

Place mustard, tarragon, garlic, salt and pepper in small bowl. Add vinegar and whisk together.

Incorporate oil in thin stream while whisking constantly. Add lemon juice and correct seasoning.

Pour dressing over salad and toss. Add eggs, toss again and serve.

1 serving	418 calories	21 g carbohydrate
7 g protein	34 g fat	5.6 g fibre

Alsatian Salad

serves 4

2	slices ham, 5 mm (¼ *in*) thick, cut into julienne
2	cooked beetroots, peeled and cut into julienne
2	cooked potatoes, peeled and sliced
15 ml	(*1 tbsp*) chopped fresh parsley
½	red pepper, cut into julienne
30 ml	(*2 tbsp*) mayonnaise
5 ml	(*1 tsp*) olive oil
1	whole chicken breast, cooked, skinned and cut into julienne
	salt and pepper
	juice ½ lemon

Place ham, beetroots, potatoes, parsley and red pepper in large bowl. Season well and toss together.

Add mayonnaise and sprinkle in lemon juice; mix well.

Sprinkle in olive oil and correct seasoning. Mix again.

Top with chicken and serve.

1 serving	*234 calories*	*14 g carbohydrate*
22 g protein	*10 g fat*	*2.1 g fibre*

Cubed Potatoes with Soured Cream   *serves 4*

30 ml	(*2 tbsp*) melted butter
1	medium onion, finely chopped
4	cooked potatoes, peeled and cubed, still hot
300 ml	(*¹/₂ pt*) soured cream
	salt and pepper
dash	paprika

Heat butter in large frying pan. Add onion and cover; cook 3 minutes over low heat.

Add potatoes and season. Cook 8 to 10 minutes, uncovered, over medium heat. Stir once or twice.

Add soured cream and gently mix in. Continue cooking 3 minutes over low heat.

Sprinkle with paprika and serve.

1 serving	277 calories	26 g carbohydrate
5 g protein	17 g fat	3.0 g fibre

Creamy Cucumber Salad

serves 4

1	**seedless cucumber, peeled**
½	**red pepper, sliced**
1	**small celery stick, sliced**
1	**apple, cored, peeled and sliced**
90 g	**(3 oz) cooked frozen green peas**
5 ml	**(1 tsp) horseradish**
45 ml	**(3 tbsp) soured cream**
	salt and pepper
	juice 1 lemon

Cut cucumber into 2 lengthways and then slice. Place in bowl and season with salt; let stand 15 minutes.

Drain cucumber and transfer to another bowl. Add red pepper, celery, apple and peas.

Sprinkle in lemon juice and season well. Mix in horseradish; then add soured cream and mix until evenly coated.

Correct seasoning. If desired, serve over shredded cabbage and decorate with fresh radishes.

1 serving	86 calories	15 g carbohydrate
2 g protein	2 g fat	3.9 g fibre

Fresh Tomato Salad

serves 4

4	tomatoes, washed
2	shallots, finely chopped
15 ml	(*1 tbsp*) chopped fresh parsley
2	hard-boiled eggs, chopped
30 ml	(*2 tbsp*) wine vinegar
45 ml	(*3 tbsp*) olive oil
	juice ½ lemon
	salt and pepper

Set tomatoes on cutting board, core side down. Slice in half vertically. Place cut side of tomato on cutting board and slice.

Place slices in bowl with shallots, parsley and eggs.

Sprinkle in vinegar, oil and lemon juice; season generously. Toss, correct seasoning and serve.

1 serving	*166 calories*	*6 g carbohydrate*
4 g protein	*14 g fat*	*1.9 g fibre*

Pan-Fried Tomato Rounds

serves 4

4	large tomatoes, cored and sliced 2 cm (*3/4 in*) thick
30 ml	(*2 tbsp*) olive oil
45 ml	(*3 tbsp*) soy sauce
2	garlic cloves, smashed and chopped
150 g	(*5 oz*) flour
45 ml	(*3 tbsp*) melted butter
	salt and pepper
	chopped fresh parsley

Season tomato slices with salt and pepper and place them on large plate.

Mix oil with soy sauce and garlic; pour over tomatoes and let stand 15 minutes.

Turn tomato slices over and let stand another 15 minutes.

Lightly dredge tomato slices in flour. Heat butter in large frying pan and when hot add tomato slices; cook 3 minutes over medium heat.

Turn slices over and continue cooking 3 to 4 minutes or until lightly browned.

Serve sprinkled with fresh parsley.

1 serving	*253 calories*	*21 g carbohydrate*
4 g protein	*17 g fat*	*2.9 g fibre*

Mixed Cucumber Salad

serves 4

1	seedless cucumber, sliced
12	large fresh mushrooms, cleaned
½	red pepper, thinly sliced
15 ml	(*1 tbsp*) chopped fresh parsley
60 g	(*2 oz*) diced Jarlsberg cheese
30 g	(*1 oz*) sliced bamboo shoots
30 ml	(*2 tbsp*) soured cream
15 ml	(*1 tbsp*) olive oil
30 g	(*1 oz*) chopped walnuts
	juice 1 lemon
	paprika to taste
	salt and pepper

Place cucumber in large bowl. Peel off thin skin from mushrooms, starting just beneath the cap, and discard. Slice mushrooms and add to bowl.

Sprinkle in lemon juice. Add red pepper, parsley and paprika; season well.

Add cheese and bamboo shoots; mix well.

Spoon in soured cream and oil; mix well and season to taste.

Sprinkle walnuts over salad and serve.

1 serving	203 calories	10 g carbohydrate
7 g protein	15 g fat	2.5 g fibre

Vibrant Rice Salad

serves 4

3	small plum tomatoes, cubed
1	yellow banana pepper, seeded and chopped
30 g	(*1 oz*) sliced bamboo shoots
5 ml	(*1 tsp*) chopped fresh parsley
350 g	(*¾ lb*) cooked rice
2	hard-boiled eggs, chopped
15 ml	(*1 tbsp*) Dijon mustard
1	garlic clove, smashed and chopped
45 ml	(*3 tbsp*) tarragon wine vinegar
125 ml	(*4 fl oz*) olive oil
15 ml	(*1 tbsp*) lemon juice
	salt and pepper

Place tomatoes, yellow pepper, bamboo shoots, parsley and rice in bowl; mix well.

Season and add chopped eggs; mix and set aside.

Place mustard and garlic in second bowl; season well. Pour in wine vinegar and whisk well.

Incorporate oil in thin stream while mixing with whisk. Sprinkle in lemon juice, mix well and correct seasoning.

Pour vinaigrette over salad and toss until evenly coated. Serve with fresh lettuce if desired.

1 serving	428 calories	29 g carbohydrate
6 g protein	32 g fat	1.8 g fibre

Cumin Pasta Salad

serves 4

600 g	(*1¼ lb*) cooked penne noodles
3	spring onions, sliced
1	shallot, chopped
1	carrot, peeled and grated
30 ml	(*2 tbsp*) mayonnaise
45 ml	(*3 tbsp*) cottage cheese
5 ml	(*1 tsp*) cumin powder
6	rashers crisp-cooked bacon, chopped
5 ml	(*1 tsp*) wine vinegar
	salt and pepper
	juice ½ lemon

Place noodles, spring onions, shallot and carrot in large bowl. Season well and mix.

In small bowl, mix together mayonnaise, cottage cheese and cumin powder. Sprinkle in lemon juice and mix again.

Pour dressing over salad, season and mix until completely incorporated.

Add bacon, mix well and sprinkle with vinegar. Mix again and serve.

Chick Pea Salad

serves 4

450 g	(*1 lb*) canned chick peas, drained
150 g	(*5 oz*) cooked cauliflower florets
15 ml	(*1 tbsp*) chopped fresh parsley
30 ml	(*2 tbsp*) Dijon mustard
1	shallot, finely chopped
1	garlic clove, smashed and chopped
30 ml	(*2 tbsp*) tarragon wine vinegar
30 ml	(*2 tbsp*) olive oil
	salt and pepper
	lettuce leaves, washed and dried

Place chick peas, cauliflower, parsley and mustard in bowl; season well.

Add shallot and garlic; mix well. Sprinkle in vinegar and mix again.

Add oil, mix and correct seasoning.

Serve on lettuce leaves.

1 serving	148 calories	14 g carbohydrate
5 g protein	8 g fat	4.2 g fibre

Mushrooms, Onions and Peas

serves 4

15 g	(*½ oz*) butter
125 g	(*¼ lb*) fresh mushrooms, cleaned and halved
1	onion, cut into 6
1 ml	(*¼ tsp*) tarragon
50 ml	(*2 fl oz*) chicken stock, heated
225 g	(*½ lb*) cooked frozen green peas
5 ml	(*1 tsp*) cornflour
30 ml	(*2 tbsp*) cold water
	salt and pepper

Melt butter in deep frying pan. Add mushrooms and onion; season well. Cook 3 to 4 minutes over high heat.

Add tarragon and chicken stock; season well and bring to boil. Continue cooking 1 minute.

Stir in peas and cook another minute.

Mix cornflour with cold water; incorporate into sauce and cook 1 more minute. Serve.

1 serving	*99 calories*	*14 g carbohydrate*	
4 g protein	*3 g fat*	*9.0 g fibre*	

White Mushrooms

serves 4

30 g	(*1 oz*) butter
450 g	(*1 lb*) fresh mushrooms, cleaned and sliced
1	shallot, finely chopped
300 ml	(*½ pt*) white sauce, heated
15 ml	(*1 tbsp*) chopped fresh parsley
	salt and pepper
	few drops lemon juice
dash	paprika

Melt butter in frying pan over medium heat. Add mushrooms and shallot; season well. Cook, partly covered, 8 to 10 minutes.

Pour in white sauce and mix well. Cook 2 to 3 minutes over low heat.

Sprinkle in parsley, lemon juice and paprika; correct seasoning. Mix well and serve at once.

1 serving	185 calories	12 g carbohydrate
5 g protein	13 g fat	3.3 g fibre

Mushrooms à l'Orange

serves 4

30 g	(*1 oz*) butter
15 ml	(*1 tbsp*) olive oil
450 g	(*1 lb*) large, fresh mushrooms*, cleaned and sliced into 3
30 ml	(*2 tbsp*) finely chopped orange zest
1	shallot, finely chopped
2	garlic cloves, smashed and chopped
15 ml	(*1 tbsp*) chopped fresh parsley
30 g	(*1 oz*) homemade croutons
	salt and pepper

Heat butter and oil in frying pan. When hot, add mushrooms and season; cook 2 minutes on each side over high heat.

Stir in orange zest, shallot and garlic. Continue cooking 2 to 3 minutes.

Add parsley and croutons; sprinkle with a little more oil if needed. Cook 2 minutes over high heat and serve at once.

* There are a variety of cultivated mushrooms to choose from. Look for mushrooms that are white and firm. Avoid mushrooms that have caps spreading and starting to separate from the stem. This is an indication of age. Clean mushrooms by brushing with a special brush or rubbing with a clean dish towel or sheet of absorbent kitchen paper.

1 serving	162 calories	14 g carbohydrate
4 g protein	10 g fat	3.3 g fibre

Mixed Vegetables Chinese Style

serves 4

30 ml	(*2 tbsp*) vegetable oil
1	celery stick, sliced on angle
1	Italian aubergine*, cut into sticks
1	carrot, peeled and thinly sliced on angle
1/2	red pepper, thinly sliced
1	small courgette, sliced on angle
1/2	seedless cucumber, sliced on angle
300 ml	(*1/2 pt*) chicken stock, heated
5 ml	(*1 tsp*) soy sauce
30 ml	(*2 tbsp*) chopped fresh ginger
30 ml	(*2 tbsp*) grated lemon zest
15 ml	(*1 tbsp*) cornflour
30 ml	(*2 tbsp*) cold water
	salt and pepper

Heat oil in large frying pan over high heat. When very hot, add celery, aubergine and carrot; cook 7 to 8 minutes, mixing occasionally.

Add red pepper, courgette and cucumber; season well. Continue cooking 5 to 6 minutes over high heat.

Pour in chicken stock and cook 3 to 4 minutes over medium heat.

Mix in soy sauce, ginger and lemon zest; continue cooking 3 to 4 minutes.

Mix cornflour with cold water; incorporate into sauce and continue cooking 2 minutes.

Serve at once.

* Italian aubergines are the short purple variety.

1 serving	115 calories	11 g carbohydrate
2 g protein	7 g fat	3.0 g fibre

1. Cook celery, aubergine and carrot in hot oil for 7 to 8 minutes. Be sure to mix occasionally.

2. Add red pepper, courgette and cucumber; season well. Continue cooking 5 to 6 minutes over high heat.

3. Reduce heat to medium and pour in chicken stock; cook 3 to 4 minutes.

4. Mix in soy sauce, ginger and lemon zest; continue cooking 3 to 4 minutes.

Gingered Bok Choy and Greens

serves 4

2	small Italian aubergines, unpeeled
30 ml	(*2 tbsp*) vegetable oil
1	onion, cut into 6
1	bok choy, washed and sliced 2.5 cm (*1 in*) wide on angle
½	red pepper, sliced
30 ml	(*2 tbsp*) chopped fresh ginger
400 ml	(*⅔ pt*) chicken stock, heated
15 ml	(*1 tbsp*) cornflour
45 ml	(*3 tbsp*) cold water
15 ml	(*1 tbsp*) soy sauce
	salt and pepper

Slice aubergines in half lengthways; then cut into pieces about 2.5 cm (*1 in*) long.

Heat oil in large frying pan over high heat. Add aubergines and onion; season well. Cook 3 to 4 minutes.

Add bok choy and red pepper; mix well. Sprinkle in ginger and season. Continue cooking 5 to 6 minutes over high heat.

Pour in chicken stock, stir and bring to boil. Correct seasoning.

Mix cornflour with water; incorporate into sauce. Sprinkle in soy sauce, mix and finish cooking 5 to 6 minutes over low heat.

1 serving	*118 calories*	*12 g carbohydrate*
4 g protein	*6 g fat*	*5.9 g fibre*

1. Before beginning the recipe, prepare the ingredients as directed. Be sure to wash the bok choy especially well.

2. Cook aubergines and onion in hot oil for 3 to 4 minutes over high heat.

3. Add remaining vegetables.

4. Add ginger and season well. Continue cooking 5 to 6 minutes, still over high heat.

Brussels Sprouts

700 g	**(1½ lb) Brussels sprouts***
15 g	**(½ oz) butter**
2	**rashers back bacon, diced**
	salt and pepper

Wash Brussels sprouts in plenty of cold water. Using a small knife, trim stems and make an incision in the shape of a cross on the base of each sprout — this will encourage even, rapid cooking.

Place sprouts in salted boiling water and cover. Cook 8 minutes or longer, depending on size. Sprouts should be tender but still a little firm when cooked. They should not be mushy.

When done, place pan under cold running water for several minutes. Drain well.

Heat butter in frying pan. Add bacon and sprouts; cook 3 to 4 minutes over high heat.

Correct seasoning and serve.

* When choosing fresh Brussels sprouts, look for those with a bright green colour and feel for a definite firmness. Avoid discoloured sprouts or those with a ragged appearance. Select sprouts of uniform size for ease in cooking.

1 serving	*137 calories*	*13 g carbohydrate*
10 g protein	*5 g fat*	*5.0 g fibre*

Spinach in White Sauce

serves 4

600 g	(*1¼ lb*) fresh spinach*
600 ml	(*1 pt*) cold water
15 g	(*½ oz*) butter
400 ml	(*⅔ pt*) white sauce, heated
	salt

Fill sink with plenty of cold water and add spinach. Agitate to remove dirt and sand from leaves. Drain and refill; repeat until no trace of grit remains.

Drain spinach well and snip off stems.

Pour cold water into large saucepan and add some salt. Cover and bring to boil.

Add spinach, season with more salt and cover. Cook 3 to 4 minutes over high heat, stirring once during cooking.

Remove spinach from pan and drain well in colander. Press spinach with back of spoon to remove excess water.

Melt butter in large frying pan. Add spinach and cook 1 minute over medium-high heat.

Stir in white sauce and cook 3 minutes. Serve.

* Look for dark green leaves and a very crisp appearance.

1 serving	192 calories	13 g carbohydrate
8 g protein	12 g fat	5.5 g fibre

Baked Leeks with Gruyère

serves 4

½	lemon, cut into 2 pieces
4	leeks
30 g	(*1 oz*) butter
30 ml	(*2 tbsp*) flour
500 ml	(*17 fl oz*) milk, heated
60 g	(*2 oz*) grated Gruyère cheese
15 ml	(*1 tbsp*) breadcrumbs
	salt and white pepper
dash	paprika
pinch	nutmeg

Preheat oven to 200°C (*400°F, gas mark 6*).

Fill large saucepan with water and add lemon pieces. Add sprinkling of salt and bring to boil over high heat.

Meanwhile, prepare leeks as directed in the technique.

Add leeks to boiling water, cover and cook 25 to 30 minutes over medium heat. Drain well and set aside.

Melt butter in saucepan. Add flour and mix well; cook 2 minutes over low heat.

Pour in milk and incorporate by mixing well with wooden spoon. Season sauce with salt, pepper, paprika and nutmeg. Cook 8 to 10 minutes over low heat, stirring once or twice during cooking.

Mix in half of cheese and continue cooking 2 to 3 minutes.

Arrange leeks in baking dish. Pour in sauce and top with remaining cheese. Sprinkle with breadcrumbs and bake 20 minutes.

Serve with a main course.

1 serving	233 calories	19 g carbohydrate
10 g protein	13 g fat	1.1 g fibre

1. This picture shows the parts of a fresh leek. Notice that the roots are still intact and that the base (stalk) is white and straight. Begin by rinsing leeks in cold water.

2. Next, cut off and discard the roots and the top green portion of the stalk. (The green leaves can be used for flavouring soups.)

3. Slit the white portion, making sure to leave about 1 cm (½ in) of uncut leek at the base; otherwise it will fall apart. Turn the leek and slit lengthways once more. This will enable you to wash the leek well, which is your next step.

4. With all traces of sand and dirt removed, leeks are ready to be cooked. Add them to boiling water with a hint of lemon juice and cook, covered, for 25 to 30 minutes over medium heat.

Broccoli with Old-Fashioned Cheddar Sauce *serves 4*

15 ml	(*1 tbsp*) white vinegar
1	head broccoli*, well washed and split from stem into several pieces
30 g	(*1 oz*) butter
30 ml	(*2 tbsp*) flour
600 ml	(*1 pt*) milk, heated
60 g	(*2 oz*) grated medium-aged Cheddar cheese
	salt and white pepper
dash	paprika
dash	nutmeg

Bring plenty of salted water and vinegar to boil in large saucepan.

Add broccoli, cover and cook 5 minutes over high heat. Depending on size of stalks, time may need adjustment. Cooked broccoli should be tender but still retain a little crispness.

When broccoli is cooked, place saucepan under cold running water to stop cooking process. Drain well and set aside.

Melt butter in small saucepan over low heat. Add flour and mix well; cook 2 minutes.

Pour in milk and incorporate by mixing with wooden spoon. Season sauce with salt, pepper, paprika and nutmeg. Cook 8 to 10 minutes over low heat, stirring several times during cooking.

Stir in cheese and continue cooking 2 to 3 minutes over low heat.

Arrange broccoli on serving platter, top with Cheddar sauce to taste and serve.

* When choosing a fresh head of broccoli, look for tight green florets and sturdy stalks with crisp leaves.

1 serving	262 calories	20 g carbohydrate
14 g protein	14 g fat	7.3 g fibre

Sautéed Cauliflower with Croutons

serves 4

50 ml	(*2 fl oz*) milk
1	head cauliflower
30 g	(*1 oz*) butter
7 to 8	fresh mushrooms, cleaned and quartered
1	spring onion, sliced
	salt and pepper
	chopped fresh parsley
	homemade croutons

Fill large saucepan with cold water and add sprinkling of salt. Pour in milk and bring to boil.

Meanwhile, cut off most of base from cauliflower and remove tough outer leaves surrounding head. Using small knife, make an incision in the shape of a cross at the base.

Place cauliflower in boiling liquid and cover; cook 8 minutes over medium heat. Depending on size of cauliflower, you may need to adjust time.

When cooked, place saucepan under cold running water for several minutes. Then drain well and set cauliflower on cutting board. Remove the rest of the base and separate into florets.

Heat butter in saucepan. Add cauliflower and mushrooms; season well. Cook 3 to 4 minutes over high heat.

Add spring onion and chopped parsley to taste; finish cooking 3 to 4 minutes. Serve with croutons.

1 serving	143 calories	15 g carbohydrate
5 g protein	7 g fat	4.0 g fibre

Golden Cauliflower

serves 4

50 ml	(*2 fl oz*) milk
1	medium head cauliflower
15 ml	(*1 tbsp*) melted butter
1	onion, chopped
1	celery stick, finely diced
1	garlic clove, smashed and chopped
5 ml	(*1 tsp*) chopped fresh parsley
30 ml	(*2 tbsp*) curry powder
600 ml	(*1 pt*) white sauce, heated
	salt and pepper

Fill large saucepan about ¾ full with hot salted water. Bring to boil.

Meanwhile, prepare cauliflower by cutting off most of base and removing tough outer leaves surrounding head. Using small knife, make an incision in the shape of a cross at the base.

Pour milk into boiling water. When boiling resumes, add cauliflower and cover; cook 10 to 15 minutes, depending on size. Adjust time if needed.

When cooked, drain cauliflower, reserving 125 ml (*4 fl oz*) of liquid. Set cauliflower aside but keep hot.

Place melted butter in deep frying pan over medium heat. When hot, add onion, celery, garlic and parsley; cook 3 to 4 minutes.

Season and add curry powder; mix well and cook 6 to 7 minutes over low heat.

Pour in white sauce and mix very sell. Add reserved cooking liquid from cauliflower and season to taste.

Cook sauce 10 minutes over low heat, pour over cauliflower and serve at once.

1 serving	247 calories	20 g carbohydrate
8 g protein	15 g fat	2.9 g fibre

1. Cut off most of base and remove tough outer leaves as shown in the background. Make an incision in the shape of a cross at the base. This will promote even, rapid cooking.

2. Cook cauliflower whole in large saucepan containing boiling salted water with milk added. The milk helps the vegetable retain its colour.

3. Either after cauliflower is cooked or just before, start preparing curry sauce. Cook onion, celery, garlic and parsley 3 to 4 minutes in hot butter.

4. Add curry powder, mix well, and continue cooking 6 to 7 minutes over low heat.

Spaghetti Squash au Naturel

serves 2

1	spaghetti squash
30 g	(*1 oz*) butter
	freshly ground pepper

Preheat oven to 180°C (*350°F, gas mark 4*).

Cut squash in half lengthways. Remove and discard seeds.

Spread butter over each half and place, flesh side down, on baking sheet. Bake 1 hour.

Using spoon, loosen flesh into spaghetti-like strands and serve with freshly ground pepper and butter, if desired.

1 serving	217 calories	23 g carbohydrate
2 g protein	13 g fat	4.9 g fibre

Baked Butternut Squash

serves 2

1	**butternut squash**
30 g	(*1 oz*) **butter**
15 ml	(*1 tbsp*) **brown sugar**
	salt and pepper

Preheat oven to 200°C (*400°F, gas mark 6*).

Slice squash in half lengthways, remove seeds and place cut-side-up on baking sheet. Divide butter and brown sugar between cavities and season well.

Bake 40 minutes in oven or until done.

Stuffed Courgettes

serves 4

2	**large courgettes**
30 g	(*1 oz*) **butter**
1	**onion, chopped**
225 g	(*½ lb*) **fresh mushrooms, cleaned and finely chopped**
2	**garlic cloves, smashed and chopped**
1 ml	(*¼ tsp*) **thyme**
2 ml	(*½ tsp*) **tarragon**
30 ml	(*2 tbsp*) **breadcrumbs**
	salt and pepper
	melted butter for basting

Preheat oven to 200°C (*400°F, gas mark 6*).

Slice each courgette in half lengthways. Scoop out most of pulp to make room for stuffing.

Place courgettes in salted boiling water and blanch for 5 to 6 minutes over medium heat. Drain well and set aside.

Heat 30 g (*1 oz*) butter in saucepan. Add onion, mushrooms, garlic and seasonings. Cook 7 to 8 minutes over medium heat.

Stir in breadcrumbs to bind stuffing. Spread mixture into courgette halves and press stuffed halves together to form whole courgette again. Tie with kitchen string.

Place stuffed courgettes in baking dish and baste with melted butter. Finish cooking 10 minutes in oven.

Carefully remove string and slice each courgette into 6 pieces. Serve at once.

1 serving	*209 calories*	*18 g carbohydrate*
5 g protein	*13 g fat*	*6.0 g fibre*

Creamy Curried Carrots

serves 4

4	large carrots, peeled and thinly sliced
15 g	(*½ oz*) butter
30 ml	(*2 tbsp*) curry powder
90 g	(*3 oz*) sliced bamboo shoots
300 ml	(*½ pt*) white sauce, heated
pinch	sugar
	salt and pepper

Cook carrots in salted boiling water until tender. Cool under cold running water and drain well.

Heat butter in frying pan over medium heat. Add carrots and cook 2 minutes to brown lightly.

Mix in curry powder and continue cooking 2 minutes.

Add bamboo shoots and sugar; cook 3 to 4 minutes over low heat. Season to taste.

Pour in white sauce, stir and simmer 3 to 4 minutes before serving.

Sprinkle with chopped parsley or chives, if desired.

1 serving	*181 calories*	*21 g carbohydrate*
4 g protein	*9 g fat*	*1.6 g fibre*

Baked Acorn Squash

serves 4

2	**acorn squash**
20 ml	(*4 tsp*) **butter**
15 ml	(*1 tbsp*) **brown sugar**

Preheat oven to 180°C (*350°F, gas mark 4*).

Place squash in roasting tin and drop 5 ml (*1 tsp*) butter in each cavity. Cover with foil and bake 1 hour.

Remove squash from oven and sprinkle with brown sugar. Grill 5 minutes; then serve at once.

1 serving	*120 calories*	*18 g carbohydrate*
3 g protein	*4 g fat*	*2.5 g fibre*

Vegetables in Curry Sauce

serves 4–6

30 ml	(*2 tbsp*) olive oil
2	onions, diced large
1	garlic clove, smashed and chopped
30 ml	(*2 tbsp*) curry powder
2	carrots, peeled and thinly sliced on an angle
400 ml	(*⅔ pt*) chicken stock, heated
1	head broccoli, well washed and in florets
1	red pepper, diced large
5 ml	(*1 tsp*) cornflour
30 ml	(*2 tbsp*) cold water
	salt and pepper

Heat oil in large frying pan over medium heat. Add onions and cook 6 minutes.

Add garlic and curry powder; mix well. Cook 4 minutes over low heat. Stir in carrots and cook another 5 minutes, stirring occasionally.

Pour in chicken stock and bring to boil. Cook 4 minutes over medium heat. Add all remaining vegetables and season well; cook 4 minutes over low heat.

Mix cornflour with cold water; stir into mixture until well incorporated. Cook 2 minutes over medium heat and serve.

1 serving	102 calories	10 g carbohydrate
2 g protein	6 g fat	3.0 g fibre

Ratatouille Parmesan

serves 4

60 ml	(*4 tbsp*) olive oil
1	large aubergine, cubed with skin
1	onion, finely chopped
2	garlic cloves, smashed and chopped
15 ml	(*1 tbsp*) chopped fresh parsley
2 ml	(*½ tsp*) oregano
1 ml	(*¼ tsp*) thyme
2 ml	(*½ tsp*) basil
1 ml	(*¼ tsp*) crushed chillies
1	courgette, halved lengthways and thinly sliced
4	fresh plum tomatoes, diced
30 g	(*1 oz*) grated Parmesan cheese
	salt and pepper
dash	paprika

Heat 45 ml (*3 tbsp*) of oil in large, deep frying pan. When very hot, add aubergine and season well. Cover and cook 15 to 20 minutes over medium-low heat, stirring 2 to 3 times during cooking.

Add onion, garlic and parsley; mix well and correct seasoning. Cover and continue cooking 7 to 8 minutes.

Add seasonings, courgette, tomatoes and remaining 15 ml (*1 tbsp*) of oil. Mix, cover and cook 35 minutes over medium-low heat.

Add cheese, mix, and finish cooking 7 to 8 minutes, uncovered.

Serve with main course.

1 serving	220 calories	14 g carbohydrate
5 g protein	16 g fat	5.1 g fibre

1. Cook aubergine in hot oil for 15 to 20 minutes over medium-low heat. Be sure pan is covered and stir several times during cooking.

2. Add onion, garlic and parsley; mix well and correct seasoning. Cover and continue cooking 7 to 8 minutes.

3. Add seasonings, courgette, tomatoes and remaining oil. Mix, cover and cook 35 minutes.

4. Mix in cheese and finish cooking 7 to 8 minutes, uncovered.

Helen's Vegetables au Jus

serves 4

1.2 litres	(2¼ pt) homemade beef stock
2	potatoes, peeled and halved
4	carrots, peeled and cut into 2
½	turnip, peeled and cut into 4
½	head cabbage, cut into 4
3	celery sticks, cut into 2
	salt and pepper
	oil and vinegar to taste
	chopped parsley to taste

Bring beef stock to boil in large saucepan. Add all vegetables and cook over medium heat; season to taste.

Monitor each vegetable when cooked, remove from beef stock and set aside. Be careful not to overcook.

When all vegetables are done, return to saucepan with beef stock and reheat 2 minutes.

Serve vegetables moistened with a bit of cooking liquid. Add oil and vinegar to taste and garnish with chopped parsley.

1 serving	236 calories	28 g carbohydrate
4 g protein	12 g fat	4.9 g fibre

Potato Carrot Purée

serves 4

4	**peeled carrots, cooked and still hot**
4	**potatoes, cooked in skins, peeled and still hot**
15 ml	(*1 tbsp*) **garden mint sauce (commercial)**
50 ml	(*2 fl oz*) **milk, heated**
15 g	(*½ oz*) **butter**
	salt and pepper

Purée cooked vegetables through vegetable mill or potato ricer into bowl.

Add mint sauce and incorporate with wooden spoon.

Pour in milk and mix well. Add butter, season and mix again.

Serve.

1 serving	*180 calories*	*32 g carbohydrate*	
4 g protein	*4 g fat*	*3.1 g fibre*	

Castle Potatoes

serves 4

5	potatoes, peeled and washed
45 g	(1½ oz) butter
2	egg yolks
60 ml	(4 tbsp) double cream
	salt and pepper
dash	paprika

Cook potatoes in plenty of salted boiling water until done. Drain well and let stand 5 minutes in saucepan to dry.

Purée potatoes using vegetable mill or potato ricer.

Add butter and season; mix thoroughly with wooden spoon.

Incorporate egg yolks; then stir in cream. Add paprika and mix until well combined.

Preheat oven to 200°C (400°F, gas mark 6).

Spoon potatoes into piping bag fitted with large star nozzle. Squeeze out mounds of potato on baking sheet.

Cook 10 to 12 minutes in oven or until lightly browned.

Serve at once with meat or poultry.

1 serving	277 calories	26 g carbohydrate
5 g protein	17 g fat	3.0 g fibre

1. Force cooked potatoes through vegetable mill or potato ricer to purée them. If you mash by hand it is very difficult to remove all the lumps.

2. After butter, salt and pepper have been incorporated, add egg yolks and continue mixing with wooden spoon.

3. Add cream and paprika and mix until well combined.

4. Using a piping bag, squeeze out mounds of potato.

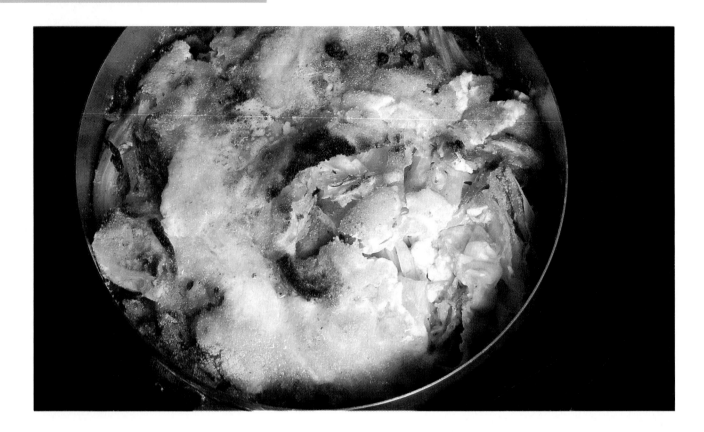

Baked Cabbage with Onions

serves 6

1	cabbage, cut into 4
45 g	*(1½ oz)* butter
4	onions, thinly sliced
600 ml	*(1 pt)* soured cream
60 ml	*(4 tbsp)* breadcrumbs
30 ml	*(2 tbsp)* melted butter
	salt and pepper
dash	paprika

Place cleaned cabbage in large saucepan containing plenty of boiling salted water. Cover and cook 18 minutes over medium heat. Drain cabbage well and set aside.

Preheat oven to 180°C (*350°F, gas mark 4*).

Heat 45 g (*1½ oz*) butter in large, deep frying pan. When hot, add onions and season; cook 15 to 18 minutes over low heat. Stir several times during cooking.

Add cabbage to frying pan and mix in soured cream. Correct seasoning and cover; bake 30 minutes in oven.

Remove cover and sprinkle top with breadcrumbs and melted butter. Change oven setting to grill and brown for 4 minutes.

Serve sprinkled with a dash of paprika.

1 serving	486 calories	34 g carbohydrate
11 g protein	34 g fat	6.0 g fibre

Quick Potato Sauté

serves 4

30 ml	(*2 tbsp*) olive oil
1	large onion, thinly sliced
4	large potatoes, cooked in skins
15 g	(*½ oz*) butter
1 ml	(*¼ tsp*) savory
	salt and pepper
	chopped fresh parsley

Heat oil in large frying pan over medium heat. Add onion and cover; cook 4 minutes.

Peel potatoes and cut in slices 1 cm (½ *in*) thick. Add to pan with butter and savory; season well.

Cook potatoes 15 minutes over medium-high heat, stirring as needed.

Sprinkle with parsley and serve.

Ultimate Jacket-baked Potatoes

serves 4

4	medium-size baking potatoes, scrubbed

"ULTIMATE" GARNISH IDEAS:

	soured cream and chives
	soured cream and pimiento
	strips of back bacon and chopped spring onions
	sautéed mushrooms and shallots
	melted butter and crisp crumbled bacon
	grated Parmesan cheese and paprika

Preheat oven to 200°C (*400°F, gas mark 6*).

Prick potatoes 2 to 3 times with a wooden skewer to allow steam to escape during cooking. Wrap in foil, prick again and place on oven rack. Bake about 1 hour, depending on size.

Just before potatoes are cooked, have ready your choice of "ultimate" garnish.

Remove cooked potatoes, discard foil and slit top in a cross about 2 cm (¾ in) deep. Press sides to open and generously top with garnish.

Serve at once.

1 serving	246 calories	52 g carbohydrate
5 g protein	2 g fat	3.1 g fibre

1. If you enjoy eating the skin, remember to wash potatoes well and scrub if necessary. Prick potatoes 2 to 3 times with a wooden skewer to allow steam to escape during cooking.

2. Wrap potatoes in foil. You can purchase potatoes already wrapped in foil, but it is difficult to determine their quality. Remember to prick several times through foil.

3. After potatoes are baked, slit top in a cross about 2 cm (¾ *in*) deep.

4. Press sides to open. Remember to discard foil for the final presentation.

Potatoes Provençale

serves 4

4	large potatoes, cooked in skins and still hot
60 g	(*2 oz*) butter
45 ml	(*3 tbsp*) grated Parmesan cheese
5 ml	(*1 tsp*) chervil
15 ml	(*1 tbsp*) double cream
	salt and pepper

Peel and cube potatoes. Force through vegetable mill or potato ricer and purée.

Add 45 g (*1½ oz*) butter and potatoes and season well. Mix in cheese and then chervil.

Incorporate cream and shape mixture into patties.

Heat remaining butter in large frying pan. Cook potato patties 6 to 7 minutes on each side over medium heat. Season once during cooking. When the first side is well browned, turn patties over.

Serve at once.

1 serving	231 calories	20 g carbohydrate
4 g protein	15 g fat	2.4 g fibre

French-Fried Potatoes

serves 4

4	large potatoes
	salt
	peanut oil for frying

Preheat plenty of peanut oil in electric deep-fryer set at 180°C (*350°F*).

Peel potatoes and square ends and sides. Slice potatoes lengthways into pieces about 5 mm (*¼ in*) thick. Cut into uniform sticks.

Place potato sticks in large bowl and place under cold running water for 2 minutes. Stir potatoes several times to help remove starch.

Drain well and pat dry with a clean dish towel.

Place potato sticks in deep-fryer basket and cook in hot oil for 6 minutes.

Remove basket and set chips aside. Increase heat of oil to 190°C (*375°F*).

When ready, return chips to hot oil and continue cooking until golden brown.

Remove from deep-fryer and drain on absorbent kitchen paper. Sprinkle with salt to taste and serve.

1 serving	211 calories	25 g carbohydrate
3 g protein	11 g fat	3.0 g fibre

Potato Croquettes

serves 4

4	**large potatoes, cooked in skins**
30 g	**(*1 oz*) butter**
1	**egg yolk**
1	**egg**
1 ml	**(*¼ tsp*) nutmeg**
2 ml	**(*½ tsp*) tarragon**
3	**beaten eggs**
125 g	**(*4 oz*) breadcrumbs**
	salt and pepper
	peanut oil for frying

Peel and cube potatoes. Force through vegetable mill or potato ricer and purée.

Add butter to potatoes and season well. Mix to incorporate.

Add egg yolk and 1 whole egg; mix well with wooden spoon. Add nutmeg and tarragon; mix again.

Spread potato mixture flat on dinner place. Cover with cling film and refrigerate 3 hours.

Preheat plenty of peanut oil in electric deep-fryer set at 190°C (*375°F*).

Shape potato mixture into croquettes (cylindrical-shaped rolls). Dip in beaten egg to coat completely and roll in breadcrumbs.

Deep-fry 3 to 4 minutes.

1 serving	*565 calories*	*45 g carbohydrate*
13 g protein	*37 g fat*	*3.5 g fibre*

FOOD FROM
OUR NEIGHBOURS

*Delightful dishes
from
many cultures*

Potato Salad à la Poire (*French*)

serves 4

3	large potatoes, cooked in skins and still hot
8	slices salami, cut into julienne
2	shallots, chopped
30 ml	(*2 tbsp*) chopped fresh parsley
15 ml	(*1 tbsp*) chopped fresh chives
15 ml	(*1 tbsp*) Dijon mustard
45 ml	(*3 tbsp*) wine vinegar
75 ml	(*5 tbsp*) olive oil
3	chicory heads, leaves well cleaned, sliced into 2.5-cm (*1-in*) pieces
1/2	pear, peeled and sliced
15 ml	(*1 tbsp*) wine vinegar
30 ml	(*2 tbsp*) olive oil
	salt and pepper
	lemon juice
	romaine lettuce leaves

Cut peeled potatoes into large cubes and place in bowl. Add salami, shallots, parsley and chives; season well.

Place mustard in smaller bowl and season well. Pour in 45 ml (3 tbsp) vinegar and 75 ml (5 tbsp) oil; whisk together until smooth. Add lemon juice to taste, mix and correct seasoning.

Pour dressing over potatoes in bowl and gently toss to coat evenly. Spoon onto platter and set aside.

Place chicory and sliced pear in bowl. Season and sprinkle with a bit of lemon juice. Sprinkle with remaining vinegar and oil; mix well.

Serve chicory mixture with potatoes and decorate platter with lettuce leaves.

1 serving	429 calories	25 g carbohydrate
8 g protein	33 g fat	3.3 g fibre

Tomato and Feta Plate (*Greek*)

serves 4

2	large ripe tomatoes
125 g	(*4 oz*) feta cheese, sliced
60 g	(*2 oz*) chopped feta cheese
1	sprig lovage, coarsely chopped
45 ml	(*3 tbsp*) wine vinegar
75 ml	(*5 tbsp*) olive oil
	washed and dried romaine lettuce leaves
	salt and pepper
	juice ¼ lemon

Core tomatoes, cut in half and slice. Arrange lettuce leaves on platter and alternate tomato with slices of feta cheese. Set aside.

Place chopped cheese in bowl and pepper well. Add lovage and vinegar; mix well.

Add oil and lemon juice; mix very well with whisk. Correct seasoning.

Pour dressing over platter and serve.

1 serving	294 calories	8 g carbohydrate
7 g protein	26 g fat	2.0 g fibre

401

Italian Salad (*Italian*)

serves 4

2	tomatoes, cored, halved and sliced
20	stoned black olives
6	stuffed green olives
1	yellow pepper, thinly sliced
1	head romaine lettuce, well washed, dried and in bite-size pieces
1/2	head cooked broccoli, in florets
125 g	(*1/4 lb*) cooked French beans
30 ml	(*2 tbsp*) grated Parmesan cheese
15 ml	(*1 tbsp*) Dijon mustard
45 ml	(*3 tbsp*) wine vinegar
105 ml	(*7 tbsp*) olive oil
15 ml	(*1 tbsp*) chopped fresh parsley
2 ml	(*1/2 tsp*) chopped fresh basil
4	hard-boiled eggs, chopped
	few drops lemon juice
	salt and pepper

Place tomatoes, both types of olives, yellow pepper, lettuce, broccoli and beans in large salad bowl. Set aside.

In smaller bowl place cheese and mustard. Add vinegar and whisk together.

Incorporate oil in thin stream while whisking constantly. Sprinkle in parsley and basil; whisk very well. Add lemon juice and season.

Mix in chopped eggs and pour dressing over salad. Toss until evenly coated and serve. If desired, decorate portions with sliced hard-boiled eggs.

1 serving	493 calories	11 g carbohydrate
11 g protein	45 g fat	7.8 g fibre

1. Place cheese and mustard in small bowl.

2. Add vinegar and whisk together.

3. Incorporate oil in thin stream while whisking; then sprinkle in parsley and basil. Whisk very well. Add lemon juice and season.

4. Mix in chopped eggs and prepare to pour over salad.

Gena's Cold Lamb Salad Plate (*Greek*)   *serves 4*

450 g	(*1 lb*) leftover cooked sliced lamb
½	yellow pepper, thinly sliced
½	red pepper, thinly sliced
½	green pepper, thinly sliced
8	stoned black olives
½	head broccoli, in florets, blanched
6	fresh mint leaves, chopped
1	large potato, cooked in skin, peeled and sliced
30 ml	(*2 tbsp*) red wine vinegar
45 ml	(*3 tbsp*) olive oil
125 g	(*4 oz*) chopped feta cheese
	salt and pepper
	few drops lemon juice

Place lamb in large bowl with peppers and olives; toss and season well. Add broccoli, mint and potato; toss again.

Pepper well and sprinkle with vinegar and oil. Add cheese, toss again and correct seasoning.

Sprinkle with lemon juice and serve on large platter decorated with lettuce leaves and extra slices of cheese, if desired.

1 serving	407 calories	14 g carbohydrate
27 g protein	27 g fat	6.3 g fibre

Aubergine Spread (*Greek*)

serves 4–6

2	large aubergines
15 ml	(*1 tbsp*) chopped fresh oregano
3	blanched garlic cloves, smashed
60–75 ml	(*4–5 tbsp*) olive oil
	salt and pepper
	assorted crackers and toasted rounds of bread

Preheat oven to 220°C (*425°F, gas mark 7*).

Score aubergines 3 to 4 times with small knife. Place whole in roasting tin and cook 45 minutes in oven.

Remove aubergines from oven, peel and chop flesh. Place in bowl.

Add oregano and garlic; mix well and season. Incorporate olive oil, whisking constantly.

Serve on crackers and toast.

1 serving	190 calories	21 g carbohydrate
4 g protein	10 g fat	2.7 g fibre

Croque-Monsieur aux Oeufs Sauerkraut (*French*) serves 4

15 ml	(*1 tbsp*) olive oil
½	onion, chopped
1	garlic clove, smashed and chopped
225 g	(*½ lb*) sauerkraut, well rinsed
8	thick slices French bread
12	slices Black Forest ham
175 g	(*6 oz*) grated Swiss cheese
50 ml	(*2 fl oz*) water
4	beaten eggs
30 g	(*1 oz*) butter
	extra butter
	pepper

Heat oil in frying pan. Add onion and garlic; cook 5 to 6 minutes over medium-low heat.

Add sauerkraut, mix and cover; continue cooking 15 to 20 minutes, stirring occasionally.

Meanwhile, spread extra butter over slices of bread. Make 4 sandwiches each containing 3 slices of ham and grated cheese.

Mix water into beaten eggs and pepper well.

Heat butter in large frying pan. Dip sandwiches one at a time in beaten egg mixture to coat well; then place in hot butter.

Cook sandwiches 3 minutes each side over medium heat. Outsides should be nicely browned and cheese inside should be soft if not melted.

Cut sandwiches in half and serve with sauerkraut. A delicious treat before or after an evening show!

1 serving	578 calories	33 g carbohydrate
35 g protein	34 g fat	2.8 g fibre

Chunky Avocado Vegetable Dip (*Mexican*)   *serves 4*

1	**cucumber, peeled, seeded and diced small**
1	**large tomato, skinned, seeded and diced**
2	**spring onions, chopped**
150 g	**(*5 oz*) canned refried beans**
50 ml	**(*2 fl oz*) chicken stock**
2 ml	**(*½ tsp*) Maggi seasoning**
15 ml	**(*1 tbsp*) chopped seeded jalapeño pepper**
1	**ripe avocado, peeled and flesh puréed**
5 ml	**(*1 tsp*) olive oil salt and pepper**
	juice 1 lemon
	lettuce leaves for decoration

Place cucumber, tomato and spring onions in bowl; season well. Set aside.

Heat refried beans with chicken stock in small saucepan. Add to vegetables in bowl and mix well.

Add Maggi seasoning and jalapeño pepper. Mix in avocado and lemon juice until well incorporated.

Sprinkle with olive oil and chill dip 20 minutes.

Serve on bed of lettuce with a variety of dipping chips (nachos) and crackers.

1 serving	*118 calories*	*14 g carbohydrate*
2 g protein	*6 g fat*	*3.6 g fibre*

Avocado Soup (*Mexican*)

serves 4

1	ripe avocado
150 ml	(¼ *pt*) whipped cream
500 ml	(17 *fl oz*) chicken stock
2 ml	(½ *tsp*) Maggi seasoning
	juice ½ lemon
	salt and pepper
	soured cream
	chopped fresh chives
	paprika

Peel avocado and cut flesh into small pieces. Purée in food processor.

Transfer avocado to bowl and whisk in whipped cream. Pour in chicken stock while mixing.

Sprinkle in lemon juice and Maggi seasoning; add salt and pepper to taste.

Chill soup 1 hour.

To serve, garnish portions with dollop of soured cream and sprinkle with chives and paprika.

1 serving	153 calories	7 g carbohydrate
2 g protein	13 g fat	1.2 g fibre

Aubergine with Lima Beans (*Mexican*)   *serves 4*

1	aubergine, skin pierced
15 ml	(*1 tbsp*) oil
1	onion, chopped
30 ml	(*2 tbsp*) sliced jalapeño pepper
1	garlic clove, smashed and chopped
1	tomato, peeled and chopped
400 g	(*14 oz*) canned lima (butter) beans, drained
	salt and pepper

Preheat oven to 200°C (*400°F, gas mark 6*).

Place pierced whole aubergine in roasting tin. Bake 45 minutes.

Remove from oven and cube aubergine with skin. Heat oil in large frying pan over high heat. Add aubergine, onion, jalapeño pepper and garlic; cook 3 to 4 minutes.

Mix well and add tomato; season. Continue cooking 4 to 5 minutes.

Add lima beans, mix well and correct seasoning. Cook 3 to 4 minutes and serve.

1 serving	144 calories	22 g carbohydrate
5 g protein	4 g fat	4.5 g fibre

Prawn Dish (*Mexican*)

serves 4

700 g	(*1½ lb*) jumbo prawns
15 ml	(*1 tbsp*) oil
1	red pepper, cut into large strips
2	spring onions, sliced
5 ml	(*1 tsp*) chopped jalapeño pepper
300 ml	(*½ pt*) Mexican piquant sauce
150 g	(*5 oz*) canned refried beans
125 ml	(*4 fl oz*) chicken stock, heated salt and pepper

Shell prawns, wash and devein.

Heat oil in large frying pan over medium-high heat. Add prawns and cook 2 minutes.

Add red pepper, spring onions and jalapeño pepper; continue cooking 2 to 3 minutes. Correct seasoning.

Remove prawns and set aside.

Add piquant sauce and refried beans to frying pan; mix well and pour in chicken stock. Cook 4 to 5 minutes.

Return prawns to frying pan and simmer 1 minute to reheat.

1 serving	198 calories	13 g carbohydrate
23 g protein	6 g fat	1.6 g fibre

1. Add prawns to hot oil in frying pan and cook 2 minutes over medium-high heat.

2. Add red pepper, green onions and chopped jalapeño pepper; continue cooking 2 to 3 minutes. Correct seasoning.

3. Remove prawns; add piquant sauce to vegetables.

4. Add refried beans and pour in chicken stock. Cook 4 to 5 minutes.

Minced Meat Picadillo (*Mexican*)

serves 4

15 ml	(*1 tbsp*) oil	
225 g	(*½ lb*) lean minced beef	
1	small onion, chopped	
1	spring onion, chopped	
2	garlic cloves, smashed and chopped	
90 g	(*3 oz*) chopped stuffed green olives	
1	small marinated green pepper, seeded and chopped	
15 ml	(*1 tbsp*) chopped fresh chives	
30 ml	(*2 tbsp*) canned refried beans	
150 ml	(*¼ pt*) Mexican piquant sauce	
150 ml	(*¼ pt*) taco sauce	
4	tostada shells	
125 g	(*4 oz*) grated Cheddar cheese	
	salt and pepper	

Heat oil in large frying pan over high heat. Add beef and season; cook 3 to 4 minutes, stirring several times.

Add both types of onions, garlic, olives, green pepper and chives; mix well. Correct seasoning and continue cooking 3 to 4 minutes.

Mix in refried beans and cook another 2 minutes.

Incorporate piquant and taco sauces; let simmer 5 minutes over low heat.

Arrange tostada shells on large ovenproof platter. Spoon meat mixture on each and top with cheese.

Grill until cheese is melted.

1 serving	434 calories	25 g carbohydrate
25 g protein	26 g fat	3.7 g fibre

Chicken Pepper Tacos (*Mexican*)   *serves 4*

15 ml	(*1 tbsp*) oil
½	green pepper, cut into julienne
½	red pepper, cut into julienne
½	onion, sliced
2	spring onions, chopped
½	courgette, cut into julienne
2	whole chicken breasts, skinned, boned and cut into strips
45 ml	(*3 tbsp*) canned refried beans
50 ml	(*2 fl oz*) chicken stock
30 ml	(*2 tbsp*) taco sauce
4	taco shells
	salt and pepper

Heat oil in large frying pan over high heat. Add peppers, both types of onions and courgette; mix well and season. Cook 4 minutes over medium-high heat.

Add chicken strips to pan, season and continue cooking 7 to 8 minutes. Stir once.

Mix in refried beans, chicken stock and taco sauce; correct seasoning. Cook 2 more minutes; then fill taco shells. Serve at once.

1 serving	268 calories	19 g carbohydrate
30 g protein	8 g fat	2.1 g fibre

Chicken Burrito Dinner (*Mexican*)

serves 4

15 ml	(*1 tbsp*) oil
2	whole chicken breasts, skinned, boned and cut into thin strips
1	yellow pepper, cut into julienne
8	stuffed green olives, finely chopped
1	large tomato, peeled, seeded and chopped
1	marinated hot green pepper, chopped
175 ml	(*6 fl oz*) taco sauce
150 g	(*5 oz*) canned refried beans
4	soft tortillas
	paprika
	salt and pepper

Heat oil in large frying pan over medium-high heat. Add chicken strips and cook 2 to 3 minutes.

Add yellow pepper and olives; season with paprika. Continue cooking 3 to 4 minutes.

Season well and add tomato and marinated chopped pepper; mix well.

Add taco sauce, mix and add refried beans; correct seasoning. Cook 3 to 4 minutes over low heat; serve in tortillas.

1 serving	*329 calories*	*22 g carbohydrate*
31 g protein	*13 g fat*	*4.3 g fibre*

1. Cook chicken strips in hot oil for 2 to 3 minutes over medium-high heat. Add yellow pepper and olives; season with paprika. Continue cooking 3 to 4 minutes.

2. Season well and add tomato and marinated chopped pepper; mix well.

3. Add taco sauce and mix.

4. Add refried beans, correct seasoning and cook 3 to 4 minutes over low heat.

Green Rice (*Mexican*)

serves 4

15 ml	(*1 tbsp*) vegetable oil
3	spring onions, sliced
1	large green pepper, chopped
15 ml	(*1 tbsp*) chopped jalapeño pepper
2	garlic cloves, smashed and chopped
90 g	(*3 oz*) chopped stoned olives
350 g	(*¾ lb*) cooked white rice, hot
15 ml	(*1 tbsp*) olive oil
15 ml	(*1 tbsp*) chopped fresh parsley
	salt and pepper

Heat vegetable oil in saucepan over medium heat. Add spring onions, green and jalapeño peppers, garlic and olives; season well. Cook 4 to 5 minutes.

Transfer contents to food processor; blend until puréed.

Mix green purée with hot rice; season with olive oil and parsley. Correct seasoning, mix again and serve.

1 serving	238 calories	29 g carbohydrate
3 g protein	12 g fat	3.4 g fibre

Pork and Vegetable Strips in Bean Sauce (*Oriental*)   *serves 4*

15 ml	(*1 tbsp*) oil
2	butterflied pork chops, trimmed of fat and cut into strips
15 ml	(*1 tbsp*) chopped fresh ginger
2	garlic cloves, smashed and chopped
30 ml	(*2 tbsp*) soy sauce
1	red pepper, thinly sliced
1½	yellow peppers, thinly sliced
1	courgette, thinly sliced
150 g	(*5 oz*) seedless green grapes
300 ml	(*½ pt*) chicken stock, heated
60 ml	(*4 tbsp*) Chinese bean sauce
15 ml	(*1 tbsp*) cornflour
45 ml	(*3 tbsp*) cold water
	pepper

Heat oil in wok or frying pan over high heat. When hot, add pork, ginger and garlic; cook 2 minutes over medium heat.

Turn pieces over, season with pepper and cook 1 more minute.

Add soy sauce and cook 1 more minute. Remove meat from wok; set aside.

Add vegetables and grapes to wok. Stir-fry 4 minutes over medium-high heat.

Pour in chicken stock and bean sauce; mix well. Bring to boil and cook 1 minute.

Mix cornflour with cold water; stir into sauce until well incorporated. Cook 2 minutes.

Reheat pork in mixture several seconds and serve at once over rice, if desired.

1 serving	378 calories	18 g carbohydrate
36 g protein	18 g fat	2.2 g fibre

Steamed Vegetables (*Oriental*)

serves 4

20	**mangetouts, topped and tailed**
1/2	**red pepper, sliced into strips**
1/2	**courgette, halved lengthways and sliced**
1	**celery stick, sliced**
1/2	**head broccoli, in florets**
125 g	**(1/4 lb) French beans, pared**
	salt and pepper

Place bamboo steamer in wok and pour in enough water to reach bottom of basket.

Add vegetables, placing larger pieces on bottom and season well. Cover basket and steam.

When vegetables are tender (crisp and not overcooked)*, remove from basket and serve.

Serve with a variety of dishes, or as is for a truly healthy light meal.

* Check the vegetables for doneness several times until you become accustomed to the timing.

1 serving	44 calories	8 g carbohydrate
3 g protein	0 g fat	4.4 g fibre

1. An authentic bamboo steamer and a stainless steel wok are a good investment and will allow you to prepare a wide variety of Oriental dishes. You will find these kitchen utensils handy for other types of cooking too.

2. The principle of vegetable steaming is the same for all vegetables. Begin by placing steamer in wok and pour in enough water to reach bottom of basket. Add desired vegetables, cover basket and steam.

3. Be sure to place the larger pieces of vegetable in bottom of basket, with the thinner strips on top. Season well before covering.

4. When tender but still a little crisp, remove vegetables and serve.

Szechuan Pork with Dipping Sauce (*Oriental*)   *serves 4*

2	**butterflied pork chops, fat trimmed and cut in strips**
15 ml	(*1 tbsp*) **chopped fresh ginger**
2	**garlic cloves, smashed and chopped**
3	**pickled Tabasco peppers, finely chopped**
5 ml	(*1 tsp*) **sesame oil**
5 ml	(*1 tsp*) **soy sauce**
400 ml	(*⅔ pt*) **chicken stock, heated**
30 ml	(*2 tbsp*) **bean sauce**
15 ml	(*1 tbsp*) **plum sauce**
2 ml	(*½ tsp*) **cornflour**
15 ml	(*1 tbsp*) **cold water**
15 ml	(*1 tbsp*) **vegetable oil**
	pepper

Place pork strips in bowl and season with pepper. Add ginger, half of garlic and half of Tabasco peppers. Sprinkle with sesame oil and soy sauce; mix well. Pour in 200 ml (*⅓ pt*) chicken stock and marinate 15 minutes.

Meanwhile, pour bean and plum sauces in small saucepan. Add remaining chicken stock and mix well. Add remaining Tabasco peppers and garlic; bring to boil over high heat. Continue cooking 8 to 10 minutes over low heat.

Drain pork, reserving 50 ml (*2 fl oz*) liquid; set both aside.

Mix cornflour with cold water; incorporate to mixture in saucepan. Pour in reserved marinade from meat and cook 1 to 2 minutes over low heat.

Heat vegetable oil in frying pan over high heat. Add pork and cook 3 minutes. Turn strips over, season with pepper and cook another 2 minutes.

Serve at once with dipping sauce and accompany with mild-flavoured fruit such as cantaloupe melon wedges.

1 serving	*335 calories*	*7 g carbohydrate*
34 g protein	*19 g fat*	*0.9 g fibre*

Vegetable Rice (*Oriental*)

serves 4

30 ml	(*2 tbsp*) vegetable oil
1	celery stick, sliced on angle
¹/₂	onion, chopped
¹/₂	courgette, cut into sticks
6	large fresh mushrooms, cleaned and diced
¹/₂	red pepper, chopped
20	mangetouts, topped and tailed
15 ml	(*1 tbsp*) chopped fresh ginger
15 ml	(*1 tbsp*) soy sauce
350 g	(*³/₄ lb*) cooked white rice
	salt and pepper
	few drops sesame oil

Heat vegetable oil in large frying pan. Add celery, onion and courgette; cook 3 to 4 minutes over high heat.

Add mushrooms, red pepper and mangetouts; season and sprinkle with sesame oil. Add ginger and mix well; cook 3 to 4 minutes.

Sprinkle in soy sauce and cook 1 more minute.

Mix in rice and finish cooking 3 to 4 minutes. Serve.

1 serving	216 calories	31 g carbohydrate
5 g protein	8 g fat	5.2 g fibre

Sake Teriyaki Beef (*Oriental*)

serves 4

600 g	(*1¼ lb*) beef sirloin, very thinly sliced
30 ml	(*2 tbsp*) soy sauce
15 ml	(*1 tbsp*) teriyaki sauce
45 ml	(*3 tbsp*) sake wine
3	garlic cloves, smashed and chopped
15 ml	(*1 tbsp*) brown sugar
30 ml	(*2 tbsp*) peanut oil
	juice ½ lemon
	pepper

Arrange slices of beef on large platter. Sprinkle with soy sauce, teriyaki sauce, lemon juice and sake. Spread garlic over meat and pepper well — do not salt.

Sprinkle with brown sugar, cover and refrigerate 4 hours.

Heat peanut oil in large frying pan over high heat. Add meat and sear 1 minute. Turn slices over and sear 1 more minute.

Serve with rice and soup.

1 serving	298 calories	7 g carbohydrate
36 g protein	14 g fat	0 g fibre

Orange Beef Sirloin Stir-Fry (*Oriental*)   *serves 4*

600 g	(*1¼ lb*) sirloin steak, cut into strips
2	pickled Tabasco peppers, chopped
15 ml	(*1 tbsp*) soy sauce
5 ml	(*1 tsp*) sesame oil
10 ml	(*2 tsp*) cornflour
30 ml	(*2 tbsp*) vegetable oil
½	onion, sliced
1	celery stick, sliced on angle
1	yellow pepper, thinly sliced
4	water chestnuts, sliced
30 ml	(*2 tbsp*) white vinegar
30 ml	(*2 tbsp*) brown sugar
250 ml	(*8 fl oz*) orange juice
15 ml	(*1 tbsp*) cold water
	salt and pepper

Place meat in bowl with Tabasco peppers; sprinkle with soy sauce and sesame oil. Mix well. Add 5 ml (*1 tsp*) cornflour and toss; marinate 15 minutes.

Heat 15 ml (*1 tbsp*) vegetable oil in large frying pan over high heat. Add meat and sear 1 minute. Turn strips over, season and sear 1 more minute.

Remove meat from pan and set aside.

Add onion and celery to frying pan and sprinkle in remaining vegetable oil. Cook 8 to 10 minutes over high heat.

Add yellow pepper and water chestnuts; season and cook 4 minutes over medium-high heat.

Mix in vinegar and brown sugar; cook 3 to 4 minutes over high heat. Add orange juice, mix well and bring to boil.

Mix remaining cornflour with cold water; incorporate to sauce and season. Cook 2 minutes over low heat.

Place meat with juices in sauce; heat 2 minutes and serve. Decorate with slices of orange.

1 serving	367 calories	21 g carbohydrate
37 g protein	15 g fat	1.4 g fibre

Sesame Seed Meatballs (*Oriental*)

serves 4

350 g	(*¾ lb*) lean minced beef
30 ml	(*2 tbsp*) brown sugar
1	garlic clove, smashed and chopped
15 ml	(*1 tbsp*) chopped fresh ginger
30 ml	(*2 tbsp*) sesame seeds
1	egg
15 ml	(*1 tbsp*) soy sauce
15 ml	(*1 tbsp*) vegetable oil
	few drops sesame oil
	pepper
	bean sauce

Place beef, brown sugar, garlic, ginger, 15 ml (*1 tbsp*) sesame seeds, egg, soy sauce and sesame oil in bowl of food processor; pepper well and blend until incorporated.

Remove meat and shape mixture into small meatballs.

Heat vegetable oil in large frying pan over high heat. Add meatballs and cook 4 minutes over medium heat. Turn over, pepper well and cook another 4 minutes or until done.

Sprinkle with remaining sesame seeds and cook 1 more minute.

Serve meatballs with an arrangement of garnishes such as sliced oranges, sections pears, etc. Accompany with bean sauce.

1 serving	264 calories	8 g carbohydrate
22 g protein	16 g fat	0.1 g fibre

Korean Beef Steak (*Oriental*)

serves 4

700 g	(*1½ lb*) beef sirloin, thinly sliced against the grain
60 ml	(*4 tbsp*) soy sauce
30 ml	(*2 tbsp*) brown sugar
2	garlic cloves, smashed and chopped
30 ml	(*2 tbsp*) peanut oil
	few drops sesame oil
	juice ½ lemon
	sesame seeds

Place meat in bowl and sprinkle with soy sauce and sesame oil. Add brown sugar, lemon juice and garlic; mix well. Chill 3 hours, covered.

Heat peanut oil in wok over high heat. Add meat and sear 1 minute on each side or adjust time depending on thickness.

Remove meat from wok to serving platter and quickly sprinkle with sesame seeds. Serve at once.

Grilled Pork Fillet (*Oriental*)

serves 2

1	pork fillet, trimmed of fat
45 ml	(*3 tbsp*) olive oil
2	garlic cloves, smashed and chopped
15 ml	(*1 tbsp*) chopped fresh lovage
5 ml	(*1 tsp*) chopped fresh marjoram
5 ml	(*1 tsp*) chopped fresh rosemary
1	courgette, cut into 3 lengthways and again into 3 across width
15 ml	(*1 tbsp*) Dijon mustard
	salt and pepper

Open fillet lengthways butterfly-style. Mix olive oil with garlic and brush some over meat.

Spread fresh seasonings over inside of meat and brush again with oil mixture. Close meat and brush outside with oil. Set aside.

Brush courgette pieces with oil.

Preheat barbecue grill to high. Cook courgette 3 to 4 minutes each side.

Reopen fillet butterfly-style and place on hot grill. Cook 4 to 5 minutes.

Turn meat over, season and brush with mustard. Cook 4 to 5 minutes.

Turn over once more and cook another 4 to 5 minutes or adjust time according to size.

Serve with courgette.

1 serving	668 calories	7 g carbohydrate
61 g protein	44 g fat	2.5 g fibre

Spaghetti Primavera (*Italian*)

serves 4

30 ml	(*2 tbsp*) olive oil
½	head broccoli, well cleaned and in florets
½	green pepper, thinly sliced
½	red pepper, thinly sliced
1	courgette, halved lengthways and sliced
1	celery stick, sliced
20	mangetouts, topped and tailed
1	garlic clove, smashed and chopped
4	portions cooked spaghetti, hot
60 ml	(*4 tbsp*) grated Parmesan cheese
	salt and pepper

Heat oil in large frying pan over medium heat. Add broccoli, peppers, courgette, celery and mangetouts; mix well. Add garlic and season well. Cover and cook 4 to 5 minutes.

Mix in spaghetti, correct seasoning and cook, covered, 2 minutes.

Sprinkle in cheese; cover and cook 1 minute. Serve at once.

1 serving	358 calories	54 g carbohydrate
13 g protein	10 g fat	8.5 g fibre

Calf Liver Lyonnaise (*French*)

serves 4

30 g	(*1 oz*) butter
2	red onions, thinly sliced
1	garlic clove, smashed and chopped
4	large slices calf liver
	salt and pepper
	seasoned flour
	juice ½ lemon

Melt half of butter in frying pan over medium heat. Add onions and garlic; season. Cook 10 to 15 minutes.

Meanwhile, trim fat from liver. Dredge in flour.

Heat remaining butter in frying pan over medium heat. Add liver slices and cook 2½ minutes over medium-low heat.

Turn pieces over, season and continue cooking 2 to 3 minutes or adjust time depending on taste.

Deglaze onions with lemon juice by cooking 1 minute over high heat.

Serve liver with onions.

1 serving	316 calories	18 g carbohydrate
34 g protein	12 g fat	1.4 g fibre

Wild Mushroom Fantasy (*French*)

serves 4

30 g	(*1 oz*) butter
2	shallots, chopped
900 g	(*2 lb*) white mushrooms, cleaned and quartered
225 g	(*½ lb*) edible wild mushrooms, cleaned
15 ml	(*1 tbsp*) chopped fresh parsley
15 ml	(*1 tbsp*) chopped fresh chives
45 ml	(*3 tbsp*) dry white wine
25 ml	(*1½ tbsp*) flour
375 ml	(*13 fl oz*) hot milk
	salt and pepper
	paprika
	toasted French bread

Melt butter in large frying pan over medium-high heat. Add shallots and white mushrooms; cook 5 to 6 minutes.

Add wild mushrooms, parsley and chives; season. Sauté 2 to 3 minutes.

Add wine and continue cooking 3 minutes. Mix in flour and cook 1 minute.

Mix in hot milk and cook 3 to 4 minutes over medium heat.

Sprinkle with paprika and spoon over toasted French bread.

1 serving	*282 calories*	*36 g carbohydrate*
12 g protein	*10 g fat*	*7.5 g fibre*

Strip Steaks Mama Mia (*Italian*)

serves 2

45 ml	(*3 tbsp*) olive oil
1	small aubergine, cubed with skin
1	green pepper, thinly sliced
1	banana pepper, chopped
½	yellow pepper, thinly sliced
1	large tomato, cored and cubed
15 ml	(*1 tbsp*) chopped fresh oregano
5 ml	(*1 tsp*) chopped fresh thyme
2	garlic cloves, smashed and chopped
2	225-g (*8-oz*) strip loin steaks
	salt and pepper

Heat 30 ml (*2 tbsp*) oil in large frying pan over high heat. Add aubergine, cover and cook 10 minutes over medium heat.

Mix in peppers, tomato, oregano, thyme and half of garlic; season well. Continue cooking 6 to 7 minutes, partly covered.

Meanwhile, mix remaining oil with remaining garlic; brush over meat.

Preheat barbecue to high.

Cook meat 3 minutes on each side; adjust time depending on thickness. Serve with vegetables.

1 serving	639 calories	14 g carbohydrate
58 g protein	39 g fat	4.3 g fibre

Osso Bucco (*Italian*)

serves 4

8	veal shanks, 4 cm (*1½ in*) thick
25 ml	(*1½ tbsp*) oil
1	onion, chopped
3	garlic cloves, smashed and chopped
250 ml	(*8 fl oz*) dry white wine
800 g	(*1¾ lb*) canned tomatoes, drained and chopped
30 ml	(*2 tbsp*) tomato purée
125 ml	(*4 fl oz*) beef gravy, heated
2 ml	(*½ tsp*) oregano
1 ml	(*¼ tsp*) thyme
1	bay leaf, chopped
	seasoned flour
	salt and pepper
pinch	sugar

Preheat oven to 180°C (*350°F, gas mark 4*). Dredge veal in flour.

Heat oil in large ovenproof casserole. Sear veal (in two batches) for 3 to 4 minutes on each side over medium-high heat. Season well when turning.

Set seared veal aside. Add onion and garlic to casserole; mix and cook 3 to 4 minutes over medium heat.

Pour in wine and cook 4 minutes over high heat.

Mix in tomatoes, tomato purée and gravy. Add seasonings and sugar; correct seasoning to taste. Bring to boil.

Return veal to casserole. Cover and cook 2 hours in oven.

When veal is cooked, remove from casserole and set aside. Cook sauce over high heat 3 to 4 minutes.

Correct seasoning and pour over veal.

1 serving	499 calories	25 g carbohydrate
48 g protein	23 g fat	2.8 g fibre

Veal alla Vista (*Italian*)

serves 4

30 ml	(*2 tbsp*) melted butter
2	large slices veal shoulder, about 2.5 cm (*1 in*) thick, cubed
1	onion, finely chopped
1	green pepper, diced large
3	tomatoes, skinned, seeded and diced large
15 ml	(*1 tbsp*) tomato purée
150 ml	(*¼ pt*) chicken stock, heated
2 ml	(*½ tsp*) tarragon
3	spring onions, chopped
	salt and pepper

Preheat oven to 180°C (*350°F, gas mark 4*).

Heat melted butter in frying pan. Add veal and brown on all sides over medium heat. Transfer meat to ovenproof casserole and set aside.

Add chopped white onion and green pepper to frying pan; season well. Cook 4 minutes over medium heat.

Stir in tomatoes, tomato purée and chicken stock; season well. Add tarragon and bring to boil. Cook 3 to 4 minutes over high heat.

Mix well, correct seasoning and pour over veal in casserole. Cover and cook 1 hour in oven.

Top with spring onions before serving. Accompany with pasta, if desired.

1 serving	670 calories	10 g carbohydrate
72 g protein	38 g fat	2.7 g fibre

Chicken Florence (*Italian*)

serves 4

30 ml	(*2 tbsp*) olive oil
1.8 kg	(*4 lb*) roasting chicken, cleaned, skinned and cut into 8 pieces
1	red onion, chopped
1	garlic clove, smashed and chopped
1	red pepper, cubed
1	green pepper, cubed
1	broccoli stalk, sliced
6	large fresh mushrooms, cleaned and quartered
	seasoned flour
	salt and pepper

Heat oil in large frying pan over medium-high heat. Meanwhile, dredge chicken pieces in flour.

When oil is hot, sear chicken 8 minutes on one side. Turn pieces over, season and add onion and garlic. Reduce heat to medium and continue cooking 6 minutes.

Add both peppers, sliced broccoli stalk and mushrooms; correct seasoning. Cover and finish cooking 10 to 12 minutes over low heat.

1 serving	543 calories	22 g carbohydrate
62 g protein	23 g fat	4.1 g fibre

Oregano-Seasoned Veal Chops (*Italian*)   serves 2

2	veal chops, about 2 cm (3/4 *in*) thick, trimmed of fat
15 ml	(*1 tbsp*) olive oil
8	large fresh mushrooms, cleaned and sliced
15 g	(*1/2 oz*) butter
15 ml	(*1 tbsp*) chopped fresh oregano
50 ml	(*2 fl oz*) double cream
	seasoned flour
	salt and pepper
	juice 1/2 lemon

Dredge chops in flour. Heat oil in large frying pan over high heat.

When hot, add chops and cook 4 minutes over medium-high heat. Turn chops over, season and continue cooking 5 minutes over medium heat.

Turn over once more and finish cooking 3 minutes or adjust time depending on size. Remove chops to heated platter and set aside.

Add mushrooms to hot frying pan and sprinkle with lemon juice. Add butter and oregano; cook 3 to 4 minutes over high heat.

Stir in cream and correct seasoning; cook 2 to 3 minutes over medium heat.

Pour sauce over veal chops and serve with noodles.

1 serving	498 calories	20 g carbohydrate
28 g protein	34 g fat	3.1 g fibre

1. Choose the freshest meat and produce available.

2. After dredging meat in flour, sear in hot oil 4 minutes over medium-high heat. Continue cooking for about 8 minutes at reduced heat, turning chops over twice. Time will vary according to size of chops and pan — use your judgment.

3. Add mushrooms to hot pan. Sprinkle with lemon juice, add butter and oregano; cook 3 to 4 minutes over high heat.

4. Pour in cream and mix well; correct seasoning. Cook 2 to 3 minutes over medium heat before serving veal.

White Beans de l'Amour (*French*)

serves 4–6

5 ml	(*1 tsp*) olive oil
1	large red onion, diced large
1	celery stick, diced large
1	garlic clove, smashed and chopped
350 g	(*¾ lb*) dry white beans, soaked overnight
800 g	(*1¾ lb*) canned tomatoes, with juice
1 litre	(*1¾ pt*) chicken stock, heated
	fresh seasonings to taste: thyme, oregano, basil, parsley
	salt and pepper

Heat oil in large casserole over medium-high heat. Add onion, celery and garlic; cook 5 to 6 minutes.

Add beans and remaining ingredients; mix well. Correct seasoning, cover and bring to boil.

Reduce heat to low and continue cooking, covered, for 3 hours.

1 serving	174 calories	30 g carbohydrate
9 g protein	2 g fat	8.2 g fibre

Sausages with Gruyère Potatoes (*French*)   *serves 2*

5 ml	(*1 tsp*) olive oil
2	large veal sausages
½	onion, chopped
15 ml	(*1 tbsp*) peanut oil
2	large potatoes, cooked in skins, peeled and sliced thick
30 g	(*1 oz*) grated Gruyère cheese
250 ml	(*8 fl oz*) leftover tomato sauce or substitute
	salt and pepper

Heat olive oil in frying pan. Add sausages and cook 3 to 4 minutes over medium heat. Turn over, season and continue cooking 3 minutes.

Add onion and cook with sausages for 25 to 30 minutes, depending on size, over medium-low heat. Turn sausages several times.

Meanwhile, heat peanut oil in frying pan over medium-high heat. Add potatoes, season and cook 16 to 18 minutes. Turn slices over often.

Add grated cheese and cook 3 more minutes over medium heat.

Mix tomato sauce into pan containing sausages and cook 4 to 5 minutes.

Serve at once with potatoes.

1 serving	691 calories	48 g carbohydrate
28 g protein	43 g fat	4.5 g fibre

Veal Shanks Lizanne (*French*)

serves 4

4	veal shanks, about 2.5 cm (*1 in*) thick, trimmed of fat
15 ml	(*1 tbsp*) oil
1	large red onion, in small wedges
2	garlic cloves, smashed and chopped
500 ml	(*17 fl oz*) dry red wine
2	tomatoes, cored and cut in wedges
30 ml	(*2 tbsp*) tomato purée
1	sprig thyme, chopped
1	sprig oregano, chopped
1	sprig lovage, chopped
15 g	(*½ oz*) butter
225 g	(*½ lb*) fresh mushrooms, cleaned and quartered
	seasoned flour
	salt and pepper

Preheat oven to 180°C (*350°F, gas mark 4*). Dredge meat in flour.

Heat oil in large deep frying pan over high heat. Add veal and sear 8 minutes on each side over medium heat.

Add onion and garlic; cook 3 to 4 minutes.

Pour in wine, add tomatoes and tomato purée; season well. Add fresh chopped herbs, cover and cook 1½ hours in oven.

Just before end of cooking time, melt butter in frying pan. Sauté mushrooms 3 minutes; season well.

Add mushrooms to veal, cover and continue cooking 1½ hours in oven. Serve.

1 serving	319 calories	20 g carbohydrate
26 g protein	15 g fat	4.0 g fibre

_1._ Dredge veal in seasoned flour. This will help the searing process.

_2._ Begin by searing first side for 8 minutes. During this time, do not disturb the meat.

_3._ Turn shanks over to sear second side.

_4._ Add onion and garlic; continue cooking 3 to 4 minutes.

Souvlaki (*Greek*)

700 g	(*1½ lb*) cubed lamb from the leg
60 ml	(*4 tbsp*) olive oil
30 ml	(*2 tbsp*) chopped fresh mint
2	garlic cloves, smashed and chopped
3	spring onions, cut into 5-cm (*2-in*) lengths
	salt and pepper
	juice 1 lemon

Place lamb, oil, pepper and lemon juice in bowl. Add mint and garlic; season again and mix. Cover with sheet of cling film and marinate 3 hours in refrigerator.

Alternate lamb and spring onion on metal skewers. Grill in preheated oven or on preheated grill 3 to 4 minutes on each side over high heat.

Serve on pitta bread, if desired.

1 serving	*392 calories*	*4 g carbohydrate*
40 g protein	*24 g fat*	*0.6 g fibre*

Scallop Skewers (*Greek*)

serves 4

700 g	(*1½ lb*) medium-size scallops
30 ml	(*2 tbsp*) olive oil
1	garlic clove, smashed and chopped
15 ml	(*1 tbsp*) chopped fresh oregano
	juice ½ lemon
	white pepper

Place scallops in bowl with all ingredients; mix and cover with cling film. Refrigerate 2 to 3 hours.

Thread scallops on wet wooden skewers. Place on preheated grill or under preheated oven grill. Cook 1 minute on each side over high heat.

Serve with fresh vegetables and lemon.

1 serving	*213 calories*	*1 g carbohydrate*	**441**
32 g protein	*9 g fat*	*0 g fibre*	

Herbed Lamb Chops (*Greek*)

serves 4

8	**2-cm (¾-*in*) thick lamb chops**
2	**garlic cloves, peeled and cut into pieces**
8	**parsley sprigs**
8	**oregano sprigs**
8	**thyme sprigs**
2	**garlic cloves, smashed and chopped**
15 ml	**(*1 tbsp*) chopped fresh parsley**
5 ml	**(*1 tsp*) chopped fresh rosemary**
45 ml	**(*3 tbsp*) olive oil**
	juice 1 lemon
	salt and pepper

Preheat barbecue to high.

Trim excess fat from chops and discard. Insert garlic pieces in meat.

Tuck fresh herbs in fold of each chop and carefully thread on skewers. Set aside.

Place chopped garlic, parsley, rosemary and lemon juice in small bowl; mix well. Incorporate oil using whisk and season.

Brush over both sides of chops and pepper meat well — do not salt. Cook on preheated barbecue 3 minutes.

Turn skewers over; cook another 3 to 4 minutes depending on taste. Remove from skewers before serving.

1 serving	309 calories	3 g carbohydrate
27 g protein	21 g fat	0.1 g fibre

_1._ Trim excess fat from chops.

_2._ Tuck fresh herbs in the fold of each chop; then carefully thread on skewers. This technique will make chops easier to handle during barbecuing.

_3._ Baste chops on both sides with garlic herb marinade.

_4._ Pepper well but do not salt.

Paprika Chicken Stew (*Hungarian*)

serves 4–6

1.8 kg	(*4 lb*) chicken, cleaned
15 ml	(*1 tbsp*) olive oil
15 g	(*½ oz*) butter
1	red onion, cubed
25 ml	(*1½ tbsp*) paprika
800 g	(*1¾ lb*) canned tomatoes, with juice
2	blanched garlic cloves, smashed
1	sprig lovage, chopped
1	green pepper, cubed and sautéed
	seasoned flour
	salt and pepper

Preheat oven to 180°C (*350°F, gas mark 4*).

Cut chicken into 8 pieces as shown on facing page. Skin and dredge meat in seasoned flour.

Heat oil in large ovenproof casserole over high heat. Add chicken pieces and sear 4 minutes over medium-high heat.

Add butter to pan, turn chicken pieces over and continue searing 4 minutes.

Add onion and paprika; cook another 6 to 7 minutes. Add tomatoes with juice and garlic; mix well.

Add lovage, season and bring to boil. Cover and finish cooking 30 minutes in oven.

Add sautéed green pepper to casserole; cover and resume cooking for 15 minutes.

1 serving	367 calories	17 g carbohydrate
41 g protein	15 g fat	2.0 g fibre

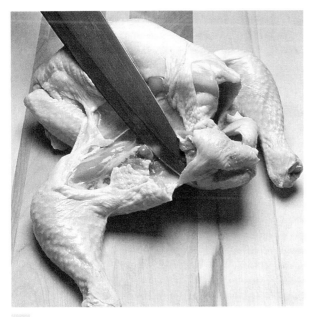

1. Begin cutting chicken by removing legs from body. Once detached, cut each into 2 pieces at the joint.

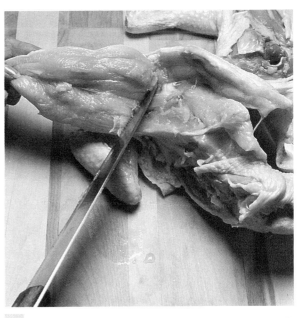

2. Remove breasts without the bone and set aside. Finish by cutting off wings, being sure to snip off tips. You should have 8 pieces.

3. Skin chicken pieces, dredge in flour and sear in hot oil 4 minutes on each side. This will seal in the juices.

4. Add onion and paprika; cook another 6 to 7 minutes before adding remaining ingredients.

Veal on a Bun (*Hungarian*)

serves 4

45 g	(*1½ oz*) butter
2	small onions, cut in wedges
15 ml	(*1 tbsp*) paprika
45 ml	(*3 tbsp*) flour
750 ml	(*1¼ pt*) chicken stock, heated
1	red pepper, cubed
350 g	(*¾ lb*) leftover cooked veal, sliced, trimmed of fat
½	cucumber, peeled and sliced
	salt and pepper
	English muffins, toasted

Melt 30 g (*1 oz*) butter in saucepan over medium heat. Add onions; cover and cook 4 minutes.

Sprinkle in paprika and flour; mix very well. Cook, uncovered, 2 to 3 minutes over low heat.

Pour in chicken stock, mix well and season. Bring to boil and cook sauce 12 minutes over medium-low heat.

Before sauce is done, melt remaining butter in frying pan. Add red pepper, veal and cucumber; sauté 3 minutes over medium-high heat.

Transfer veal mixture to sauce and simmer 2 to 3 minutes.

Serve over toasted muffins.

1 serving	*436 calories*	*37 g carbohydrate*
27 g protein	*20 g fat*	*1.8 g fibre*

Soured Cream Meat Loaf (*Hungarian*)   serves 6–8

450 g	(*1 lb*) lean minced beef
225 g	(*½ lb*) lean minced pork
1	small onion, grated
45 g	(*1½ oz*) coarse breadcrumbs
250 ml	(*8 fl oz*) milk
2 ml	(*½ tsp*) ground cloves
5 ml	(*1 tsp*) basil
2 ml	(*½ tsp*) marjoram
1	egg, slightly beaten
45 ml	(*3 tbsp*) soured cream
15 ml	(*1 tbsp*) flour
125 ml	(*4 fl oz*) chicken stock
	salt and pepper
	paprika

Preheat oven to 180°C (*350°F, gas mark* 4).

Place both meats and onion in large bowl. Mix and season well.

Soak breadcrumbs in milk for 10 minutes, and then add to meat; incorporate well. Sprinkle in cloves, basil and marjoram; mix well.

Mix in beaten egg and pack mixture into buttered 24 x 14-cm (*9½ x 5½-in*) loaf tin. Set in roasting tin with 2.5 cm (*1 in*) hot water and cook 30 minutes in oven.

Mix soured cream, flour and chicken stock together. Pour mixture over meat loaf still in pan and season well; sprinkle with paprika.

Return to oven and continue baking 15 minutes. Serve with a sauce, if desired.

1 serving	226 calories	11 g carbohydrate
23 g protein	10 g fat	0.6 g fibre

Veal Cutlets (*Hungarian*)

serves 4

4	150-g (*5-oz*) veal cutlets, flattened thin
2	beaten eggs
225 g	(*8 oz*) seasoned breadcrumbs
15 ml	(*1 tbsp*) oil
15 g	(*½ oz*) butter
	juice 1½ lemons
	salt and pepper

Preheat oven to 190°C (*375°F, gas mark 5*).

Place cutlets in dish and squeeze in lemon juice; marinate, covered, 1 hour in refrigerator.

Dip veal in beaten eggs; then dredge in breadcrumbs. Redip veal in eggs and finish with final coating of breadcrumbs. Season well.

Heat oil and butter in large frying pan. Add cutlets and brown 2 to 3 minutes over medium heat.

Turn cutlets over, season and transfer to oven; cook 8 minutes.

Serve with soured cream and your choice of fresh vegetable.

1 serving	567 calories	42 g carbohydrate
39 g protein	27 g fat	1.8 g fibre

HAPPY ENDINGS

Irresistible sweets,
cakes, pies and pastries—
pure pleasure!

Flambéed Peaches

serves 6

45 ml	(*3 tbsp*) syrup*
6	peaches, peeled and halved
30 ml	(*2 tbsp*) vodka
5 ml	(*1 tsp*) cornflour
30 ml	(*2 tbsp*) cold water
150 g	(*5 oz*) strawberries, washed and hulled

Heat syrup in large frying pan over medium heat. Add peaches and cook 2 minutes on each side. Pour in vodka and continue cooking 2 minutes. Flambé.

Remove peaches and set aside.

Mix cornflour with cold water; stir into sauce until incorporated. Cook 1 minute.

Return peaches to pan, add strawberries and cook 1 more minute. Serve warm.

* See Rainbow Tartlets, page 484.

1 serving	80 calories	19 g carbohydrate
1 g protein	0 g fat	1.8 g fibre

Peach Pudding

serves 4–6

550 g	(*19 oz*) canned sliced peaches, drained
15 ml	(*1 tbsp*) brown sugar
2	large eggs
2	large egg yolks
50 g	(*1¾ oz*) granulated sugar
60 g	(*2 oz*) white breadcrumbs
375 ml	(*13 fl oz*) hot milk

Preheat oven to 180°C (*350°F, gas mark 4*). Butter 20-cm (*8-in*) square x 5-cm (*2-in*) deep baking dish; set aside.

Place peaches in frying pan with brown sugar; cook 3 minutes over medium heat. Set aside.

Beat all eggs with granulated sugar; set aside.

Place breadcrumbs in large bowl and pour in hot milk. Mix well and let stand 3 minutes.

Add beaten eggs to breadcrumbs and mix well. Stir in peaches and pour batter into prepared baking dish.

Set dish in roasting tin with 2.5 cm (*1 in*) hot water and bake 35 to 40 minutes in oven.

Transfer baking dish to counter top and let cook before serving. If desired, serve with whipped cream, ice cream or maple syrup.

1 serving	244 calories	35 g carbohydrate
8 g protein	8 g fat	1.9 g fibre

Pineapple Fruit Salad

serves 6

1	**fresh pineapple**
300 g	**(*11 oz*) strawberries, washed, hulled and halved**
½	**cantaloupe melon**
250 ml	**(*8 fl oz*) double cream**
75 g	**(*2½ oz*) toasted almonds**
	juice 1 lemon
	salt and white pepper

Cut off top from pineapple. With fruit standing upright on cutting board, core centre then proceed to slice off spiny bark cutting from top to bottom. Try to follow fruit's shape. When done, finish by cutting out brown eyes.

Dice pineapple and place in bowl with strawberries; set aside.

Using melon-ball scoop, remove flesh from cantaloupe half; add to bowl.

Place lemon juice in small bowl; add salt and pepper. Mix until salt disintegrates. Incorporate double cream by beating to obtain thick mixture.

Pour cream over fruits and mix well. Top with toasted almonds and serve.

1 serving	*325 calories*	*30 g carbohydrate*
4 g protein	*21 g fat*	*3.5 g fibre*

Fresh Fruit Bite

serves 2

2	slices muskmelon
1	prickly pear, halved
2	large wedges pawpaw
½	grapefruit
1	pear, halved and hollowed
4	thin slices mango
1	apricot, halved and pitted
	fresh strawberries for decoration
	ricotta cheese (optional)

These quantities are ample for two and can be stretched to serve more diners, depending on your menu. The most important thing is to choose fresh fruit — if one kind in not available, substitute something that is.

Second, the arrangement of the fruit will be a deciding factor in how appealing your presentation is; use the picture for guidance.

Mixed Fruit Compote

serves 8–10

12	**peaches, peeled and sectioned**
45 ml	(*3 tbsp*) **syrup***
30 ml	(*2 tbsp*) **vodka**
1	**mango, peeled, sliced and diced**
1	**pawpaw, cubed**
225 g	(*½ lb*) **whole strawberries, washed and hulled**
2	**kiwis, peeled and sliced**
15 ml	(*1 tbsp*) **cornflour**
30 ml	(*2 tbsp*) **cold water**

Place peaches and syrup in large frying pan. Add vodka and cook 3 to 4 minutes over medium heat.

Mix in mango; continue cooking 3 to 4 minutes.

Add remaining fruit, cover and cook another 3 to 4 minutes.

Mix cornflour with cold water; stir into fruit until well incorporated. Simmer 2 to 3 minutes.

Serve warm.

* See Rainbow Tartlets, page 484.

1 serving	*116 calories*	*28 g carbohydrate*
1 g protein	*0 g fat*	*2.6 g fibre*

1. Place peaches with syrup in large frying pan.

2. Pour in vodka and cook 3 to 4 minutes over medium heat.

3. Add mango; mix and continue cooking 3 to 4 minutes.

4. Add remaining fruit, cover and cook 3 to 4 minutes more.

Honeymooners' Heaven

serves 2

200 g	(7 oz) fresh raspberries, washed
50 ml	(2 fl oz) syrup*
5 ml	(1 tsp) orange liqueur
12	strawberries, washed and hulled
125 ml	(4 fl oz) egg custard sauce**
1	large scoop vanilla ice cream
	whipped cream
	blackberries

Force raspberries through fine sieve into small saucepan. Add syrup and liqueur; mix well. Bring to boil; continue cooking 1 to 2 minutes. Cool before using.

To assemble sundae, begin by choosing a very large glass that can hold at least 750 ml (1¼ pt) water.

Place most of strawberries in bottom of glass. Ladle in some of raspberry sauce and egg custard sauce.

Add scoop of ice cream, surround with remaining strawberries and drizzle in remaining raspberry sauce and egg custard sauce.

Decorate with whipped cream and blackberries. Serve with two very long spoons.

* See Rainbow Tartlets, page 484.
** See Dessert on Broadway, page 457.

1 serving	506 calories	78 g carbohydrate
8 g protein	18 g fat	3.2 g fibre

Dessert on Broadway

serves 4

EGG CUSTARD SAUCE:

4	**large egg yolks**
100 g	**(3¹/₂ oz) caster sugar**
250 ml	**(8 fl oz) scalded milk, still hot**
1 ml	**(¹/₄ tsp) vanilla**

Have ready saucepan half-filled with hot water.

Using electric hand beater, mix egg yolks and sugar in large stainless steel bowl until light and frothy.

Slowly incorporate milk with vanilla while whisking. Place bowl over saucepan on stove with heat set at low. Cook cream until thick enough to coat back of a spoon. You must whisk constantly!

Remove bowl from saucepan and whisk a little more to cool. Then set aside to finish cooling; cover with greaseproof paper so that it touches surface. For best consistency, refrigerate 6 hours before using.

ASSEMBLY:

350 g	**(³/₄ lb) fresh raspberries, washed**
30 ml	**(2 tbsp) syrup***
4	**slices white cake, preferably square, about 1 cm (¹/₂ in) thick**
4	**scoops vanilla ice cream**
150 g	**(5 oz) blackberries, washed**
	icing sugar

Place half of raspberries in food processor; blend to purée. Transfer to small saucepan and mix in syrup; bring to boil and continue cooking 2 minutes. Remove, strain and set aside to cool.

When ready to serve, arrange ingredients on counter.

Begin by placing slice of cake on each of 4 plates. Ladle egg custard sauce and raspberry purée onto opposite sides of cake. Set scoop of ice cream on cake and decorate with remaining berries. Sift icing sugar lightly over each plate and serve at once.

* See Rainbow Tartlets, page 484.

1 serving	*550 calories*	*88 g carbohydrate*
9 g protein	*18 g fat*	*6.6 g fibre*

The Ultimate Trifle

serves 8–12

1	**Génoise cake*, cut into 1-cm (*½-in*) thick square pieces**
300 g	**(*11 oz*) halved fresh strawberries**
225 g	**(*½ lb*) mixed berries (in season)**
1	**recipe egg custard sauce****
250 ml	**(*8 fl oz*) double cream, whipped**
	vodka
	whole strawberries for decoration

This trifle takes some imagination on your part. You can reduce the quantities for a smaller group or add and substitute at will. The following is the basic assembly procedure.

Choose an attractive trifle bowl. Have all your ingredients ready on counter.

Begin by placing one third of cake squares in bottom of bowl. Follow with sprinkling of vodka, one-third of halved strawberries and same amount of mixed berries.

Ladle in some of egg custard sauce and add dollops of whipped cream.

Repeat twice and finish with a topping of whole strawberries. Chill slightly to firm cream (if you can resist waiting) or serve at once. No calorie counting, please!

* See Basic Génoise Cake, page 498.

** See Dessert on Broadway, page 457.

1 serving	325 calories	37 g carbohydrate
6 g protein	16 g fat	2.1 g fibre

Ladies' Luncheon Strawberry Maria
serves 4

450 g	**(*1 lb*) fresh strawberries, washed and hulled**
75 ml	**(*5 tbsp*) caster sugar**
60 ml	**(*4 tbsp*) Tia Maria**
30 ml	**(*2 tbsp*) orange juice**
5 ml	**(*1 tsp*) lemon juice**

Place all ingredients in bowl, toss lightly and marinate 2 to 3 hours at room temperature.

Dish out into glass bowls and decorate with freshly whipped cream and additional berries of your choice.

Serve with strong coffee.

1 serving	*128 calories*	*27 g carbohydrate*
1 g protein	*0 g fat*	*2.6 g fibre*

Baked Peach Halves

serves 4

6	**peaches, halved and peeled**
45 ml	(*3 tbsp*) **syrup***
50 ml	(*2 fl oz*) **water**
60 g	(*2 oz*) **brown sugar**
75 g	(*2½ oz*) **plain flour**
15 ml	(*1 tbsp*) **cinnamon**
75 g	(*2½ oz*) **butter, softened**

Preheat oven to 180°C (*350°F, gas mark 4*).

Place peaches, cut side up, in one layer in large baking dish. Sprinkle each first with syrup, then with water.

Mix brown sugar and flour together in small bowl. Add cinnamon and mix.

Cream in butter using finger tips. Sprinkle mixture in hollows of peach halves and bake 20 minutes. Do not cover.

* See Rainbow Tartlets, page 484.

1 serving	*363 calories*	*54 g carbohydrate*
3 g protein	*15 g fat*	*2.4 g fibre*

Peaches à la Saint-Germain

serves 4

4	ripe peaches, halved and peeled
45 ml	(*3 tbsp*) syrup*
45 ml	(*3 tbsp*) Cointreau liqueur
250 ml	(*8 fl oz*) puréed raspberries
	ice cream
	blanched sliced almonds
	icing sugar

Place peaches, syrup, liqueur and raspberries in frying pan; cover and cook 5 minutes over low heat.

Remove peaches from sauce and set aside to cool. Continue cooking sauce 3 minutes over high heat. Remove and cool.

To serve dessert, arrange peaches with ice cream on serving platter or individual plates.

Top with fruit sauce and garnish with almonds and decorate with icing sugar.

* See Rainbow Tartlets, page 484.

1 serving	*318 calories*	*52 g carbohydrate*
5 g protein	*10 g fat*	*4.9 g fibre*

Caramel Custard

serves 6

100 g	(3½ oz) granulated sugar
50 ml	(2 fl oz) cold water
75 ml	(5 tbsp) cold water
100 g	(3½ oz) granulated sugar
4	large eggs
2	large egg yolks
5 ml	(1 tsp) vanilla
500 ml	(17 fl oz) scalded milk, still hot

Preheat oven to 180°C (350°F, gas mark 4).

Place 100 g (3½ oz) sugar and 50 ml (2 fl oz) water in small saucepan. Set over medium-high heat to caramelize sugar. Stir once at the beginning to help sugar melt but do not stir again. You can brush sides of saucepan with a little more cold water to prevent loose granules from burning.

When sugar is at caramel stage, quickly add 75 ml (5 tbsp) cold water and continue cooking 30 seconds.

Immediately pour into 6 ramekin dishes, rotating each to coat evenly. Set dishes aside in roasting tin.

Begin making custard by placing remaining measure of sugar in large stainless-steel bowl. Add all eggs and vanilla.

Incorporate ingredients well by mixing gently with whisk. Try to avoid foaming.

Slowly pour in milk while whisking; when incorporated, strain custard before pouring into dishes.

Add enough hot water to roasting tin to measure 2.5 cm (1 in) and place in oven; bake for 45 minutes.

Cool custard on counter; then refrigerate until thoroughly chilled.

To serve, run knife around inside edge of moulds and invert each on dessert plate.

1 serving	251 calories	39 g carbohydrate
8 g protein	7 g fat	0 g fibre

1. Once the sugar/water mixture starts to change colour it will caramelize quite quickly, so keep a sharp eye on it to avoid burning. This mixture is just about ready for the next step, which is...

2. ... adding 75 ml (5 *tbsp*) cold water. It might be wise to stand back a little while doing this. Without stirring, continue cooking caramel 30 seconds before pouring into ramekin dishes.

3. It is important to rotate each dish immediately after you have poured in caramel, as the sugar will start to set very quickly.

4. While caramel is hardening in dishes, begin making custard.

Chocolate Custard Caramel

serves 6

100 g	(*3½ oz*) granulated sugar
50 ml	(*2 fl oz*) cold water
75 ml	(*5 tbsp*) cold water
100 g	(*3½ oz*) granulated sugar
4	large eggs
2	egg yolks
5 ml	(*1 tsp*) Tia Maria liqueur
60 g	(*2 oz*) semi-sweet chocolate, melted
500 ml	(*17 fl oz*) scalded milk, still hot

Preheat oven to 180°C (*350°F, gas mark 4*).

The caramel is optional for this recipe — the custard will be tasty without it. Place 100 g (*3½ oz*) sugar and 50 ml (*2 fl oz*) water in small saucepan. Set over medium-high heat to caramelize sugar, stirring once at beginning to help melt sugar.

When sugar is at caramel stage*, quickly add 75 ml (*5 tbsp*) cold water and cook 30 seconds more.

Immediately pour into ramekin dishes, rotating each to coat evenly. Set dishes aside in roasting tin.

To make custard, place remaining sugar, all eggs and Tia Maria in stainless steel bowl. Whisk until thoroughly incorporated but not foaming.

Place melted chocolate in another stainless steel bowl and whisk in hot milk.

Incorporate chocolate milk to egg mixture, whisking constantly. Pass mixture through fine sieve and pour into ramekin dishes.

Add enough hot water to roasting tin to measure 2.5 cm (*1 in*) and place in oven; bake for 45 minutes.

Cool on counter; then refrigerate until thoroughly chilled.

To serve, run knife around inside edge of moulds and invert each on dessert plate. If made without caramel, decorate with whipped cream.

* See pictures of Caramel Custard, page 463.

1 serving	312 calories	42 g carbohydrate
9 g protein	12 g fat	0.2 g fibre

Raspberry Custard

serves 6

175 g	(*6 oz*) fresh raspberries, washed
30 ml	(*2 tbsp*) liqueur of your choice
30 ml	(*2 tbsp*) caster sugar
4	large eggs
2	large egg yolks
100 g	(*3½ oz*) granulated sugar
500 ml	(*17 fl oz*) scalded milk, still hot

Preheat oven to 180°C (*350°F, gas mark 4*).

Marinate raspberries in liqueur and caster sugar for 10 minutes.

Meanwhile, place all eggs in large stainless steel bowl. Incorporate granulated sugar while whisking gently, being careful that mixture does not foam

Slowly pour in milk while whisking until incorporated. Strain custard.

Divide raspberries into 6 ramekin dishes and place in roasting tin. Pour in custard and add enough hot water to pan to measure 2.5 cm (*1 in*). Bake 45 minutes in oven.

Cool on counter; then refrigerate until thoroughly chilled.

To serve, run knife around inside edge of mould and invert onto plate. You can ladle a little egg custard sauce* into bottom of plates, if desired, and perhaps top with more berries.

* See Dessert on Broadway, page 457.

1 serving	*235 calories*	*26 g carbohydrate*
8 g protein	*11 g fat*	*1.9 g fibre*

Decadent Chocolate Mousse

serves 4–6

4	large eggs, separated
50 g	(1¾ oz) caster sugar, sifted
60 g	(2 oz) unsweetened chocolate
250 ml	(8 fl oz) double cream, whipped

Place egg yolks in stainless steel bowl and add sugar. Using whisk, mix together and set bowl over saucepan half-filled with simmering water.

Cook over low heat while whisking constantly to prevent eggs from cooking — mixture should thicken in about 2 to 3 minutes.

Remove saucepan from heat; with bowl still on saucepan, continue whisking for about 5 minutes.

Place chocolate in another stainless steel bowl; melt over saucepan half-filled with hot water set over medium heat. Cool chocolate in bowl on counter.

Mix melted chocolate into egg mixture until well incorporated; set aside.

Beat egg whites until they form soft peaks; set aside.

Fold whipped cream into chocolate mixture.

Using spatula, begin folding beaten whites into mixture. They should be well incorporated, but you can leave a trace of white for a marbled effect.

Spoon mousse into individual glass dishes and chill 2 to 3 hours before serving.

1 serving	275 calories	11 g carbohydrate
6 g protein	23 g fat	0.2 g fibre

1. Place egg yolks and sugar in stainless steel bowl.

2. With bowl set over saucepan half-filled with simmering water, cook mixture over low heat while whisking constantly.

3. Incorporate cooled chocolate to egg mixture.

4. Beat whites until they form soft peaks.

Chocolate Filling Cream

150 g	(5 oz) semi-sweet chocolate
4	egg yolks
100 g	(3½ oz) icing sugar
75 ml	(5 tbsp) double cream
225 g	(½ lb) unsalted butter, softened

Melt chocolate in stainless steel bowl placed over saucepan half-filled with hot water set over low heat.

Remove bowl and add egg yolks, sugar and cream. Place bowl over saucepan again and beat mixture while cooking for 6 to 7 minutes. Water in saucepan should be simmering.

Remove and place in refrigerator to cool.

When cooled, whisk in butter until thick and smooth.

1 recipe	3488 calories	128 g carbohydrate
24 g protein	320 g fat	3.2 g fibre

Butter Cream Frosting

225 g	(¹/₂ *lb*) unsalted butter, at room temperature
150 g	(*5 oz*) icing sugar
2	egg yolks
	liqueur to taste

Cream butter and beat until light and fluffy.

Sift icing sugar and gradually add to butter while mixing with electric hand beater at low speed.

Beat in first egg yolk. Add second yolk and beat again until smooth.

Add liqueur to taste and beat once more. Use as a frosting or filling for gâteaux.

1 recipe	2544 calories	160 g carbohydrate	**469**
8 g protein	208 g fat	0 g fibre	

Country Rice Pudding

serves 6

750 ml	(*1¼ pt*) water
150 g	(*5 oz*) long-grain rice, rinsed
900 ml	(*1½ pt*) hot milk
75 g	(*2½ oz*) granulated sugar
45 g	(*1½ oz*) golden seedless raisins
45 g	(*1½ oz*) sultana raisins
1	egg
2	egg yolks
50 ml	(*2 fl oz*) double cream
pinch	salt
	grated zest 1 orange
	grated zest 1 lemon

Preheat oven to 180°C (*350°F, gas mark 4*). Butter 2-litre (*3½-pt*) soufflé mould and sprinkle sides and bottom with brown sugar; set aside.

Bring water with pinch of salt to boil in saucepan over high heat. Add rice, stir to loosen and cook, covered, 10 minutes over medium heat.

Drain well and set rice aside to cool.

Mix hot milk with sugar. Stir in rice, raisins and fruit zests. Pour into prepared mould and bake 1 hour.

Mix all eggs with cream in a bowl. Remove soufflé mould from oven and incorporate egg mixture to pudding.

Return to oven and resume cooking 15 minutes.

Serve pudding warm or cold.

1 serving	*292 calories*	*46 g carbohydrate*
9 g protein	*8 g fat*	*1.1 g fibre*

1. Add rinsed rice to boiling salted water. Cook, covered, 10 minutes over medium heat.

2. Mix hot milk with sugar.

3. It is important to drain rice well before adding it to milk mixture.

4. After 1 hour of cooking, incorporate egg mixture to pudding and resume cooking 15 minutes.

Bananas in their Skins

serves 4

4	ripe bananas
30 ml	(*2 tbsp*) syrup*
45 ml	(*3 tbsp*) jam of your choice
30 ml	(*2 tbsp*) Tia Maria liqueur
	Italian meringue**

Preheat oven to 200°C (*400°F, gas mark 6*).

Slash skins lengthways once and remove bananas. Set skins aside.

Place bananas in baking dish and score each several times. Brush with syrup and jam. Sprinkle with Tia Maria liqueur. Bake 6 to 7 minutes.

Carefully replace bananas in their skins and decorate with Italian meringue piped through piping bag. Place in ovenproof platter or pan and bake until golden brown. The skins will become quite dark.

* See Rainbow Tartlets, page 484.
** See Italian Meringue Crunch Biscuits, page 473.

1 serving	425 calories	99 g carbohydrate
5 g protein	1 g fat	4.1 g fibre

Italian Meringue Crunch Biscuits

200 g	(7 oz) caster sugar
4	large egg whites (with no trace of yolks)
2 ml	(½ tsp) vanilla
	cocoa for dusting

Preheat oven to 110°C (225°F, gas mark ¼). Butter and flour baking sheets; set aside.

Sift sugar into stainless steel bowl. Place over saucepan half-filled with hot water over low heat.

Add egg whites and vanilla to bowl. With water simmering, begin beating mixture at low speed. When it starts to take shape, increase speed to medium and continue beating steadily.

Just before meringue starts to peak, increase speed to high and continue beating. Test meringue by turning bowl upside-down. Egg whites should remain firmly in place.

Remove bowl from saucepan and continue to beat at high speed until meringue is cold.

Spoon some of meringue into piping bag fitted with plain nozzle. Squeeze out different shapes (fingers, mushroom caps, etc.) onto baking sheets.

Use soup spoon to drop lumps of meringue on some cookies, which will give uneven textures.

Place baking sheets in oven and bake 3 hours.

Remove to cool on counter and sprinkle with cocoa.

1 recipe	1008 calories	228 g carbohydrate
24 g protein	0 g fat	0 g fibre

Pastry Cream

30 ml	(*2 tbsp*)	Cointreau liqueur
5 ml	(*1 tsp*)	vanilla
3		large eggs
2		large egg yolks
225 g	(*8 oz*)	granulated sugar
75 g	(*2½ oz*)	sifted plain flour
500 ml	(*17 fl oz*)	scalded milk, still hot
15 g	(*½ oz*)	unsalted butter

Place liqueur, vanilla, all eggs and sugar in large stainless-steel bowl. Beat with electric hand whisk at high speed until light and fluffy — about 1½ minutes.

Sift flour over mixture and incorporate with wooden spoon.

Pour in milk while whisking; then transfer cream to heavy bottomed saucepan.

Cook over medium heat while mixing constantly with whisk or wooden spoon. Cream will become very thick, forming ribbons.

Transfer cream to bowl, quickly whisk in butter, and let cool before covering with greaseproof paper. Refrigerate until use (up to 2 days).

1 recipe	1800 calories	294 g carbohydrate
48 g protein	48 g fat	2.4 g fibre

Paradise Islands

serves 4

4	egg whites
100 g	(3½ oz) caster sugar
500 ml	(17 fl oz) milk
	egg custard sauce*

Beat egg whites until firm, then add sugar and continue beating 1 minute.

Pour milk into large, deep saucepan and bring to boiling point. Reduce heat to allow milk to simmer.

Dip ice cream scoop into meringue and gently drop mounds in simmering milk. Depending on the size of your pan, you may have to do this in several batches to avoid crowding. Poach meringues for 1 to 2 minutes on each side.

Using slotted spoon, remove meringues to absorbent kitchen paper to drain.

Ladle a small amount of egg custard sauce into bottom of dessert plate. Set meringues on top and serve. If desired, decorate with caramel.

* See Dessert on Broadway, page 457.

1 serving	331 calories	58 g carbohydrate
9 g protein	7 g fat	0 g fibre

Icy Strawberry Soufflé

serves 4–6

450 g	(*1 lb*) fresh strawberries, washed and hulled
1	small envelope unflavoured gelatine
75 ml	(*5 tbsp*) hot water
5	large eggs, separated
100 g	(*3½ oz*) granulated sugar
250 ml	(*8 fl oz*) double cream, whipped

Prepare mould as directed in technique; set aside.

Place strawberries in food processor and purée; set aside.

Sprinkle gelatine into small bowl with hot water, mix and set aside.

Place egg yolks and granulated sugar in stainless steel bowl. Whisk together and place over saucepan half-filled with hot water set over low heat. Cook about 2 to 3 minutes, whisking constantly.

Remove bowl from pan and whisk in gelatine mixture. Quickly whisk in puréed berries and chill until mixture starts to solidify around edges.

While mixture is chilling, beat egg whites until stiff; set aside.

Remove bowl from refrigerator and gently whisk in whipped cream. Then, using spatula, fold in beaten whites.

Pour into prepared mould and freeze 6 to 8 hours.

1 serving	308 calories	25 g carbohydrate
7 g protein	20 g fat	1.8 g fibre

1. Choose a 1- litre (*1¾-pt*) straight-sided mould. Using two thicknesses of foil, make a collar long enough to wrap around mould. It should be at least 10 cm (*4 in*) high. Tape securely to mould as shown in picture.

2. Place whole berries in bowl of food processor and prepare to purée.

3. Whisk puréed berries into egg mixture until well incorporated. Chill.

4. After whipped cream has been incorporated, gently fold in beaten egg whites before transferring mixture to prepared mould for freezing.

Poached Pears au Chocolat

serves 4

4	pears, cored from bottom and peeled
50 ml	(2 fl oz) syrup*
125 ml	(4 fl oz) water
125 g	(4 oz) icing sugar
60 g	(2 oz) bitter chocolate
5 ml	(1 tsp) vanilla
45 ml	(3 tbsp) milk
1	egg yolk
4	crêpes**

Place pears in saucepan. Pour syrup over pears and add water; cover and cook 3 to 4 minutes over medium heat.

Turn pears over; cover and continue cooking 3 to 4 minutes.

Remove pears from saucepan and set aside.

Place sugar, chocolate, vanilla and milk in stainless steel bowl. Place over saucepan half-filled with hot water and melt over low heat.

Mix well and remove bowl from saucepan. Mix in egg yolk and let stand several minutes.

Meanwhile, partly wrap pears in crêpes (a little syrup will help hold crêpe) and place on dishes.

When chocolate is tepid, ladle over pears and serve.

* See Rainbow Tartlets, page 484.
** See Sunrise-Filled Crêpes, page 480.

1 serving	*566 calories*	*92 g carbohydrate*
9 g protein	*18 g fat*	*3.9 g fibre*

Pears in Syrup

serves 4

4	**pears, cored, peeled and halved**
60 g	**(*2 oz*) granulated sugar**
300 ml	**(*½ pt*) water**
15 ml	**(*1 tbsp*) lemon juice**
15 ml	**(*1 tbsp*) grated lemon zest**
5 ml	**(*1 tsp*) vanilla**
5 ml	**(*1 tsp*) cornflour**
30 ml	**(*2 tbsp*) cold water**

Place first 6 ingredients in saucepan and bring to boil. Reduce heat to medium and continue cooking 5 minutes.

Remove saucepan from heat and let stand 10 minutes.

Transfer pears to serving platter. Return saucepan to stove and bring liquid to boil. Cook 3 to 4 minutes over high heat.

Mix cornflour with cold water; stir into sauce until well incorporated. Cook 1 more minute.

Pour syrup over pears and cool before serving. If desired, garnish with dollop of whipped cream.

1 serving	*161 calories*	*37 g carbohydrate*
1 g protein	*1 g fat*	*2.9 g fibre*

Sunrise-Filled Crêpes

serves 4

CRÊPE BATTER:

45 ml	(*3 tbsp*)	granulated sugar
150 g	(*5 oz*)	plain flour
3		large eggs
250 ml	(*8 fl oz*)	milk
125 ml	(*4 fl oz*)	warm water
45 ml	(*3 tbsp*)	melted butter, lukewarm
pinch		salt

Place sugar, flour, salt, eggs and milk in large bowl; mix together using whisk until well incorporated.

Whisk in warm water. Add melted butter and whisk again.

Pour batter through sieve into clean bowl and refrigerate 1 hour.

Make crêpes. (Refer to Allumettes, page 117, for directions, if needed.)

FILLING:

150 g	(*5 oz*)	strawberries, washed and hulled
125 g	(*4 oz*)	raspberries, washed
30 ml	(*2 tbsp*)	syrup*
15 ml	(*1 tbsp*)	liqueur of your choice
250 ml	(*8 fl oz*)	whipped cream

Place strawberries and raspberries in bowl and add syrup and liqueur; marinate 10 minutes.

Gently mix whipped cream with berries.

Have 8 crêpes ready (you can easily freeze the rest); spread berry filling over each crêpe. Fold over lengthways and serve at once.

* See Rainbow Tartlets, page 484.

1 serving	*494 calories*	*54 g carbohydrate*
11 g protein	*26 g fat*	*4.4 g fibre*

Quick Raspberry Crêpes

serves 4

400 g	(*14 oz*) raspberries, washed
30 ml	(*2 tbsp*) syrup*
5 ml	(*1 tsp*) cornflour
30 ml	(*2 tbsp*) cold water
4	crêpes**
4	scoops frozen raspberry yogurt
	few drops lemon juice

Purée raspberries in food processor.

Transfer berries to small saucepan with syrup and lemon juice; mix well. Bring to boil, and then simmer 8 to 10 minutes. Stir occasionally.

Mix cornflour with cold water; incorporate to fruit and cook 1 minute.

Pour fruit sauce into bowl and set aside to cool.

When ready to serve, arrange opened crêpes on plates. Spread some of fruit sauce over each and set a scoop of frozen yogurt in middle. Wrap crêpe around yogurt and garnish with remaining sauce.

Serve at once.

* See Rainbow Tartlets, page 484.
** See Sunrise-Filled Crêpes, page 480.

1 serving	353 calories	59 g carbohydrate
9 g protein	9 g fat	7.8 g fibre

Fresh Strawberry Coupe

serve 4

450 g	(*1 lb*) fresh strawberries, washed and hulled
15 ml	(*1 tbsp*) grated lemon zest
75 ml	(*5 tbsp*) water
75 g	(*2½ oz*) granulated sugar
75 ml	(*5 tbsp*) Tia Maria liqueur

Place strawberries in bowl with lemon zest; set aside.

Pour water into small saucepan and add sugar. Cook over high heat until mixture reaches temperature of 110°C (*230°F*).

Pour syrup over strawberries, mix and add Tia Maria; mix again. Marinate 30 minutes before scrving.

1 serving	137 calories	31 g carbohydrate
1 g protein	1 g fat	2.6 g fibre

Strawberry Cream Pie

serves 6

300 g	(*11 oz*) fresh strawberries, washed and hulled
30 ml	(*2 tbsp*) sugar
250 ml	(*8 fl oz*) pastry cream* or whipped cream
1	precooked sweet dough** shell in 23-cm (*9-in*) loose-bottomed tart tin
	juice 1 orange

Place strawberries, sugar and orange juice in saucepan. Cover and cook 2 minutes over medium-high heat. Remove from heat and set aside to cool.

Spread pastry cream or whipped cream in bottom of sweet dough crust.

Neatly arrange berries so that they are standing up in cream. Pour juice from saucepan over berries and chill 1 hour before serving.

* See Pastry Cream, page 474.
** See Cream-Filled Fruit Flan, page 493.

1 serving	357 calories	53 g carbohydrate
7 g protein	13 g fat	1.9 g fibre

483

Rainbow Tartlets

serves 4–6

SYRUP:

450 g	**(1 lb) granulated sugar**
250 ml	**(8 fl oz) cold water**

Place sugar and water in small saucepan. Set over medium heat, stir gently and boil until temperature reaches 100°C (212°F).

Remove syrup from heat, let cool and store in glass jar. Use as a glaze for fruit-topped desserts.

ASSEMBLY:

sweet dough*
pastry cream**
sliced fresh peaches (canned may be substituted; drained)
sliced kiwi
halved strawberries
beaten egg

Bring prepared dough to room temperature; use half for this recipe. Store leftover dough in refrigerator.

Roll out dough on floured surface using floured rolling pin and line desired number of tartlet tins. Trim off excess dough while leaving sides higher than edges of tin. Pinch edges with fingertips and chill 30 minutes.

Preheat oven to 200°C (400°F, gas mark 6).

Prick bottom and sides of dough with fork and brush with beaten egg. Precook in oven about 8 to 10 minutes or until cooked and brown in colour. Cool.

Arrange tartlets on serving platter and spoon some pastry cream in bottom of each. Artfully arrange fruit on top and glaze with syrup.

Chill before serving.

* See Cream-Filled Fruit Flan, page 493.

** See Pastry Cream, page 474.

1 serving	123 calories	61 g carbohydrate
8 g protein	15 g fat	1.6 g fibre

Raspberry Peach Tartlets

serves 4

2	ripe peaches, halved and peeled
30 ml	(*2 tbsp*) syrup*
30 ml	(*2 tbsp*) vodka
125 g	(*4 oz*) raspberries, washed
	sweet dough** (for tartlet shells)
	chocolate sauce***

Bake tartlet shells 8 to 10 minutes in oven preheated at 200°C (*400°F, gas mark 6*).

Place 4 precooked cooled tartlets on serving platter and fill bottoms with chocolate sauce. Set aside.

Place peaches in saucepan with syrup and vodka. Cover and poach 3 to 4 minutes. Turn once during cooking.

Using slotted spoon, transfer peaches to plate; set aside to cool.

Add raspberries to syrup in saucepan and cook 2 minutes over medium heat. Do not cover.

Transfer sauce to food processor and purée; let cool.

To assemble dessert, place peach half (cut side down) in tartlet on chocolate sauce.

Spoon raspberry sauce over and serve.

* See Rainbow Tartlets, page 484.
** See Cream-Filled Fruit Flan, page 493.
*** See Poached Pears au Chocolat, page 478.

1 serving	625 calories	92 g carbohydrate
8 g protein	25 g fat	4.4 g fibre

Honey Baked Apples with Walnuts

serves 4

4	**large apples, cored**
45 ml	**(*3 tbsp*) honey**
60 g	**(*2 oz*) chopped walnuts**
30 g	**(*1 oz*) butter**
90 g	**(*3 oz*) sultanas**
375 ml	**(*13 fl oz*) water**
5 ml	**(*1 tsp*) cornflour**
30 ml	**(*2 tbsp*) cold water**
	juice ½ lemon
	juice ½ orange
	cinnamon to taste

Preheat oven to 190°C (*375°F, gas mark 5*).

Peel upper half of apples only. Coat peeled part with honey and roll in walnuts. Place apples in roasting tin.

Divide butter and sultanas between cavities. Squeeze fruit juices over apples and sprinkle with cinnamon to taste.

Pour 375 ml (*13 fl oz*) water into roasting tin and bake 40 minutes. Depending on variety of apple, cooking time may need to be adjusted.

When cooked, transfer apples to serving platter. Place roasting tin with juices over high heat and bring to boil.

Mix cornflour with cold water; stir into sauce until well incorporated. Reduce heat and continue cooking 1 minute.

Pour sauce over apples and chill. Serve cold.

1 serving	*321 calories*	*40 g carbohydrate*
2 g protein	*17 g fat*	*3.0 g fibre*

1. Coat peeled part of apples with honey then roll in chopped walnuts.

2. Place apples in roasting tin and divide butter and sultanas between cavities. Squeeze fruit juices over apples and sprinkle with cinnamon to taste.

3. Pour in 375 ml (*13 fl oz*) water and bake apples in oven.

4. When apples are cooked, remove and set aside. Place roasting tin over high heat and bring to boil. Thicken sauce with diluted cornflour and continue cooking 1 minute over reduced heat.

Fresh Blueberry Pie

serves 6–8

600	(*1¼ lb*) fresh blueberries, washed
45 ml	(*3 tbsp*) granulated sugar
45 ml	(*3 tbsp*) brown sugar
15 ml	(*1 tbsp*) grated orange zest
15 ml	(*1 tbsp*) grated lemon zest
30 ml	(*2 tbsp*) sifted cornflour
15 g	(*½ oz*) butter
	pastry dough*
	beaten egg

Preheat oven to 200°C (*400°F, mark 6*).

Roll out half of dough and line 23-cm (*9-in*) pie plate.

Place berries, both types of sugar, both zests and cornflour in bowl; toss together and pack into pie shell. Dot with butter.

Roll out other half of dough. Moisten edges of pie shell with water and carefully lay pie crust on top. Pinch edges shut and make several slits with small knife in upper crust.

Brush dough with beaten egg and place in oven; bake 40 to 45 minutes.

* See All-American Apple Pie, page 489.

1 serving	387 calories	49 g carbohydrate
5 g protein	19 g fat	6.8 g fibre

All-American Apple Pie

serves 6–8

PASTRY DOUGH:

275 g	*(10 oz)* sifted plain flour
150 g	*(5 oz)* shortening, room temperature
50 ml	*(2 fl oz)* chilled water
15 ml	*(1 tbsp)* chilled water
pinch	salt

Resift flour with salt into large bowl. Add shortening and, using pastry blender, incorporate until mixture resembles oatmeal.

Add both measures of chilled water and form dough into ball. Wrap in greaseproof paper and refrigerate 1 hour.

Before using, remove dough and let stand 1 hour at room temperature.

Cut dough in half. Flour board and rolling pin; roll out half of dough and line 23-cm (*9-in*) pie plate. Set aside.

FILLING:

7	baking apples, peeled, cored and sliced
45 ml	*(3 tbsp)* granulated sugar
45 ml	*(3 tbsp)* brown sugar
5 ml	*(1 tsp)* cinnamon
30 ml	*(2 tbsp)* sifted cornflour
15 ml	*(1 tbsp)* grated lemon zest
15 ml	*(1 tbsp)* lemon juice
15 g	*(½ oz)* butter
	beaten egg

Preheat oven to 200°C (*400°F, gas mark 6*).

Place apples, both types of sugar, cinnamon, cornflour, lemon zest and lemon juice in bowl; toss together and pack into prepared pastry shell. Dot apples with butter. Roll out other half of dough. Moisten edges of pastry shell with water and carefully lay pastry crust on top. Pinch edges shut and make several slits with small knife in upper crust. Brush dough with beaten egg and place in oven; bake 40 to 45 minutes. Serve pie plain, with cheese or with vanilla ice cream.

1 serving	*415 calories*	*56 g carbohydrate*
5 g protein	*19 g fat*	*3.6 g fibre*

Old-Fashioned Apple Crumb Pie

serves 6

30 ml	(*2 tbsp*) plain flour
5 ml	(*1 tsp*) cinnamon
90 g	(*3 oz*) brown sugar
6	large cooking apples, cored, peeled and sliced
45 g	(*1½ oz*) plain flour
75 g	(*2½ oz*) butter, softened
60 g	(*2 oz*) brown sugar
	few drops lemon juice
	pastry dough

Preheat oven to 200°C (*400°F, gas mark 6*). Have ready 9-in. (*23-cm*) pie plate lined with dough.

Mix 30 ml (*2 tbsp*) flour, cinnamon and 90 g (*3 oz*) brown sugar together in bowl. Add apples and lemon juice and toss until evenly coated.

Pack apples into pie shell. Mix remaining ingredients together and sprinkle over top.

Bake 15 minutes in oven; then reduce heat to 190°C (*375°F, gas mark 5*) and continue baking 35 minutes.

1 serving	*470 calories*	*74 g carbohydrate*
3 g protein	*18 g fat*	*4.1 g fibre*

Peach-Filled Puffs with Chantilly Cream   *serves 6*

45 ml	(*3 tbsp*) syrup*
60 ml	(*4 tbsp*) water
30 ml	(*2 tbsp*) light rum
3	ripe peaches, halved and peeled
375 ml	(*13 fl oz*) double cream, cold
5 ml	(*1 tsp*) vanilla
30 g	(*1 oz*) sifted icing sugar
6	cream puffs**

Place syrup, water, rum and peach halves in saucepan; cook 3 minutes at boil. Remove from heat and let fruit cool in syrup.

Drain peaches well and slice; set aside.

Pour cream and vanilla into stainless-steel bowl. Beat at medium speed until soft peaks form.

Add half of icing sugar; beat 45 seconds at high speed. Gently fold in remaining sugar.

Slice off tops of cream puffs. Spoon Chantilly cream into piping bag fitted with star nozzle and fill bottoms of puffs.

Arrange peach slices on cream and reassemble puffs. You may serve at once, if desired, or chill several hours until use.

* See Rainbow Tartlets, page 484.

** See Chocolate Éclairs, page 494.

1 serving	491 calories	35 g carbohydrate
9 g protein	35 g fat	1.4 g fibre

Blueberry and Peach Open Pie
serves 6

450 g	(*1 lb*) fresh blueberries, washed and stemmed
2	peaches, peeled and sliced
15 ml	(*1 tbsp*) grated lemon zest
15 ml	(*1 tbsp*) grated orange zest
15 ml	(*1 tbsp*) grated lime zest
15 ml	(*1 tbsp*) cornflour
45 ml	(*3 tbsp*) granulated sugar
1	precooked sweet dough* shell in 23-cm (*9-in*) loose-bottomed tart tin

Place all pie ingredients in saucepan. Cover and cook 5 to 6 minutes over medium-high heat. Remove and let cool.

Pour into sweet dough crust and chill 30 minutes before serving. If desired, decorate with whipped cream.

* See Cream-Filled Fruit Flan, page 493.

1 serving	298 calories	48 g carbohydrate
4 g protein	10 g fat	6.7 g fibre

Cream-Filled Fruit Flan

serves 4–6

SWEET DOUGH:

(*for tartlets, tarts and various desserts*)

250 g	(*9 oz*) sifted plain flour
125 g	(*4 oz*) unsalted butter, softened
150 g	(*5 oz*) granulated sugar
1 ml	(*¼ tsp*) vanilla
1	large egg
30 ml	(*2 tbsp*) cold water
pinch	salt
	beaten egg

Mound flour on cutting board and sprinkle in salt. Make well in middle of flour and add all of butter. Using fingertips, incorporate until mixture resembles oatmeal.

Form another well in middle and add sugar, vanilla, egg and water. Incorporate until mixture becomes dough-like and forms ball.

Knead dough 2 or 3 times only, to incorporate fully. Wrap in clean cloth and let rest 1 hour in bottom of refrigerator.

Remember to remove dough from refrigerator 1 hour before using.

For this fruit flan use half of dough. Remaining dough can be kept for several days in refrigerator.

Using floured rolling pin, roll out dough on floured surface until about 3 mm (*⅛ in*) thick. Drape dough over rolling pin and carefully unroll over medium-size flan ring or spring release pie tin. Gently line tin and trim off excess dough, leaving sides higher than edges of tin. Pinch edges with fingertips and chill 30 minutes.

Preheat oven to 200°C (*400°F, gas mark 6*).

Prick bottom and sides of dough with fork. Cut out circle of greaseproof paper to fit bottom and place on dough.

(*continued on page 494*)

Cover with baking weights or dried beans. Place in oven and precook until just brown.

Remove from oven and take out weights and paper; brush all over with beaten egg. Return to oven and continue precooking about 10 minutes.

Cool before filling.

FILLING:

170 g	(6 oz) apricot jelly or jam
30 ml	(2 tbsp) syrup*
	pastry cream**
	sliced fresh peaches (canned can be substituted; drained)
	sliced kiwi
	halved strawberries

Place apricot jelly and syrup in small saucepan; cook 2 minutes over medium heat. Strain through sieve and set aside until tepid.

Spread pastry cream in bottom of precooked shell. Arrange fruit neatly by type, starting from outside.

Brush tepid glaze mixture over fruit and chill 1 hour before serving.

* See Rainbow Tartlets, page 484.
** See Pastry Cream, page 474.

1 serving	474 calories	80 g carbohydrate
7 g protein	14 g fat	1.8 g fibre

Chocolate Éclairs

serves 4–6

CREAM PUFF DOUGH:

250 ml	(8 fl oz) water
60 g	(2 oz) unsalted butter, cut into pieces
1 ml	(¼ tsp) salt
150 g	(5 oz) plain flour
4	large eggs
	beaten egg

Preheat oven to 190°C (375°F, gas mark 5). Lightly butter and flour 2 baking sheets; set aside.

Place water, butter and salt in heavy-bottomed saucepan. Bring to boil and cook 2 minutes until butter is completely melted. Remove pan from heat.

Add all of flour, mixing rapidly with wooden spoon.

Return saucepan to stove over low heat. Dry dough 3 to 4 minutes, stirring constantly with wooden spoon. The dough should not adhere to your fingers when pinched.

Transfer dough to bowl and let cool 4 to 5 minutes. Add 4 eggs, one at a time, mixing well between additions. The dough must regain its original texture before the next egg is added.

Spoon dough into piping bag fitted with plain nozzle. Squeeze out desired shapes onto prepared baking sheets, leaving enough space between each for rising.

Brush tops with beaten egg and smooth tails with fork; set aside 20 minutes.

Place baking sheets in middle of oven and bake 35 minutes. Turn oven off, set door ajar and let dry 1 hour before filling.

ASSEMBLY:

125 g	(4 oz) unsweetened chocolate
60 ml	(4 tbsp) water
75 g	(2½ oz) granulated sugar
	whipped cream

Place chocolate in stainless steel bowl; melt over saucepan containing warm water set over low heat.

Transfer chocolate to small saucepan and add water and sugar; bring to boiling point.

Remove saucepan from heat and let cool to lukewarm; beat mixture to thicken.

Carefully slice éclairs in half lengthways and fill bottoms with whipped cream. You can use a variety of other creams such as Chocolate Filling Cream (see page 468).

Dip tops in chocolate and assemble; chill until set.

1 serving	602 calories	36 g carbohydrate
11 g protein	46 g fat	1.3 g fibre

Chocolate Bread

serves 6–8

125 g	(*4 oz*) semi-sweet chocolate
100 g	(*3½ oz*) caster sugar
125 g	(*4 oz*) butter, softened
3	large eggs
60 g	(*2 oz*) sifted cake flour
30 g	(*1 oz*) chopped walnuts (optional)
30 ml	(*2 tbsp*) blanched sliced almonds
2	egg whites, beaten stiff

Preheat oven to 180°C (*350°F, gas mark 4*). Lightly butter and flour 13 x 23-cm (*5 x 9-in*) loaf tin that is about 6 cm (*2½ in*) deep; set aside.

Place chocolate in stainless-steel bowl and set in oven to melt.

Remove bowl; add sugar and butter. Mix well with whisk.

Add whole eggs, one at a time, whisking well between additions.

Sift flour over batter and incorporate with wooden spoon.

Stir in nuts and fold in egg whites. Transfer batter to prepared loaf tin and rap bottom against cutting board to settle batter.

Bake 40 minutes in oven or until cake is done.

Remove from oven, cool slightly in tin, and unmould onto wire rack to finish cooling.

Slice as you would a loaf of bread and serve with milk.

1 serving	362 calories	25 g carbohydrate
7 g protein	26 g fat	0.9 g fibre

Nutty Chocolate Quatre-Quarts

serves 6–8

125 g	(*4 oz*) semi-sweet chocolate
75 g	(*2½ oz*) granulated sugar
30 ml	(*2 tbsp*) Tia Maria liqueur
175 ml	(*6 fl oz*) melted butter
4	large egg yolks
60 g	(*2 oz*) sifted cake flour
60 g	(*2 oz*) chopped nuts
4	large egg whites, beaten stiff

Preheat oven to 180°C (*350°F, gas mark 4*). Butter and flour 20-cm (*8-in*) square cake tin; set aside.

Place chocolate, sugar and Tia Maria in stainless-steel bowl placed over saucepan half-filled with hot water. Melt over low heat.

Remove from heat and whisk in melted butter.

Add egg yolks, one at a time, beating very well between additions with electric hand whisk.

Sift flour over batter and incorporate with wooden spoon. Fold in nuts.

Fold in egg whites until most trace of white is gone.

Pour batter into prepared cake tin and bake 30 to 35 minutes or until cake is done.

Cool slightly in tin before unmoulding onto wire rack. When completely cooled, cut into squares and serve. Although this is a rich-tasting cake, you will find it very light.

1 serving	422 calories	22 g carbohydrate
7 g protein	34 g fat	1.1 g fibre

Basic Génoise Cake

serves 6–8

170 g	(6 oz) granulated sugar
5	large eggs
150 g	(5 oz) sifted cake flour
50 ml	(2 fl oz) clarified butter, tepid
	Tia Maria liqueur
	pastry cream*
	chocolate flakes

Preheat oven to 180°C (*350°F, gas mark* 4). Lightly butter and flour 22-cm (*8½-in*) spring release cake tin.

Place sugar in stainless steel bowl set over saucepan half-filled with hot water. Add eggs. Over low heat with water simmering, whisk for 4 to 5 minutes. Use electric hand whisk if desired.

Mixture should become quite thick and expand in volume. When cream forms ribbons, transfer bowl to counter. Sift 125 g (*4 oz*) of flour over bowl; fold in using spatula until all traces are gone.

Sift in rest of flour and fold using spatula. Gradually add butter while folding. All traces of butter must be incorporated.

Pour batter into cake tin and bake in middle of oven 35 to 40 minutes or until cake is done.

Let stand 5 minutes; then unmould and finish cooling on wire rack.

When cold, slice off layer. Sprinkle Tia Maria over bottom layer and cover with pastry cream. Replace top layer, sprinkle with more liqueur and ice outside of cake with remaining cream. Top with chocolate flakes and chill 2 hours.

* See Pastry Cream, page 474.

1 serving	428 calories	57 g carbohydrate
10 g protein	16 g fat	1.0 g fibre

1. Whisk sugar and eggs together in stainless steel bowl set over saucepan with simmering water. Continue for 4 to 5 minutes — do not stop stirring.

2. The sugar and egg mixture will become considerably thicker and expand greatly in volume. Also, when it is folded with a spatula it will form ribbons — at this point, remove bowl to counter.

3. Even though flour is sifted, resift it when adding it to batter. Incorporate flour in 2 measures.

4. Incorporate butter in thin stream while continuing to fold with spatula — all trace of yellow must be gone. If needed, use wooden spoon to finish incorporating.

Vanilla Quatre-Quarts

4	large eggs
170 g	(6 oz) granulated sugar
2 ml	(½ tsp) vanilla
90 g	(3 oz) sifted cake flour
50 ml	(2 fl oz) clarified butter, tepid

Preheat oven to 180°C (350°F, gas mark 4). Butter and flour 20-cm (8-in) square cake tin; set aside.

Beat eggs with sugar and vanilla using electric hand whisk. Continue for 3 to 4 minutes or until foamy.

Sift flour over mixture and incorporate with spatula.

Incorporate butter with spatula. Pour batter into prepared cake tin and bake 30 minutes or until cake is done.

Cool slightly in tin before unmoulding onto wire rack. When completely cooled, cut into squares and serve. This cake is a delicious treat for school lunches.

1 serving	200 calories	28 g carbohydrate
4 g protein	8 g fat	0.4 g fibre

Almond Vodka Cake

serves 6

175 g	(*6 oz*) granulated sugar
5	large eggs, separated
1 ml	(¼ *tsp*) vanilla
45 ml	(*3 tbsp*) vodka
225 g	(*8 oz*) powdered almonds
125 g	(*4 oz*) sifted cake flour
50 ml	(*2 fl oz*) melted clarified butter

Preheat oven to 180°C (*350°F, gas mark 4*). Butter and flour 22-cm (*8½-in*) spring release cake tin; set aside.

Place sugar, egg yolks, vanilla and vodka in large bowl; beat with electric hand whisk until light and frothy.

Beat egg whites until stiff; set aside.

Sift half of powdered almonds and half of flour; add half of beaten whites to sugar/yolk mixture in large bowl. Fold to incorporate using spatula.

Add remaining almonds, flour and whites using same procedure.

Incorporate butter in thin stream while folding constantly until well incorporated.

Pour batter into cake tin and bake 30 to 35 minutes or until cake is done.

Cool slightly on counter before unmoulding, and then let stand on wire cake rack until cold.

This cake can be served plain or decorated, depending on the occasion. Use your imagination.

1 serving	543 calories	51 g carbohydrate
15 g protein	31 g fat	1.7 g fibre

Super-Rich Double Cheesecake

serves 10–12

450 g	(*1 lb*) **full fat soft cheese, at room temperature**
525 g	(*18 oz*) **ricotta cheese, at room temperature**
100 g	(*3½ oz*) **granulated sugar**
3	**large eggs**
3	**egg yolks**
30 ml	(*2 tbsp*) **vodka**
250 ml	(*8 fl oz*) **whipped cream**
400 g	(*14 oz*) **raspberries, washed**
30 ml	(*2 tbsp*) **syrup***
5 ml	(*1 tsp*) **cornflour**
30 ml	(*2 tbsp*) **cold water**
	graham crumb crust**
	finely grated zest 1 orange and 1 lemon
pinch	**nutmeg**
	few drops lemon juice

Preheat oven to 160°C (*325°F, gas mark 3*).

Place soft cheese in bowl of mixer; cream until soft. Add ricotta cheese and continue mixing until incorporated. Mix in fruit zests.

Add sugar and nutmeg to bowl; mix to incorporate, scraping sides of bowl with spatula if needed.

Add whole eggs, mix thoroughly and scrape down sides as needed. Continue blending until batter is smooth. Add egg yolks and vodka; mix again. Spoon in whipped cream and blend once more. Pour batter into prepared crust, smoothing top with spatula. Bake in middle of oven for 1½ hours. Remove from oven and let cool. Chill 6 to 8 hours in cake tin before serving. At some point before serving, make fruit topping. Purée raspberries in food processor; transfer to small saucepan. Add syrup and lemon juice, mix well and bring to boil. Simmer 8 to 10 minutes, stirring occasionally. Mix cornflour with cold water; stir into mixture and cook 1 more minute. Pour fruit topping into bowl and set aside to cool. Chill before spreading over cake. If desired, decorate with whipped cream piped through piping bag.

* See Rainbow Tartlets, page 484.

** Prepare graham crumb crust according to directions on package. Use 23-cm (*9-in*) spring release cake tin. Cook as directed.

1 serving	440 calories	27 g carbohydrate
11 g protein	32 g fat	2.5 g fibre

1. Cream both cheeses with fruit zests in bowl of electric mixer.

2. Add sugar and nutmeg; mix to incorporate, scraping sides of bowl with spatula if needed.

3. Add whole eggs, mix very well and scrape down sides as needed. Continue beating until batter is smooth.

4. Add egg yolks and vodka.

Strawberry Gâteau

serves 10–12

450 g	(*1 lb*) fresh strawberries, halved
30 ml	(*2 tbsp*) caster sugar
30 ml	(*2 tbsp*) orange juice
2	Génoise cakes*
	Grand Marnier liqueur
	whipped cream

Marinate strawberries in sugar and orange juice for 30 minutes.

When ready to assemble dessert, begin by slicing Génoise cakes into 2 layers, for a total of 4 layers.

Set first layer on cake plate and soak with liqueur. Spread a layer of whipped cream over cake and arrange a layer of strawberries.

Repeat above procedure for remaining layers, ending with final topping of strawberries, artistically arranged for a pretty presentation.

If desired, choose another fruit to garnish top of cake and use leftover whipped cream piped through piping bag to decorate sides, as shown in picture.

* See Basic Génoise Cake, page 498. For this recipe use 25-cm (*10-in*) spring release cake tins. Remember to make 2!

1 serving	475 calories	54 g carbohydrate
9 g protein	23 g fat	1.8 g fibre

INDEX

507

RECIPE INDEX